VOLUME TWO

The New
World

A HISTORY OF THE
ENGLISH-SPEAKING PEOPLES

The
New
World

Winston S. Churchill

McCLELLAND & STEWART LIMITED

1956

PRINTED AND BOUND IN CANADA
T. H. Best Printing Co., Limited, Toronto

ACKNOWLEDGMENTS

I must again record my thanks to Mr F. W. Deakin and Mr G. M. Young and to Dr Keith Feiling for their assistance before the Second World War in the preparation of this work; to Mr Alan Hodge, Mr J. Hurstfield of University College, London, Mr D. H. Pennington of Manchester University, and Dr A. L. Rowse of All Souls, who have scrutinised the text in the light of subsequent advances in historical knowledge; and to Mr Denis Kelly and Mr C. C. Wood. I have also to thank many others who have read these pages and commented on them.

In composing this volume I have drawn gratefully on the writings of Gardiner, Pollard and Ranke, on the *Oxford History of England* and on the works of other scholars past and present. In the last two chapters I have, with the permission of Charles Scribner's Sons, Inc., followed in part the general character of my *Marlborough: His Life and Times*.

Preface

FAR-REACHING events took place in the two centuries
covered by this volume. The New World of the American
continent was discovered and settled by European adventure.
In the realms of speculation and belief, poetry and art, other
new worlds were opened to the human spirit. Between 1485
and 1688 the English peoples began to spread out all over the
globe. They confronted and defeated the might of Spain. Once
the freedom of the seas had been won the American colonies
sprang into being. Lively and assertive communities grew up
on the western shores of the Atlantic Ocean, which in the
course of time were to become the United States. England and
Scotland adopted the Protestant faith. The two kingdoms of
the Island became united under a Scottish dynasty. A great
civil war was fought on abiding issues of principle. The country sustained a Republican experiment under the massive personality of Oliver Cromwell. But, at the nation's demand,
the royal tradition was revived. At the end of this volume the
Protestant faith has been secured under a Dutch monarch,
Parliament is far advanced on the road to supremacy in the
affairs of State, America is fast developing, and a prolonged
and world-wide struggle with France is close at hand.

W.S.C.

Chartwell
Westerham
Kent
September 4, 1956

CONTENTS

BOOK IV

RENAISSANCE AND REFORMATION

BOOK V

THE CIVIL WAR

CONTENTS

BOOK VI

THE RESTORATION

MAPS AND GENEALOGICAL TABLE

BOOK FOUR

RENAISSANCE AND REFORMATION

The Round World

W E have now reached the dawn of what is called the sixteenth century, which means all the years in the hundred years that begin with fifteen. The name is inevitable in English, but confusing. It covers a period in which extraordinary changes affected the whole of Europe. Some had been on the move for a long time, but sprang into full operative force at this moment. For two hundred years or more the Renaissance had been stirring the thought and spirit of Italy, and now came forth in the vivid revival of the traditions of ancient Greece and Rome, in so far as these did not affect the foundations of the Christian faith. The Popes had in the meanwhile become temporal rulers, with the lusts and pomps of other potentates, yet they claimed to carry with them the spiritual power as well. The revenues of the Church were swelled by the sale of "Indulgences" to remit Purgatory both for the living and the dead. The offices of bishop and cardinal were bought and sold, and the common people taxed to the limit of their credulity. These and other abuses in the organisation of the Church were widely recognised and much resented, but as yet they went uncorrected. At the same time literature, philosophy, and art flowered under classical inspiration, and the minds of men to whom study was open were refreshed and enlarged. These were the humanists, who attempted a reconciliation of classical and Christian teachings, among the foremost of whom was Erasmus of Rotterdam. To him is due a considerable part of the credit for bringing Renaissance thought to England. Printing enabled knowledge and argument to flow through the many religious societies which made up the structure of medieval Europe, and from about 1450 onwards printing presses formed the core of a vast ever-growing domain. There were already sixty universities in the Western world, from Lisbon to Prague, and in the early part of the new century these voluntarily opened up broader paths of study and intercourse which rendered their life more fertile and informal. In the Middle Ages education had largely been confined to training the clergy; now it was steadily extended, and its purpose became to turn out not only priests but lay scholars and well-informed gentlemen. The man of many parts and accomplishments became the Renaissance ideal.

This quickening of the human spirit was accompanied by a questioning of long-held theories. For the first time in the course of the fifteenth century men began to refer to the preceding millennium as the Middle Ages. Though much that was medieval survived in their minds, men felt they were living on the brink of a new and modern age. It was an age marked not only by splendid achievements in art and architecture, but also by the beginnings of a revolution in science associated with the name of Copernicus. That the earth moved round the sun, as he conclusively proved and Galileo later asserted on a celebrated occasion, was a novel idea that was to have profound effects upon the human outlook. Hitherto the earth had been thought of as the centre of a universe all designed to serve the needs of man. Now vast new perspectives were opening.

The urge to inquire, to debate, and seek new explanations spread from the field of classical learning into that of religious studies. Greek and even Hebrew texts, as well as Latin, were scrutinised afresh. Inevitably this led to the questioning of accepted religious beliefs. The Renaissance bred the Reformation. In 1517, at the age of thirty-four, Martin Luther, a German priest, denounced the sale of Indulgences, nailed his theses on this and other matters on the door of Wittenberg Castle church, and embarked on his venturesome intellectual foray with the Pope. What began as a protest against Church practices soon became a challenge to Church doctrine. In this struggle Luther displayed qualities of determination and conviction at the peril of the stake which won him his name and fame. He started or gave an impulse to a movement which within a decade swamped the Continent, and proudly bears the general title of the Reformation. It took different forms in different countries, particularly in Switzerland under Zwingli and Calvin. The latter's influence spread from Geneva across France to the Netherlands and Britain, where it was most strongly felt in Scotland.

There are many varieties of Luther's doctrine, but he himself adhered rigorously to the principle of "salvation by faith, not works." This meant that to lead a good and upright life on earth, as many pagans had done, was no guarantee of eternal bliss. Belief in the Christian revelation was vital. The words of Holy Writ and the promptings of individual conscience, not Papal authority, were Luther's guiding lights. He himself believed in predestination. Adam sinned in the Garden of Eden because Almighty God made him do so. Hence the original sin of man. About one tenth of the human race might escape or have escaped consequential eternal damnation in the intervening years. All monks and nuns alike were however entitled to console themselves by getting married. Luther himself set the example by marrying a fugitive nun when he was forty, and lived happily ever after.

*   *   *   *   *

The Reformation affected every country in Europe, but none more than Germany. Luther's movement appealed to the nationalism of the German people who were restive under the exactions of Rome. He gave them a translation of the Bible of which they have remained rightly proud. He also gave the German princes the opportunity to help themselves to Church property. His teachings in the hands of extremists led to a social war in Southern Germany, in which scores of thousands of people perished. Luther himself was passionately on the opposite side to the masses he had inflamed. Though he had used in the coarsest terms the language which roused the mob he did not hesitate to turn on them when they responded. He would go to all lengths to fight the Pope on doctrinal issues, but the oppressed multitude who gave him his strength did not make effective appeal to him. He called them "pigs," and grosser names, and rebuked the "overlords," as he described the aristocracy and well-to-do governing powers, for their slackness in repressing the Peasants' Rebellion.

Heresies there had always been, and over the centuries feeling against the Church had often run strong in almost every country of Europe. But the schism that had begun with Luther was novel and formidable. All the actors in it, the enemies and the defenders of Rome alike, were still deeply influenced by medieval views. They thought of themselves as restorers of the purer ways of ancient times and of the early Church. But the Reformation added to the confusion and uncertainty of an age in which men and states were tugging unwillingly and unwittingly at the anchors that had so long held Europe. After a period of ecclesiastical strife between the Papacy and the Reformation, Protestantism was established over a great part of the Continent under a variety of sects and schools, of which Lutheranism covered the larger area. The Church in Rome, strengthened by the heart-searching Catholic revival known as the Counter-Reformation and in the more worldly sphere by the activities of the Inquisition, proved able to maintain itself through a long series of religious wars. The division between the assailants and defenders of the old order threatened the stability of every state in modern Europe and wrecked the unity of some. England and France came out of the struggle scarred and shaken but in themselves united. A new barrier was created between Ireland and England, a new bond of unity forged between England and Scotland. The Holy Roman Empire of the German people dissolved into a dust of principalities and cities; the Netherlands split into what we now know as Holland and Belgium. Dynasties were threatened, old loyalties forsworn. By the middle of the century the Calvinists were the spearhead of the Protestant attack, the Jesuits the shield and sword of Catholic defense and counterattack. Not for another hundred years would exhaustion and resignation put an end to the revolution that began with Luther. It ended only after Central Europe had been wrecked by the Thirty Years War, and the Peace of Westphalia in 1648 terminated a struggle whose starting-point had been almost forgotten. It was not until the nineteenth century that a greater sense of toleration based upon mutual reverence and respect ruled the souls of men throughout the Christian world.

A well-known Victorian divine and lecturer, Charles Beard, in the 1880's poses some blunt questions.

Was, then, the Reformation, from the intellectual point of view, a failure? Did it break one yoke only to impose another? We are obliged to confess that, especially in Germany, it soon parted company with free learning; that it turned its back upon culture, that it lost itself in a maze of arid theological controversy, that it held out no hand of welcome to awakening science. . . . Even at a later time it has been the divines who have most loudly declared their allegiance to the theology of the Reformation who have also looked most askance at science, and claimed for their statements an entire independence of modern knowledge. I do not know how, on any ordinary theory of the Reformation, it is possible to answer the accusations implied in these facts. The most learned, the profoundest, the most tolerant of modern theologians, would be the most reluctant to accept in their fullness the systems of Melancthon and of Calvin. . . . The fact is, that while the services which the Reformers rendered to truth and liberty by their revolt against the unbroken supremacy of medieval Christianity cannot be over-estimated, it was impossible for them to settle the questions which they raised. Not merely did the necessary knowledge fail them, but they did not even see the scope of the controversies in which they were engaged. It was their part to open the flood-gates; and the stream, in spite of their well-meant efforts to check and confine it, has since rushed impetuously on, now destroying old landmarks, now fertilising new fields, but always bringing with it life and refreshment. To look at the Reformation by itself, to judge it only by its theological and ecclasiastical development, is to pronounce it a failure; to consider it as part of a general movement of European thought, to show its essential connection with ripening scholarship and advancing science, to prove its necessary alliance with liberty, to illustrate its slow growth into toleration, is at once to vindicate its past and to promise it the future." [1]

*   *   *   *   *

While the forces of Renaissance and Reformation were gathering strength in Europe the world beyond was ceaselessly yielding its secrets to European explorers, traders, and missionaries. From the days of the ancient Greeks some men had known in theory that the world was round. Now in the sixteenth century navigations were to prove it so. The story goes back a long way. In medieval times travellers from

[1] *The Reformation of the Sixteenth Century*, by C. Beard (1927 edition), pp. 298–299.

Europe had turned their steps to the East, their imagination fired with tales of fabulous kingdoms and wealth lying in regions which had seen the birth of man—stories of the realm of Prester John, variously placed between Central Asia and the modern Abyssinia, and the later, more practical account of the travels of Marco Polo from Venice to China. But Asia too was marching against the West. At one moment it had seemed as if all Europe would succumb to a terrible menace looming up from the East. Heathen Mongol hordes from the heart of Asia, formidable horsemen armed with bows, had rapidly swept over Russia, Poland, Hungary, and in 1241 inflicted simultaneous crushing defeats upon the Germans near Breslau and upon European chivalry near Budapest. Germany and Austria at least lay at their mercy. Providentially in this year the Great Khan died in Mongolia; the Mongol leaders hastened back the thousands of miles to Karakorum, their capital, to elect his successor, and Western Europe escaped.

Throughout the Middle Ages there had been unceasing battle between Christian and infidel on the borders of Eastern and southern Europe. The people of the frontiers lived in constant terror, the infidel steadily advanced, and in 1453 Constantinople had been captured by the Ottoman Turks. Dangers of the gravest kind now jarred and threatened the wealth and economy of Christian Europe. The destruction of the Byzantine Empire and the Turkish occupation of Asia Minor imperilled the land route to the East. The road which had nourished the towns and cities of the Mediterranean and founded the fortunes and the greatness of the Genoese and the Venetians was now barred. The turmoil spread eastwards, and though the Turks wanted to preserve their trade with Europe for the sake of the tolls they levied, commerce and travel became more and more unsafe.

Italian geographers and navigators had for some time been trying to find a new sea-route to the Orient which would be unhampered by the infidel, but although they had much experience of shipbuilding and navigation from the busy traffic of the Eastern Mediterranean they lacked the capital resources for the hazard of oceanic exploration. Portugal was the first to discover a new path. Helped by English Crusaders, she had achieved her independence in the twelfth century, gradually expelled the Moors from her mainland, and now reached out to the African coastline. Prince Henry the Navigator, grandson of John of Gaunt, had initiated a number of enterprises. Exploring began from Lisbon. All through the later fifteenth century Portuguese mariners had been pushing down the west coast of Africa, seeking for gold and slaves, slowly extending the bounds of the known world, till, in 1487, Bartholomew Diaz rounded the great promontory that marked the end of the African continent. He called it "the Cape of Storms," but the King of Portugal with true insight renamed it "the Cape of Good Hope." The hope was justified; in 1498 Vasco da Gama dropped anchor in the harbour of Calicut; the sea-route was open to the wealth of India and the Farther East.

* * * * *

An event of greater moment for the future of the world was meanwhile taking shape in the mind of a Genoese named Christopher Columbus. Brooding over the dreamlike maps of his fellow-countrymen, he conceived a plan for sailing due west into the Atlantic beyond the known islands in search of yet another route to the East. He married the daughter of a Portuguese sailor who had served with the Navigator, and from his father-in-law's papers he learnt of the great oceanic ventures. In 1486 he sent his brother Bartholomew to seek English backing for the enterprise. Bartholomew was cap-

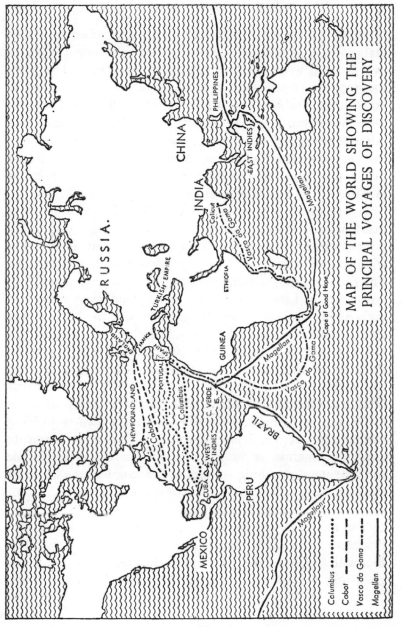

MAP OF THE WORLD SHOWING THE
PRINCIPAL VOYAGES OF DISCOVERY

Columbus ....
Cabot – – – – –
Vasco da Gama ‑ ‑ ‑ ‑ ‑
Magellan ————

RUSSIA.

CHINA

INDIA

TURKISH · EMPIRE

ETHIOPIA

PHILIPPINES

EAST INDIES

Colicut

Vasco da Gama

Magellan

Cape of Good Hope

GUINEA

Vasco da Gama

Magellan

ENGLAND

FRANCE

SPAIN

PORTUGAL

NEWFOUNDLAND

Cabot

Columbus

C. VERDE Is.

WEST INDIES

CUBA

BRAZIL

PERU

MEXICO

Magellan

tured by pirates off the French coast, and when he finally arrived in England and won the notice of Henry Tudor, the new King, it was too late. Christopher however had gathered the support of the joint Spanish sovereigns, Ferdinand of Aragon and Isabella of Castile, and under their patronage in 1492 he set sail into the unknown from Palos, in Andalusia. After a voyage of three months he made landfall in one of the islands of the Bahamas. Unwittingly he had discovered, not a new route to the East, but a new continent in the West, soon to be called America.

It was nearly a hundred years before England began to exert her potential sea-power. Her achievements during this period were by comparison meagre. The merchants of Bristol tried to seek a north-west passage beyond the Atlantic to the Far East, but they had little success or encouragement. Their colleagues in London and Eastern England were more concerned with the solid profits from trade with the Netherlands. Henry Tudor however appreciated private enterprise provided it did not involve him in disputes with Spain. He financed an expedition by John Cabot, who was a Genoese like Columbus and lived in Bristol. In 1497 Cabot struck land near Cape Breton Island. But there was little prospect of trade, and an immense forbidding continent seemed to block further advance. On a second voyage Cabot sailed down the coast of America in the direction of Florida, but this was too near the region of Spanish efforts. Upon Cabot's death the cautious Henry abandoned his Atlantic enterprise.

* * * * *

The arrival of the Spaniards in the New World, and their discovery of precious metals, had led them into wordy conflict with the Portuguese. As one of the motives of both countries was the spreading of the Christian faith into undiscovered heathen lands they appealed to the Pope, in whose hands the gift of new countries was at this time conceived to lie. By a series of Bulls in the 1490's the Borgia Pope Alexander VI drew a line across the world dividing the Spanish and Portuguese spheres. This remarkable dispensation stimulated the conclusion of a treaty between Spain and Portugal. A north–south line 370 leagues west of the Azores was agreed upon, and the Portuguese felt entitled to occupy Brazil.

Although the Portuguese were first in the field of oceanic adventure their country was too small to sustain such efforts. It is said that half the population of Portugal died in trying to hold their overseas possessions. Spain soon overtook them. In the year of Columbus's first voyage, Granada, the only Moorish city which survived on Spanish soil, had fallen to the last great Crusading army of the Middle Ages. Henceforward the Spaniards were free to turn their energies to the New World. In less than a generation a Portuguese captain, in Spanish pay, Magellan, set out on the voyage to South America and across the Pacific that was to take his ship round the globe. Magellan was killed in the Phillipines, but his chief officer brought his ship home round the Cape of Good Hope. The scattered civilisations of the world were being drawn together, and the new discoveries were to give the little kingdom in the northern sea a fresh importance. Here was to be the successor of both of Portugal and Spain, though the time for entering into the inheritance was not yet. But now the spices of the East were travelling by sea to the European market at Antwerp. The whole course of trade was shifted and revolutionised. The overland route languished; the primacy of the Italian cities was eclipsed by North-West Europe; and the future lay not in the Mediterranean, but on the shores of the Atlantic, where the new Powers, England,

France, and Holland, had ports and harbours which gave easy access to the oceans.

* * * * *

The wealth of the New World soon affected the old order in Europe. In the first half of the sixteenth century Cortes overcame the Aztec empire of Mexico and Pizarro conquered the Incas of Peru. The vast mineral treasures of these lands now began to pour across the Atlantic. By channels which multiplied gold and silver flowed into Europe. So did new commodities, tobacco, potatoes, and American sugar. The old continent to which these new riches came was itself undergoing a transformation. After a long halt its population was again growing and production on the farms and in the workshops was expanding. There was a widespread demand for more money to pay for new expeditions, new buildings, new enterprises, and new methods of government. The manipulation of finance was little understood either by rulers or by the mass of the people, and the first recourse of impoverished princes was to debase their currency. Prices therefore rose sharply, and when Luther posted his theses at Wittenberg the value of money was already rapidly falling. Under the impulse of American silver there now swept across the Continent a series of inflationary waves unparalleled until the twentieth century. The old world of landlords and peasants found it harder to carry on, and throughout Europe a new force gathered influence and honour with the overlords and began to exert its power. For merchants, traders, and bankers it was an age of opportunity. Most famous among them perhaps was the Fugger family of Germany, who gained a graceful reputation by placing their immense wealth at the service of Renaissance art. On their financial resourcefulness both Popes and Emperors at one time depended.

As ever in times of rapid inflation, there was much hardship and many difficulties in adjustment. But a strong sensation of new growth and well-being abounded, and ultimately every class benefited by the general amelioration. For a world which, a century before, had lost perhaps a third of its population by the Black Death there was a wonderful stimulus of mind and body. Men were groping their way into a larger age, with a freer interchange of more goods and services and with far greater numbers taking an effective part. The New World had opened its spacious doors, not only geographically by adding North and South America as places for Europe to live in, but by enlarging its whole way of life and outlook and the uses it could make of all it had.

The Tudor Dynasty

FOR a generation and more the English monarchy had been tossed on the rough waters of a disputed succession. On August 22, 1485, Henry Tudor, Earl of Richmond, had won a decisive victory near the small Midland town of Market Bosworth, and his rival, the usurper Richard III, was slain in the battle. In the person of Henry VII a new dynasty now mounted the throne, and during the twenty-four years of careful stewardship that lay before him a new era in English history began.

Henry's first task was to induce magnates, Church, and gentry to accept the decision of Bosworth and to establish himself upon the throne. He was careful to be crowned before facing the representatives of the nation, thus resting his title first upon conquest, and only secondly on the approbation of Parliament. At any rate, Parliament was committed to the experiment of his rule. Then he married, as had long been planned, the heiress of the rival house, Elizabeth of York.

Lack of money had long weakened the English throne, but military victory now restored to Henry most of the Crown lands alienated during the fifteenth century by confiscation and attainder, and many other great estates besides. He already possessed a valuable nucleus in the inheritance of the Lancastrian kings whose heir he was. The North Country estates of Richard, Duke of Gloucester, were his by right of conquest, and later the treason and execution of Sir William Stanley, who had been discontented with his rewards after

Bosworth, brought spacious properties in the Midlands into the royal hands. Henry was thus assured of a settled income.

But this was not enough. It was essential to regulate the titles by which land was held in England. The rapid succession of rival monarchs had produced a feeling of insecurity and legal chaos among the landowners. Execution and death in battle had shattered the power of the great feudal houses. The survivors and the mass of smaller landed gentry were in constant danger of losing their estates by actions in the law-courts started by personal enemies and based on past allegiances or treacheries. It was difficult to find a man whose family had not supported a losing side at some point or other during the civil wars. All this was extremely dangerous to Henry, for if the landowners were uncertain and insecure about the legal possession of their property they might follow another usurper if one should appear. Legislation was therefore passed stating that all who gave their allegiance to the King for the time being—that is, to the King upon the throne—should be secure in their lives and property. This idea of an actual King as distinct from a rightful King was characteristic of the new ruler. Sure of himself, he did not shrink from establishing his power upon a practical basis.

*   *   *   *   *

Then there were the frontiers. Throughout the history of medieval England there runs a deep division between North and South. In the South a more fully advanced society dwelt in a rich countryside with well-developed towns and a prosperous wool trade with Flanders and Italy. The Wars of the Roses had been a serious threat to this organised life, and it was in the South that Henry found his chief support. In the words of a chronicler, "he could not endure to see trade sick." He secured favourable terms for English merchants who traded with the Netherlands. Commerce was succoured by

peace. He put down disorder in the countryside, and representatives of the merchant classes co-operated with him in
Parliament. Henry's careful attention to this body sprang
from a real community of interests, the need for settled government. If this was despotism, it was despotism by consent.

The North was very different. Great feudal houses like the
Percys dominated the scene. The land was mountainous and
barren, the population lawless and turbulent. Communications were slow, and the King's authority was often ignored
and sometimes flouted. The long tradition of Border warfare with the Scots, the figures of the moss-troopers, and bal-
lads of cattle-raids and the burning of villages still survived.
Richard, Duke of Gloucester, had been popular in these
parts. His spirit was in harmony with the surroundings. In a
rough-and-ready fashion he had governed well, and the city
of York remained faithful to his memory even after Bosworth. Henry had not only to preserve order and authority in
these regions, but also to establish a secure frontier against
the Scots. As the new owner of the Gloucester estates he had
acquired a strategic base in the North. It was impossible to
govern England from London in the fifteenth century. The
machinery of administration was too primitive, and it was essential to delegate authority. Councils were accordingly established to administer the Northern parts and the Welsh
marches. Trusted servants were given wide powers of administration, and new officials who owed everything to their
master and were trained in the law now began to play a
decisive part in the work of government. They had always
been active in the King's household and the courts of law.
Now for the first time they had the ascendancy over the old
nobles of the feudal age. Such were men like Henry Wyatt,
the King's trusted agent in the North and captain of the key
castle of Berwick, and Edmund Dudley in the South; and

from them and their like the Sidneys, Herberts, Cecils, and Russells were descended.

The threat of internal disorder marched with the menace from beyond the sea. Henry had to keep ceaseless watch for the invasion of pretenders supported by foreign aid. His position depended upon his own political skill and judgment, and not on any hereditary sanction. The Court of Burgundy was a centre of plots against him, the Duchess being the sister of Richard III, and twice she launched pretenders against the Tudor régime. The first was Lambert Simnel, who finished ingloriously as a scullion in the royal kitchens. The second and more formidable was Perkin Warbeck, the son of a boatman and collector of taxes at Tournai, put forward as the younger of the princes murdered in the Tower. Backed by discontented Yorkist nobles in Ireland, by Burgundian money, Austrian and Flemish troops, and Scottish sympathy, Warbeck remained at large for seven years, plotting openly. Thrice he attempted to seize the English throne. But the classes who had backed the King since Bosworth stood by him. Warbeck's invasion of Kent was repulsed by the yokels before the military arrived, his attack from Scotland penetrated only four miles across the Border, and a Cornish rising in 1497 which he joined melted away. He fled to sanctuary, whence he was taken to London and kept in custody. Two years later, after two attempts at escape, he was executed, after confessing his guilt, on the scaffold at Tyburn. The affair ended in ignominy and ridicule, but the danger had been a real one.

Henry had many reasons to feel his throne shake a little beneath him. The Wars of the Roses had weakened English authority in Wales, but it was in Ireland that their effects were most manifest. The dynastic struggle had been eagerly taken up in Ireland; there were Lancastrians and Yorkists among the great Anglo-Irish families, and there were Lancastrian and Yorkist cities in the English Pale around Dublin and among remote outposts of the Englishry like Limerick and Galway. But all this turmoil was a mere continuation of clan feuds. The Butler family, under its hereditary chief, the Earl of Ormonde, was Lancastrian, because it had always been more loyal to the King of England than the rival house of Fitzgerald. The Fitzgeralds, led by the Earl of Kildare in Leinster and the Earl of Desmond in Munster, both having close alliances of blood and marriage with the native chiefs, were Yorkist in sympathy, because they thus hoped to promote their own aggrandisement.

In Munster the Desmond Fitzgeralds were already "more Irish than the Irish." In the Pale, Kildare, who was called "Garret More," or Great Earl, might perform his feudal duties and lead the English, but on his remoter lands on the Shannon a different rule prevailed. Lords Deputy from England found it profitless to assert their legal powers in face of Kildare's dominating local position and island-wide alliances. There was even a chance, unknown since the defeat and death of Edward Bruce, that his great house might provide a dynasty for all Ireland. But even if Kildare remained loyal to England would he adhere to a Yorkist king or a Lancastrian king? His kinsman Desmond supported Lambert Simnel; there was good reason to suspect that he himself supported Perkin Warbeck. Sir Edward Poynings, appointed Lord Deputy of Ireland in 1494, tried to limit his powers of mischief. He persuaded the Irish Parliament at Drogheda to pass the celebrated Poynings' Law, subordinating the Irish Parliament to the English, which was not repealed for three hundred years and remained a grievance till the twentieth century.

Kildare was attainted and sent over to London; but Henry was too wise to apply simple feudal justice to so mighty an offender, with his fighting clan on the outskirts of Dublin, and cousins, marriage-kin, and clients all over the island. The charges against the Great Earl were serious enough apart from his suspect favour to Perkin Warbeck. Had he not burned down the cathedral of Cashel? The Earl admitted it, but excused himself in a fashion that appealed to the King. "I did, but I thought that the Archbishop was inside." Henry VII accepted the inevitable with a dictum that is famous, if not authentic. "Since all Ireland cannot govern the Earl of Kildare, let the Earl of Kildare govern all Ireland." Kildare was pardoned, freed, married to the king's cousin, Elizabeth St John, and sent back to Ireland, where he succeeded Poynings as Lord Deputy.

Power in Ireland still rested on the ability to call out and command a sufficiency of armed men. In this the English King exercised a potent and personal influence. He could clothe with the royal insignia and status of Deputy any great noble who could muster and control the fighting men. On the other hand, by raising Butlers and Burkes the King could make it impossible for even a Kildare to control the great clan chiefs. This precarious and shifting balance was for a while the only road to establishing a central Government. No English king had yet found how to make his title of "Lord of Ireland" any more real than his title of "King of France."

But a powerful ally was at hand. Artillery, which had helped to expel the English from France, now aided their incursion into Ireland. The cannons spoke to Irish castles in a language readily understood. But the cannons came from England. The Irish could use but could not make them. Here for a time was the key to an English control over Irish affairs far beyond the outlook of Henry VII or Sir Edward Poynings. For generations the chiefs of the Fitzgeralds, from their half-Gaelic Court, had terrorised the Pale and kept to Irish eyes a more truly royal state than the harassed Deputies of the English monarch in Dublin Castle. Now in the advance of culture precedence was regulated by gunpowder.

* * * * *

Henry's dealings with Scotland are characteristic of his shrewd judgment. His first move was to shake the position of the Scottish King, James IV, by shipping armaments through Berwick to the baronial opponents of the Crown and by continual intrigues with the opposing factions. Border raids, as often in the past, troubled the peaceful relations of the two kingdoms, and an ugly situation arose when James lent his support to the Pretender Perkin Warbeck. But Henry's ultimate aims were constructive. He signed a truce with James which was confirmed by treaty. Although not obviously a man of imagination, he had his dreams. He may even have looked to the time when the everlasting fight between Scots and English would end and the ceaseless danger of a Franco-Scottish alliance which had threatened medieval England so often should be for ever broken. At any rate, Henry took the first steps to unite England and Scotland by marrying his daughter Margaret to James IV in 1502, and there was peace in the North until after his death.

With France too his policy was eminently successful. He realised that more could be gained by the threat of war than by war itself. Henry summoned Parliament to consent to taxation for a war against France, and proceeded to gather together a small army, which crossed to Calais in 1492 and besieged Boulogne. At the same time he entered into negotiations with the French king, who, unable to face Spain, the Holy Roman Emperor, and England simultaneously, was compelled to buy him off. Henry gained both ways. Like Edward IV, he pocketed not only a considerable subsidy from France, which was punctually paid, but also the taxes collected in England for war.

The most powerful new monarchy in Europe was Spain, recently forged into a strong state by the united efforts of Ferdinand of Aragon and Isabella of Castile and their successful warfare against the Moors. Their marriage marked the unification of the country. From 1489, when Henry's eldest son, Arthur, was betrothed to their daughter, the Infanta Catherine, England and Spain worked steadily together to secure booty from France—Spain in the form of territory, Henry as an annual tribute in cash, which amounted in the earlier years to about a fifth of the regular revenues of the Crown.

Henry VII as a statesman was imbued with the new, ruthless political ideas of Renaissance Europe. His youth, as an exile in foreign Courts with a price upon his head, had taught him much. He had watched marriage negotiations, treaties, the hire of professional men-at-arms to fight the battles of Louis XI and Charles of Burgundy, the regulation of trade, the relations between the national monarchies of France and the territorial nobility, between Church and State. Weighing and discussing the problems of the day, he sharpened his Welsh shrewdness with the refinements and exact analysis of practical politics, which were then reaching a high development among the Latin races.

He strove to establish a strong monarchy in England, moulded out of native institutions. Like his contemporary, Lorenzo de' Medici in Florence, Henry worked almost always by adaptation, modifying old forms ever so slightly, rather than by crude innovation. Without any fundamental constitutional change administration was established again on a firm basis. The King's Council was strengthened. It was given Parliamentary authority to examine persons with or without oath, and condemn them, on written evidence alone, in a manner foreign to the practice of the Common Law. The Court of the Star Chamber met regularly at Westminster, with the two

Chief Justices in attendance. It was originally a judicial committee of the King's Council, trying cases which needed special treatment because of the excessive might of one of the parties or the novelty or enormity of the offense. The complaints of the weak and oppressed against the rich and mighty, cases of retainer which involved keeping private armies of liveried servants, and of embracery, which meant corruption of juries—all these became their sphere.

But the main function of the King's Council was to govern rather than to judge. The choice of members lay with the monarch. Even when chosen they could not attend of right; they could be dismissed instantly; meanwhile they could stop any action in any court in England and transfer it to themselves, arrest anyone, torture anyone. A small inner committee conducted foreign affairs. Another managed the finances, hacking a new path through the cumbrous practices of the medieval Exchequer; treasurers were now appointed who were answerable personally to the King. And at the centre was the King himself, the embodiment of direct personal government, often authorising or auditing expenditure, even the most trifling, with great sprawling initials which may still be seen at the Record Office in London. Henry VII was probably the best business man to sit upon the English throne.

He was also a remarkably shrewd picker of men. Few of his Ministers came from the hereditary nobility; many were Churchmen; almost all were of obscure origin. Richard Fox, Bishop of Winchester, Chief Minister, and the most powerful man in England after the King, had been a schoolmaster at Hereford before he met Henry in Paris and they became companions in exile. Edmund Dudley was an under-sheriff of the City of London, who came under the King's notice in connection with the regulation of the Flanders wool trade. John Stile, who invented the first diplomatic cipher and was appointed Ambassador to Spain, began his career as a grocer or a mercer. Richard Empson was the son of a sieve-maker. Henry was at first not yet strong enough to afford mistakes. Daily, in all his leisure, he made notes on political affairs, on matters which required attention, "especially touching persons," whom to employ, to reward, to imprison, to outlaw, exile, or execute.

Like the other princes of his age, his main interest, apart from an absorbing passion for administration, was foreign policy. He maintained the first permanent English envoys abroad. Diplomacy, he considered, was no bad substitute for the violence of his predecessors, and early, accurate, and regular information was essential to its conduct. A spy system was organised even in England, and the excellence of Henry's foreign intelligence is described in a dispatch of the Milanese envoy to his master Duke Ludovic: "The King has accurate information of European affairs, from his own representatives, from the subjects of other countries in his pay, and from merchants. If your Highness should desire to send news to him it should be given either in special detail or before others can convey it." And again: "The change in affairs in Italy has altered him; not so much the dispute with the Venetian about Pisa, *about which the King has letters every day*, as the league which he understands has been made between the Pope and the King of France."

Also, like other princes, Henry built and altered. His chapel at Westminster and his palace at Richmond are superb monuments of his architectural taste. Though personally frugal, he maintained a calculated pageantry; he wore magnificent clothes, superb jewels, rich and glittering collars, and moved in public under a canopy of state, waited upon by noblemen, with a Court where about seven hundred persons dined daily in the Tower at his expense, entertained by jesters, minstrels, huntsmen, and his famous leopards.

How far Henry VII was a conscious innovator, turning

his back on ancient ways, is in dispute among historians. Even during the last years of the Wars of the Roses the Yorkist sovereigns were preparing the foundations of a new, powerful, and centralised State. Under Henry VII these thwarted hopes became realities. His skill and wisdom in transmuting medieval institutions into the organs of modern rule has not been questioned.

His achievement was massive and durable. He built his power amid the ruins and ashes of his predecessors. He thriftily and carefully gathered what seemed in those days a vast reserve of liquid wealth. He trained a body of efficient servants. He magnified the Crown without losing the co-operation of the Commons. He identified prosperity with monarchy. Among the princes of Renaissance Europe he is not surpassed in achievement and fame by Louis XI of France or Ferdinand of Spain.

It is often forgotten that almost all existing portraits of Henry VII are based upon a single death-mask, accurate no doubt as to features, but tending to give him a hard and grave appearance, which does not tally with any contemporary description. Yet they seem to accord with what is known of his character and career. The picture in the National Portrait Gallery is however dated four years before his death; and here his quick, hard grey eyes look out from an arched setting. Delicate, well-kept hands rest lightly upon the bottom of the frame. His lips are set tight, with a faint smile breaking the corners. There is an air of disillusionment, of fatigue, of unceasing vigilance, and above all of sadness and responsibility. Such was the architect of the Tudor monarchy, which was to lead England out of medieval disorder into greater strength and broader times.

King Henry VIII

THE age in which the young King Henry VIII grew up was, when seen from the perspective of later centuries, one in which an old order was dying. But it scarcely seemed so to those who lived in it. The change most visible to the eyes of a ruler was the creation of the modern European state system. This novelty, menacing and baffling, was no remote phenomenon. Across the Channel the new French monarchy had emerged much strengthened from the Hundred Years War. Louis XI and his son, Charles VIII, were no longer mere heads of a loosely integrated group of feudal principalities. They ruled a united and populous France from the Channel to the Mediterranean. The most formidable of French feudatories, the King of England, had been finally expelled from the land where his predecessors had been great lords and claimants to an equality with the house of France. Only Calais remained to the heir of William the Conqueror and Henry Plantagenet.

Meanwhile the cadet branch of the French royal line, the house of Burgundy, which had for nearly a century disputed the authority of the Kings of France, had come to an end with the death of Charles the Bold in 1477. Louis XI contrived to lay hands on Burgundy itself. All the rest of the Burgundian inheritance passed through the marriage of Mary of Burgundy to the Holy Roman Emperor Maximilian. Henceforth the Habsburgs controlled the duchies, counties, lordships, and cities that the Dukes of Burgundy had, with craft and fortune, acquired in the Netherlands and Belgium.

Now Habsburg and Valois confronted one another on the north-eastern frontiers of France. It was the opening of a long struggle. But although time was to show the instability of royal authority in France, the Valois kings ruled over a unity that could be called a French state. And the head of that state had come out of the long struggle with England doubly strengthened; he could now raise taxes from non-noble classes without any need to appeal to the Estates, and he had a permanent army. With his revenues he could hire Swiss infantry, make and maintain his great artillery park, and take into his pay the ardent chivalry of France.

One medieval state seemed to defy this process of aggregation and concentration. The Holy Roman Empire was visibly in dissolution. But for two generations past the Emperor had been the head of the house of Habsburg, and what arms could not do diplomacy and luck did. As Emperor, Maximilian was for ever illustrating the difference between reach and grasp, but he had married the greatest heiress in Europe. The house of Austria thus began to act on the maxim of gaining its major victories by marriage. In the next generation the counsel was followed with even more brilliant results, for the Archduke Philip, heir of Maximilian and Mary, married an even greater heiress than his mother, the Infanta Joanna, heir to Castile, Aragon, Sicily, and Naples. It was her sister who had accelerated the rise of the house of Tudor by marrying Prince Arthur and after him King Henry VIII.

In this world of growing power the King of England had to move and act with far fewer resources than his neighbours. His subjects numbered not many more than three millions. He had smaller revenues, no standing army, no state apparatus answerable only to the royal will. And yet by the mere proximity of France and the Imperial Netherlands England was forced to play a part in European politics. Her King was involved in wars and negotiations, shifts in alliances and changes in the balance of power, of which he had had little experience and could only in a secondary degree affect.

In this changing world, where battle on land was decided by the invincible Spanish infantry of Gonsalvo de Cordova, "the Great Captain," or occasionally by the Swiss infantry and the terrible cavalry of Gaston de Foix or other generals of the French king, the old politics, the old tried recipes of war and victory that had stood English kings in good stead for so long, were of little avail. And so for a century the rulers of England had to move warily, threatened with disaster and conscious of dangerous weakness if any shift of Continental politics should leave England alone in face of France or Spain.

*　　*　　*　　*　　*

Until the death of his elder brother, Prince Arthur, Henry had been intended for the Church. He had therefore been brought up by his father in an atmosphere of learning. Much time was devoted to serious studies—Latin, French, Italian, theology, music—and also to bodily exercise, to the sport of jousting, at which he excelled, to tennis, and hunting the stag. His manner was straightforward, and he impressed one of the cleverest women of the age, Margaret of Austria, Regent of the Netherlands, as a young man on whose word reliance could be placed. Owing to his father's careful savings he had at his accession more ready money than any other prince in Christendom. The ambassadors reported favourably on him. "His Majesty is the handsomest potentate I have ever set eyes on; above the usual height, with an extremely fine calf to his leg; his complexion fair and bright, with auburn hair combed straight and short in the French fashion, and a round face so very beautiful that it would become a pretty woman; his throat rather long and thick. . . . He speaks French, English, Latin, and a little Italian, plays well on the lute and harpsichord, sings from a book at sight, draws the bow with greater strength than any man in England, and jousts marvellously." "He is fond of hunting, and never takes his diversion without tiring eight or ten horses, which he causes to be stationed beforehand along the line of country he means to cover. He is extremely fond of tennis, at which game it is the prettiest thing in the world to see him play, his fair skin glowing through a shirt of the finest texture." [1]

Henry in his maturity was a tall, red-headed man who preserved the vigour and energy of ancestors accustomed for centuries to the warfare of the Welsh marches. His massive frame towered above the throng, and those about him felt in it a sense of concealed desperation, of latent force and passion. A French ambassador confessed, after residing for months at Court, that he could never approach the King without fear of personal violence. Although Henry appeared to strangers open, jovial, and trustworthy, with a bluff good humour which appealed at once to the crowd, even those who knew him most intimately seldom penetrated the inward secrecy and reserve which allowed him to confide freely in no one. To those who saw him often he seemed almost like two men, one the merry monarch of the hunt and banquet and procession, the friend of children, the patron of every kind of sport, the other the cold, acute observer of the audience chamber or the Council, watching vigilantly, weighing arguments, refusing except under the stress of great events to speak his own mind. On his long hunting expeditions, when the courier arrived with papers, he swiftly left

[1] Quoted from A. F. Pollard: *Henry VIII* (1919), pp. 39–40.

his companions of the chase and summoned the "counsellors attendant" for what he was wont to call "London business."

Bursts of restless energy and ferocity were combined with extraordinary patience and diligence. Deeply religious, Henry regularly listened to sermons lasting between one and two hours, and wrote more than one theological treatise of a high standard. He was accustomed to hear five Masses on Church days, and three on other days, served the priest at Mass himself, was never deprived of holy bread and holy water on Sunday, and always did penance on Good Friday. His zeal in theological controversy earned him from the Pope the title of "Defender of the Faith." An indefatigable worker, he digested a mass of dispatches, memoranda, and plans each day without the help of his secretary. He wrote verses and composed music. Profoundly secretive in public business, he chose as his advisers men for the most part of the meanest origin: Thomas Wolsey, the son of a poor and rascally butcher of Ipswich, whose name appears on the borough records for selling meat unfit for human consumption; Thomas Cromwell, a small attorney; Thomas Cranmer, an obscure lecturer in divinity. Like his father he distrusted the hereditary nobility, preferring the discreet counsel of men without a wide circle of friends.

Early in his reign he declared, "I will not allow anyone to have it in his power to govern me." As time passed his wilfulness hardened and his temper worsened. His rages were terrible to behold. There was no noble head in the country, he once said, "but he would make it fly," if his will were crossed. Many heads were indeed to fly in his thirty-eight years on the throne.

This enormous man was the nightmare of his advisers. Once a scheme was fixed in his mind he could seldom be turned from it; resistance only made him more stubborn; and, once embarked, he always tended to go too far unless restrained. Although he prided himself on his tolerance of any expression of opinion by his advisers, however outspoken, it was usually unwise to continue to oppose him after he had made up his mind. "His Highness," as Sir Thomas More put it to Wolsey, "esteemeth nothing in counsel more perilous than one to persevere in the maintenance of his advice because he hath once given it." The only secret of managing him, both Wolsey and Cromwell disclosed after they had fallen, was to see that dangerous ideas were not permitted to reach him. But arrangements of this sort could not be complete. His habit was to talk to all classes—barbers, huntsmen, his "yeoman cook to the King's mouth"—and particularly anyone, however humble, connected with the sea, to ferret out opinions, and ride off on hunting expeditions which sometimes lasted for weeks. He showed himself everywhere. Each summer he went on progress through the country, keeping close to the mass of his subjects, whom he understood so well.

Almost his first act, six weeks after the death of his father in 1509, was to marry his brother Arthur's widow, Princess Catherine of Aragon. He was aged eighteen and she was five years and five months older. She had made great efforts to fascinate him, and succeeded so well that while Ferdinand and Henry VII had made plans for the match long beforehand, and had obtained from the Pope a dispensation for a marriage within the degrees of affinity prohibited by the Church, there can be no doubt that Henry was eager to complete the proceedings. Catherine was at Henry's side during the first twenty-two years of his reign, while England was becoming a force in European affairs, perilous for foreign rulers to ignore. Until she reached the age of thirty-eight she remained, apart from three or four short lapses, the mistress of his affections, restrained his follies, and in her narrow way helped to guide public affairs between the intervals of her numerous confinements. Henry settled down to married life very quickly, in spite of a series of misfortunes which would have daunted a less robust character. The Queen's first baby was born dead, just after Henry's nineteenth birthday; another died soon after birth a year later. In all there were to be five such disappointments.

*   *   *   *   *

The King continued the standing alliance with his father-in-law, Ferdinand of Aragon, which had brought honour and wealth to England. He supported the Pope, and was sent the Golden Rose, the highest distinction which could be conferred on any Christian prince. He deliberated with his father's grave counsellors—William Warham, Lord Chancellor and Archbishop of Canterbury; Richard Fox, Bishop of Winchester; Thomas Ruthal, Bishop of Durham and royal Secretary—and under their guidance pursued for a short time the policy which his father had always favoured—isolation, provided that France continued to pay tribute. But Henry was on the edge of the vortex of Europe's new politics. Should he plunge in? The richest cities of Europe had changed hands many times during the last few years, paying tribute on each occasion. Frontiers were altering almost from month to month. Ferdinand of Aragon, Catherine's father, had conquered the Kingdom of Naples, and the two French border provinces of Cerdagne and Roussillon. Other princes had done nearly as well. Amid the alluring vistas of conquest which opened up before Henry his father's aged counsellors remained osbtinately men of peace. Henry VII had only once sent English levies abroad, preferring to hire mercenaries who fought alongside foreign armies. Henry VIII now determined that this policy should be reversed.

For some time he had been watching Dean Wolsey of Lincoln, a discovery of the Marquis of Dorset, whose sons had been to Magdalen College School at Oxford when Wolsey was the master there. Dorset had liked Wolsey well enough to invite him to stay for the Christmas holidays and had provided him with several livings. The young priest then obtained a post as chaplain to the Governor of Calais. Besides academic learning Wolsey possessed a remarkable aptitude for negotiation and finance—he had been bursar of Magdalen College—and Henry VII, sensing his abilities, had taken him over from the Governor and employed him on minor official business abroad. He was promoted by Henry VIII to the Council Board in November 1509, with the office of almoner to the royal household. He was then aged thirty-six.

Two years later Wolsey's growing influence may be perceived in the decision to join the Holy League against France, for it was in the same week that Wolsey signed his first documents as an executive member of the Council. He was put in charge of preparations for the war, and his former pupil, the young Marquis of Dorset, was Commander-in-Chief. France was preoccupied with Italian adventures, and Henry planned to reconquer Bordeaux, lost sixty years before, while King Ferdinand invaded Navarre, an independent kingdom lying athwart the Pyrenees, and the Pope and the republic of Venice operated against the French armies in Italy. The year was 1512, and this was the first time since the Hundred Years War that an English army had campaigned in Europe.

The English expedition to Gascony failed. Ferdinand took the whole of Navarre, and, according to Dr William Knight, the senior English Ambassador in Spain, showed great zeal, passing his cannon across the Pyrenees and inviting the English to join him in operations against France. But the Eng-

lish found that the style of warfare they had learned in the
Wars of the Roses, with long-bows and ponderously armed
mounted men, had become obsolete on the Continent. Both
Ferdinand and the French employed professional infantry,
Swiss and Austrian, who advanced at a great pace in solid
squares with eighteen-foot pikes bristling in every direction.
The primitive firearms of the day, known as arquebuses,
were too heavy and slow-firing to inflict serious damage on
these fast-moving squares. Ferdinand sent a great deal of military advice to Henry, and suggested that he should use his
gathered wealth to procure an overwhelming professional
force of his own. But, before Henry could adopt this plan,
Dorset's army, as unaccustomed to Gascon wine as to
French tactics, and ravaged by dysentery, disintegrated. The
troops refused to obey their officers and boarded the transports for home. Dorset abandoned a fruitless campaign and
followed them. After negotiations lasting throughout the
winter of 1512–13 Ferdinand and the Venetians deserted
Henry and the Pope and made peace with France. The
Holy League, they concluded, although high-sounding in
name, had proved futile as a political combination.

In England the responsibility for these failures was cast on
the new adviser, Wolsey. In fact it was in the hard work of
administration necessitated by the war that he had first
shown his abilities and immense energy. The lay members of
the Council however had from the beginning opposed a war
policy managed by a priest and had intrigued to get rid of
him. But Henry VIII and the Pope never wavered. Pope
Julius II, who had been besieged by a French force in Rome,
had excommunicated the entire French army, and now
grew a beard, an adornment then out of fashion, and swore
he would not shave until he was revenged on the King of
France. Henry, not to be outdone, also grew a beard. It was

auburn, like his hair. He arranged to hire the Emperor Maximilian, with the Imperial artillery and the greater part of the Austrian army, to serve under the royal standard of England. The Emperor, we are told, was requested to spread his standard, but refused to do so, saying he would be the servant, for the campaign, of the King and St George.

These arrangements, though costly, were brilliantly successful. Under Henry's command, the English, with Austrian mercenaries, routed the French in August 1513 at the Battle of the Spurs, so called because of the rapidity of the French retreat. Bayard, the most famous knight in Europe, was captured, together with a host of French notables. Tournai, the richest city of all North-East France, surrendered at the mere sight of the Imperial artillery, and was occupied by an English garrison. To crown all, Queen Catherine, who had been left behind as Regent of England, sent great news from the North.

To aid their French ally the Scots in the King's absence had crossed the Tweed in September and invaded England with an army of fifty thousand men. Thomas Howard, Earl of Surrey, son of Richard III's Duke of Norfolk, slain at Bosworth, and still under the family attainder, was none the less entrusted with the command. This skilful veteran, the only experienced general left in England after Dorset's failure, knowing every inch of the ground, did not hesitate to march round the Scottish army, and, although outnumbered by two to one, placed himself between the enemy and Edinburgh. At Flodden Field a bloody battle was fought on September 9, 1513. Both armies faced their homeland. The whole of Scotland, Highland and Lowland alike, drew out with their retainers in the traditional schiltrons, or circles of spearmen, and around the standard of their King. The English archers once again directed upon these redoubtable masses a long, intense, and murderous arrow storm. Moreover, the bills or axes in the hands of English infantry were highly effective against the Scottish spears in hand-to-hand assault, while the English cavalry awaited the chance of piercing the gaps caused by slaughter. When night fell the flower of the Scottish chivalry lay in their ranks where they had fought, and among them King James IV. This was the last great victory gained by the long-bow. Surrey was rewarded by the restoration of the Norfolk dukedom. In Scotland a year-old child succeeded to the throne as James V. His mother, the Regent, was Henry's sister Margaret, and peace now descended on the Northern border for the greater part of the reign.

Fitting celebrations were arranged in Brussels by the Emperor's daughter, Margaret of Austria. Henry, now twenty-two, was permitted to spend whole nights dancing "in his shirt" with the leading beauties of the Imperial Court. "In this," the Milanese Ambassador reported, "he performs wonders, leaping like a stag." The Council had forbidden gaming and the presence of women in the English lines, but "for him," the Ambassador added, "the Austrians provide everything." His rewards were princely; he never sat down to the table without losing in a royal manner, and the chief personalities were gratified with rich presents.

Cardinal Wolsey

DURING the autumn of 1513 the French were hard-pressed from all sides. Wolsey, through the Emperor, hired a Swiss army, which invaded Burgundy by way of Besançon, the fortress capital of Franche-Comté, a part of the Burgundian inheritance that had passed into Habsburg hands. Dijon was captured. The French had no troops of their own which could resist the Swiss, and doubled their *taille* to hire fresh mercenaries from abroad. Henry had every intention of renewing his campaign in France in 1514, but his successes had not been to the liking of Ferdinand of Spain. Ferdinand now set about making a separate peace with France, into which he also tried to draw the Emperor Maximilian.

Faced with the defection of his allies, Henry was quick to launch a counter-stroke. First he looked to the defences of the realm, and took measures to strengthen his navy. Then he sought and obtained a favorable peace treaty with France, thereby securing exactly double the amount of annual tribute that had been paid to his father. The crowning event of the peace was the marriage between Henry's young sister, Mary, and Louis XII himself. She was seventeen, he was fifty-two. The story runs that she extracted from her brother the promise that if she married this time for diplomacy she would be free next time to marry for love. Promise or no promise, that is what she did. She was Queen of France for three months; then, as Queen Dowager, and to Henry's displeasure, she cut short her widowhood by marrying Charles Brandon, Duke of Suffolk. But in this case the royal wrath subsided and Henry VIII joined in the wedding festivities. The marriage ultimately bore tragic fruit: a grandchild was the Lady Jane Grey, who was for ten days to be Queen of England.

* * * * *

Among those who had crossed with the bridal retinue to France was a young girl named Mary Boleyn. She was one of three nieces of the Duke of Norfolk, all of whom successively engaged the dangerous and deadly love of Henry VIII. Mary and her sister Anne had been educated in France at an expensive academy attached to the French Court. On her return to England Mary married William Carey, a Gentleman of the Bedchamber, and before long became the King's mistress. Her father was upon this favour created Lord Rochford, while her sister, Anne, continued her studies in France.

Wolsey was richly rewarded for the foreign successes. He received the Bishopric of Lincoln during the course of the negotiations; then, after the peace terms were settled, the Archbishopric of York; and, a year later, after long negotiation by the King on his behalf, in September 1515, a cardinal's hat. This shower of ecclesiastical honours did not however give Wolsey sufficient civil authority, and in December 1515 Henry created him Lord Chancellor in place of Warham, whom he forced to resign the Great Seal.

For fourteen years Wolsey in the King's name was the effective ruler of the realm. He owed his position not only to his great capacity for business, but to his considerable personal charm. He had "an angel's wit," one of his contemporaries wrote, for beguiling and flattering those whom he wished to persuade. In the King's company he was brilliant, convivial, and "a gay seeker out of new pastimes." All this commended him to his young master. Other would-be counsellors of Henry's saw a different side of the Cardinal's character. They resented being scornfully overborne by him in debate; they detested his arrogance, and envied his evergrowing wealth and extensive patronage. At the height of his influence Wolsey enjoyed an income equivalent to about £500,000 a year in early twentieth-century money. He kept one thousand servants, and his palaces surpassed the King's in splendour. He loaded profitable favours upon his relations, including his illegitimate son, who held eleven Church appointments, and their incomes, while still a boy. These counts against him gradually added up in the course of years. But for the time being—and it was for a long time, as Chief Ministers go—he successfully held in his grasp an accumulation of power that has probably never been equalled in England.

The King's popularity rose with the achievements of his reign. There were many of course who grumbled at the war taxes imposed during the previous two years; but while pouring money into pageantry and magnificence Wolsey managed to tap new sources of revenue. Henry's subjects were taxed much as they had been under his father, which was more lightly than any other subjects in Europe. Indeed, the North of England, which had to support billeting and Border warfare, was excused taxation altogether.

Successes abroad enabled Wolsey to develop Henry VII's principles of centralised government. During the twelve years that he was Lord Chancellor Parliament met only once, for two sessions spreading over three months in all. The Court of Star Chamber grew more active. It developed new and simple methods copied from Roman law, by which the Common Law rules of evidence were dispensed with, and persons who could give evidence were simply brought in for interrogation, one by one, often without even the formality of an oath. Justice was swift, fines were heavy, and no one in England was so powerful that he could afford to flout the Star Chamber. When a common soldier of the Calais garrison

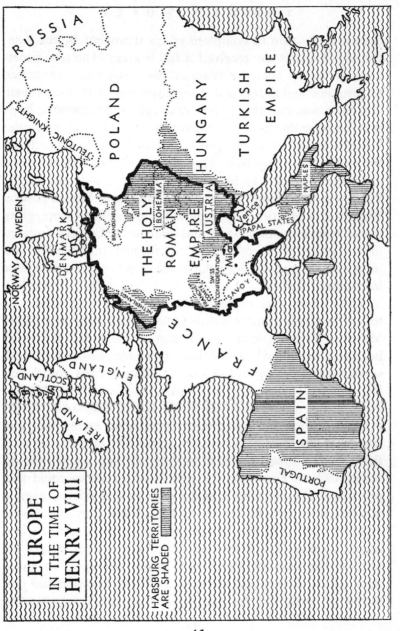

EUROPE
IN THE TIME OF
HENRY VIII

HABSBURG TERRITORIES
ARE SHADED

RUSSIA

POLAND

TEUTONIC KNIGHTS

SWEDEN

NORWAY

DENMARK

BRANDENBURG

THE HOLY ROMAN EMPIRE

BOHEMIA

HUNGARY

TURKISH EMPIRE

AUSTRIA

Venice

PAPAL STATES

NAPLES

Milan

SW. SS
CONFEDERATION

SAVOY

NETHERLANDS

FRANCE

SCOTLAND

ENGLAND

IRELAND

SPAIN

PORTUGAL

once sent his wife to complain of his treatment by the Lord Deputy of Calais she received a full hearing. The new generation grown up after the Wars of the Roses was accustomed to royal law and order, and determined that it should prevail.

Thus it was that this system of arbitrary government, however despotic in theory, however contrary to the principles believed to lie behind Magna Carta, in fact rested tacitly on the real will of the people. Henry VIII, like his father, found an institution ready to his hand in the unpaid Justice of the Peace, the local squire or landlord, and taught him to govern. Rules and regulations of remarkable complexity were given to the Justice to administer; and later in the century Justices' manuals were produced, which ran through innumerable editions and covered almost every contingency which could arise in country life.

The Tudors were indeed the architects of an English system of local government which lasted almost unchanged until Victorian times. Unpaid local men, fearless and impartial, because they could rely on help from the King, dealt with small matters, sitting in the villages often in twos and threes. Bigger matters such as roads and bridges and sheep-stealing came before quarter sessions in the appropriate town. It was a rough justice that the country gentlemen meted out, and friendship and faction often cut across the interests of both the nation and the Crown. If in the main they carried the directions of the Crown to the people, the Justices could also on occasion, by turning a deaf ear to official advice, express popular resistance to the royal will. What they did in the counties they could also sometimes do in the House of Commons. Even as Tudor rule advanced towards its climax the faithful Members of Parliament were not afraid to speak their minds. Wolsey saw the dangers of the situation and preferred to work out his policy without the unappreciative counsel of Parliament. Henry VIII and Thomas Cromwell learned to handle the Commons with discretion, though even then resistance was not unknown. But in spite of occasional friction, and even riot and rebellion in the countryside, it was on the whole a working partnership. Crown and community alike recognised what the partnership had achieved and what it had to offer.

*　*　*　*　*

Within a few years of his accession Henry embarked upon a programme of naval expansion, while Wolsey concerned himself with diplomatic manœuvre. Henry had already constructed the largest warship of the age, the *Great Harry,* of 1,500 tons, with "seven tiers one above the other, and an incredible array of guns." The fleet was built up under the personal care of the sovereign, who ordered the admiral to send word to him in minute detail "how every ship did sail," and was not content until England commanded the Narrow Seas. Wolsey's arrangements for the foreign service were hardly less remarkable. A system of couriers and correspondents was organised over Western Europe, through whom news was received in England as quickly as during the wars of Marlborough or Wellington. The diplomatic service which Henry VII had organised with such care was used as a nucleus, supplemented by the ablest products of the New Learning at Oxford, including Richard Pace, John Clerk, and Richard Sampson, the last two destined to become bishops later in the reign. The dispatches of this period, at the height of the Renaissance, are as closely knit and coloured as any in history; each event, the size of armies, rebellions in Italian cities, movements within the College of Cardinals, taxes in France, is carefully weighed and recorded. For some years at least Wolsey was a powerful factor and balancing weight in Europe.

The zenith of this brilliant period was reached at the Field of the Cloth of Gold in June 1520, when Henry crossed the Channel to meet his rival, Francis I of France, for the first time. Henry's main perplexity was, we are told, about his appearance; he could not decide how he would look best, in his beard as usual or clean-shaven. At first he yielded to Catherine's persuasion and shaved. But directly he had done so he regretted the step and grew the beard again. It reached its full luxuriance in time to create a great impression in France.

At the Field of the Cloth of Gold, near Guîsnes, the jousting and feasting, the colour and glitter, the tents and trappings, dazzled all Europe. It was the last display of medieval chivalry. Many noblemen, it was said, carried on their shoulders their mills, their forests, and their meadows. But Henry and Francis failed to become personal friends. Henry, indeed, was already negotiating with Francis's enemy, the new Emperor Charles V, who had lately succeeded his grandfather, Maximilian. At Guîsnes he attempted to outdo Francis both by the splendour of his equipment and the cunning of his diplomacy. Relying on his great physical strength, he suddenly challenged Francis to a wrestling match. Francis seized him in a lightning grip and put him on the ground. Henry went white with passion, but was held back. Although the ceremonies continued Henry could not forgive such a personal humiliation. He was, in any case, still seeking friends elsewhere. Within a month he had concluded an alliance with the Emperor, thus forfeiting the French tribute. When the Emperor declared war on Francis English wealth was squandered feverishly on an expedition to Boulogne and subsidies to mercenary contingents serving with the Emperor. Wolsey had to find the money. When Kent and the Eastern Counties rose against a species of capital levy imposed by Wolsey in the second year of war, and absurdly mis-named the "Amicable Grant," the King pretended he did not know of the taxation. The Government had to beat a retreat, and the campaign was abandoned. Wolsey now got the King's consent to make secret overtures for peace to Francis.

These overtures were Wolsey's fatal miscalculation; only six weeks later the Imperial armies won an overwhelming victory over the French at Pavia, in Northern Italy. After the battle the entire peninsula passed into the hands of the Em-peror. Italy was destined to remain largely under Habsburg domination until the invasions of Napoleon. But although Francis himself was taken prisoner and crushing terms of peace were imposed on France, England did not share in the spoils of victory. Henry could no longer turn the scales in Europe. The blame was clearly Wolsey's, and the King de-cided that perhaps the Cardinal had been given too free a hand. He insisted on visiting the great new college which Wol-sey was building at Oxford, Cardinal College, destined to be-come Christ Church, the largest and most richly endowed in the university. When he arrived he was astonished at the vast sums which were being lavished upon the masonry. "It is strange," he remarked to the Cardinal, "that you have found so much money to spend upon your college and yet could not find enough to finish my war."

Up till now he had been inseparable from Wolsey. In 1521 he had sent to the scaffold the Duke of Buckingham, son of Richard III's Buckingham, and close in line of succession to the throne. His crime had been leading the opposition of the displaced nobility to the King's chosen Chancellor. But after Pavia Henry began to have second thoughts. Perhaps, he de-cided, Wolsey would have to be sacrificed to preserve the popularity of the monarch. Then there was Queen Catherine. In 1525 she was aged forty. At the Field of the Cloth of Gold, five years before, King Francis had mocked at her behind the scenes with his courtiers, saying she was already "old and deformed." A typical Spanish princess, she had matured and aged rapidly; it was clear that she would bear Henry no male heir. Either the King's illegitimate son, the Duke of Richmond, now aged six, would have to be appointed by Act of Parliament, or perhaps England might accept Catherine's child, Mary, now aged nine, as the first Queen of England in her own right since Matilda. It was still doubtful if a woman could succeed to the throne by English law. Would England tolerate being ruled by a woman? Might Mary not turn out very like her Spanish mother, narrow and bigoted, a possible queen perhaps in Spain, or France, or Austria, countries full of soldiers, but not acceptable to the free English, who had obeyed Henry VII and Henry VIII because they wished to obey, and although there was no central army except the Beef-eaters in the Tower? Would Mary be able to rule in the Tudor manner, by favour and not by force?

The long clash of the Wars of the Roses had been a nightmare to the nation which a disputed succession might revive. To the monarch these great questions of State were also questions of conscience, in which his sensual passions and his care for the stability of the realm were all fused together. They perplexed Henry for two more years. The first step, clearly, was to get rid of Catherine. In May 1527 Cardinal Wolsey, acting as Papal Legate and with the collusion of the King, held a secret ecclesiastical court at his house in Westminster. He summoned Henry to appear before him, charged with having married his deceased brother's wife within the degrees of affinity prohibited by the laws of the Church. Henry's authority had been a Bull of dispensation obtained by Ferdinand and Henry VII in 1503, which said in effect that since the marriage between Catherine and Arthur had not been consummated Catherine was not legally Henry's deceased brother's wife and Henry could marry Catherine. Although Catherine, on the advice of successive Spanish ambassadors, maintained to her dying day that her marriage with Arthur had not been consummated, nobody was convinced. She had lived under the same roof with Prince Arthur for seven months.

After hearing legal argument for three days the court decided that the point should be submitted to a number of the most learned bishops in England. Several bishops replied however that provided Papal dispensation had been secured such a marriage was perfectly lawful. Henry then tried to persuade Catherine herself that he and she had never been legally married, that they had lived in mortal sin for eighteen years. He added that as he intended to abstain from her company in future he hoped she would retire far from Court. Catherine burst into tears and firmly refused to go away.

About a fortnight later Wolsey crossed the Channel to conduct prolonged negotiations for a treaty of alliance with France. While Wolsey was away Henry became openly infatuated with Anne Boleyn. Since she had returned from school in France Anne had grown into a vivacious, witty woman of twenty-four, very slender and frail, with beautiful black eyes and thick black hair so long that she could sit on it, which she wore flowing loose over her shoulders. "Mistress Anne," wrote the Venetian Ambassador, "is not the handsomest woman in the world. She is of middle height, dark-skinned, long neck, wide mouth, rather flat-chested." She had a fiery temper, was outspoken and domineering, and although not generally liked soon gained a small following, many of them noted for their leanings towards the new religious doctrines of Luther. We first hear of Anne Boleyn at Court in a dispatch of the Imperial Ambassador dated August 16, 1527, four months after Henry had begun proceedings for the annulment of his marriage. Did he plan the divorce and then find Anne? Or had he arranged to marry Anne from the beginning? We shall never know, for Henry was very secretive in his private matters. "Three may keep counsel," he observed a year or two later, "if two be away; and if I thought my cap knew my counsel I would cast it into the fire and burn it." His love letters were secured by Papal agents, and are now in the Vatican library, but, while prettily phrased, they are undated, and disclose little except that Anne Boleyn kept him waiting for nearly a year.

Henry had been carefully guarded by Wolsey and Catherine. He had had mistresses before, but never openly. The appearance at Court of a lady with whom he spent hours at a time created an extraordinary stir. Together Anne and Henry arranged to send a special royal ambassador to Pope Clement VII, independently of the resident ambassador chosen by Wolsey, to seek not only annulment of the King's marriage, but also a dispensation to marry again at once. Dr William Knight, now over seventy, was brought forth from retirement to undertake this delicate mission. Two entirely different sets of instructions were prepared for Knight. One made no mention of the proposed new marriage and was to be shown to Wolsey as he passed through Compiègne on his way to Rome; the other was the one on which Knight was to act. Wolsey was shown the dummy instructions as arranged, and at once saw that they had been drafted by ignorant laymen. He hurried home to have the instructions altered, and thus learned all. But although he now took over the management of the negotiations every expedient proved fruitless. The Papal Legate, Cardinal Campeggio, who was sent to England to hear the case used all possible pretexts to

postpone a decision. Now that Italy had fallen to the Habsburgs the Pope was at the mercy of the Imperial soldiery.
In 1527 they shocked Europe by seizing and sacking Rome.
The Pope was now practically a prisoner of Charles V, who
was determined that Henry should not divorce his aunt.

This broke Wolsey. New counsellors were called in. A follower of the Duke of Norfolk, Dr Stephen Gardiner, was appointed Secretary to the King. Soon after this appointment
Dr Cranmer, a young lecturer in divinity at Cambridge and
a friend of the Boleyns, made a helpful new suggestion to
Gardiner, that the question whether the King had ever been
legally married should be withdrawn from the lawyers and
submitted to the universities of Europe. The King at once took
up the idea. Cranmer was sent for and complimented. Letters
and messengers were dispatched to all the universities in
Europe. At the same time the King had the writs sent out for a
Parliament, the first for six years, to strengthen his hand in the
great changes he was planning. Norfolk and Gardiner, not
Wolsey, completed the arrangements. Wolsey retired in disgrace to his diocese of York, which he had never visited. On
one occasion he came to Grafton to see the King. But when
he entered he found that Anne was there, Norfolk insulted
him to his face, and he was dismissed without an audience.

On October 9, 1529, Wolsey's disgrace was carried a step
farther by an indictment in the King's Bench under one of
the Statutes of Præmunire, passed in the reign of Richard II.
These Acts of Parliament were designed to uphold the jurisdiction of the royal courts against the Church courts, and
had been one of Wolsey's favourite instruments for exacting
money for the King for technical offences. They provided
that anyone who obtained in the court of Rome or elsewhere
any transfers of cases to Rome, processes, sentences of excommunication, Bulls, instruments, or "any other things

whatsoever which touch, the King, against him, his crown and regalty, or his realm," should lose the royal protection and forfeit all his goods to the King. While the proceedings were going forward in King's Bench, Norfolk and Suffolk came to Wolsey to take away the Great Seal as a mark that he was no longer Lord Chancellor. But Wolsey protested, saying that he had been made Chancellor for life. Next day they came again, bearing letters signed by the King. When they had gone with the seal the great Cardinal broke down, and was found seated, weeping and lamenting his misfortunes.

Anne was determined however to ruin him. She had set her heart on York Place, the London residence of the Archbishops of York, which was, she decided, of a convenient size for her and Henry; large enough for their friends and entertainments, yet too small to permit Queen Catherine to live there also. Anne and her mother took the King to inspect the Cardinal's goods in York Place, and Henry was incensed by the wealth which he found. The judges and learned counsel were summoned and the King asked how he could legally obtain possession of York Place, which had been regarded as belonging to the Archbishops of York in perpetuity. The judges advised that Wolsey should make a declaration handing over York Place to the King and his successors. A judge of the King's Bench was accordingly sent to Wolsey. A member of his household, George Cavendish, has left an account of the Cardinal's last days. According to him Wolsey said, "I know that the King of his own nature is of a royal stomach. How say you, Master Shelley? May I do it with justice and conscience, to give that thing away from me and my successors which is none of mine?" The judge explained how the legal profession viewed the case. Then said the Cardinal, "I will in no wise disobey, but most gladly fulfil and accomplish his princely will and pleasure in all things, and in especial in this matter, inasmuch as ye, the fathers of the law, say that I may lawfully do it. Howbeit I pray you show his Majesty from me, that I most humbly desire his Highness to call to his most gracious remembrance that *there is both Heaven and Hell.*"

Henry cared nothing for the fulminations of a Cardinal. Threats merely made him take more sweeping measures. The charge under Præmunire was supplemented by a charge of traitorous correspondence with the King of France, conducted without the King's knowledge. Five days after Wolsey had been found guilty under Præmunire the Earl of Northumberland came to the castle of the Archbishop of York at Cawood, near York, and, trembling, said in a very faint and soft voice, "My lord, I arrest you of high treason." "Where is your commission?" quoth the Cardinal. "Let me see it." "Nay, sir, that you may not," replied the Earl. "Well, then," said the Cardinal, "I will not obey your arrest." Even as they were debating this matter there came in Councillor Walshe, and then said the Cardinal, "Well, there is no more to do. I trow, gentleman, ye be one of the King's privy chamber; your name, I suppose, is Walshe; I am content to yield unto you, but not to my Lord of Northumberland without I see his commission. And also you are a sufficient commissioner yourself in that behalf, inasmuch as ye be one of the King's privy chamber; for the worst person there is a sufficient warrant to arrest the greatest peer of this realm by the King's only commandment, without any commission."

As Wolsey journeyed back to London, where the cell in the Tower used by the Duke of Buckingham before his execution was again being placed in readiness, he fell ill, and when he neared Leicester Abbey for the night he told the monks who came out to greet him, "I am come to leave my bones among you." About eight in the morning two days later he sank into a last decline, murmuring to those gathered at the bedside, "If I had served God as diligently as I have done the King He would not have given me over in my grey hairs." Soon afterwards he died; and they found next to his body a shirt of hair, beneath his other shirt, which was of very fine linen holland cloth. This shirt of hair was unknown to all his servants except his chaplain.

Wolsey's high offices of State were conferred on a new administration: Gardiner secured the Bishopric of Winchester, the richest see in England; Norfolk became President of the Council, and Suffolk the Vice-President. During the few days that elapsed until Wolsey was replaced by Sir Thomas More as Lord Chancellor the King applied the Great Seal himself to documents of State. With the death of the Cardinal political interests hitherto submerged made their bid for power. The ambition of the country gentry to take part in public affairs in London, the longing of an educated, wealthy Renaissance England to cast off the tutelage of priests, the naked greed and thirst for power of rival factions, began to shake and agitate the nation. Henry was now thirty-eight years old.

The Break with Rome

CRANMER'S idea of an appeal to the universities about Henry's marriage to Catherine had proved a great success, and the young lecturer was rewarded with an appointment as Ambassador to the Emperor. Even the University of Bologna in the Papal States declared that the King was right and that the Pope could not set aside so fundamental a law. Many others concurred: Paris, Toulouse, Orleans, Padua, Ferrara, Pavia, Oxford, and Cambridge. The King had known all along that he was right, and here, it seemed, was final proof. He determined to mark his displeasure with the Pope by some striking measure against the power of the Church of England. Why, he asked, was the right of sanctuary allowed to obstruct the King's justice? Why were parsons permitted to live far away from their parishes and hold more than one living while underpaid substitutes did the work for the absentees? Why did Italians enjoy the revenues of English bishoprics? Why were the clergy demanding fees for probate on wills and gifts on the death of every parishioner? The King would ask his learned Commons to propose reforms.

Some years earlier, in 1515, a celebrated case had shaken the Church in England. A London merchant tailor, Richard Hunne, had stood out against Church fees, and the dispute had expanded into a bold challenge to ecclesiastical authority.

As a result Hunne was arrested, and imprisoned by the clergy in the Lollards' Tower, where he was subsequently found hanged. Was it suicide or murder? Opposition in Parliament and the City grew in volume, and reached up to the Bishop of London himself. But these early rumblings of a Reformation had been silenced by the then immovable power of Wolsey. Now the Commons eagerly resumed their interrupted task. A committee was formed of all the lawyers in the House, and they drafted the necessary Bills in record time. The House of Lords, where the bishops and abbots still had more votes than the lay peers, agreed to the Bills reforming sanctuaries and abolishing mortuary fees, which affected the lower clergy only, but when the Probate Bill came up to the Lords the Archbishop of Canterbury "in especial," and all the other bishops in general, both frowned and grunted. Fisher, Bishop of Rochester, a representative of the old school, warned the Lords that religious innovation would bring social revolution in its train. He pointed to the national Czech revolt led by John Huss.

"My lords," he said, "you see daily what Bills come here from the Commons house, and all is for the destruction of the Church. For God's sake see what a realm the kingdom of Bohemia was; and when the Church went down, then fell the glory of the kingdom. Now with the Commons is nothing but *down with the Church*, and all this meseemeth is for lack of faith only."

The Commons soon heard of this bold speech, and Members pointed out the implication of the last words—that laws the Commons made were laws made by pagans and heathen people and not worthy to be kept. They formed a deputation of thirty leading Members, headed by the Speaker, and went off to complain to the King. Henry summoned the offending bishops and asked Fisher to explain. Fisher shuffled. He had only meant, he declared, that the Bohemians lacked faith, not the Commons. With this interpretation the other bishops agreed. "But this bland excuse," we are told, "pleased the Commons nothing at all." Sharp exchanges took place before the Probate Bill could be forced through the Lords, and rancour grew. Thus from the outset the Reformation House of Commons acquired a corporate spirit, and during its long life, longer than any previous Parliament, eagerly pursued any measure which promised revenge against the bishops for what it deemed their evasion and duplicity over the Probate Bill. Hostility to the Episcopate smouldered, and marked the Commons for more than a hundred years.

The King was already delighted with what they had done, and went about telling everybody, including the Imperial Ambassador. "We have issued orders," he said, "for the reform of the clergy in our kingdom. We have already clipped their claws considerably by taking away from them several taxes imposed by their own excessive authority on our subjects. We are now about to undertake the Annates [the first year's income which the bishops paid to Rome on consecration] and prevent ecclesiastics from holding more than one benefice." But he made it clear at once that he remained fully orthodox in matters of doctrine, that he was merely adhering to the principle of Colet and other leading divines whom he had known in his youth, that men could be Catholic though critical of Papal institutions. "If Luther," he declared, "had confined himself to denouncing the vices, abuses, and errors of the clergy, instead of attacking the sacraments of the Church and other divine institutions, we should all have followed him and written in his favour." After this blunt though reasoned statement the negotiations in Rome for annulling the King's marriage encountered even greater obstacles. But Henry all his life was only spurred by opposition, and he determined to show he was in earnest.

During December 1530 the Attorney-General charged the whole body of the clergy with breaking the fourteenth-century Statutes of Præmunire and Provisors which had been passed to limit the powers of the Pope. This they had done by acquiescing in Wolsey's many high-handed actions in his rôle as Papal Legate. Henry, after defeating the bishops in the matter of probate by enlisting the support of Parliament, knew that Convocation would not defy him. When the Papal Nuncio intervened to stiffen them against the King all the clergy present were astonished and scandalised. Without allowing him even to open his mouth they begged him to leave them in peace, since they had not the King's leave to speak with him. In return for a pardon for contravening Præmunire and Provisors the King extracted large sums from Convocation, £100,000 from the province of Canterbury and £19,000 from York, which was much more than at first they were prepared to pay. After further negotiation he also obtained a new title. On February 7, 1531, the clergy acknowledged that the King was "their especial Protector, one and supreme lord, and, as far as the law of Christ allows, even supreme head."

Parliament, which had been prorogued from month to month since the great doings about probate in 1529, was now recalled to hear and disseminate the royal view on the divorce. Lord Chancellor More came down to the House and said, "There are some who say that the King is pursuing a divorce out of love for some lady, and not out of any scruple of conscience; but this is not true," and he read out the opinions of twelve foreign universities and showed a hundred "books" drawn up by doctors of strange regions, all agreeing that the King's marriage was unlawful. Then the Lord Chancellor said, "Now you of this Commons house may report in your counties what you have seen and heard, and then all men shall openly perceive that the King hath not attempted this matter of will or pleasure, as some strangers report, but only for the discharge of his conscience and surety of the succession of his realm."

Throughout these proceedings Queen Catherine remained at Court. The King, although he rode and talked openly with Anne, left Catherine in charge of his personal wardrobe, including supervision of the laundry and the making of his linen. When he required clothes he continued to apply to Catherine, not Anne. Anne was furiously jealous, but for months the King refused to abandon his old routine. A new attempt was then made by the Boleyn party to persuade Catherine to renounce her rights. On June 1, 1531, she was waited on by Norfolk, Suffolk, and Gardiner, Anne's father, now Earl of Wiltshire, Northumberland, and several others. As before she refused to renounce anything. Finally, about the middle of July, Anne took the King on a long hunting expedition, away from Windsor Castle, longer than any they had ever made together. Catherine waited, day after day, until a month had gone by, but still there was no news of the King's return. At last the messenger came: the King would come back. But his Majesty did not wish to see the Queen; she was commanded to retire instantly to Wolsey's former palace at Moor, in Hertfordshire. Henceforward she and her daughter Mary were banished from Court.

*　　*　　*　　*　　*

The winter of 1531–32 was marked by the tensest crisis of Henry's reign. A form of excommunication, or even interdict, had been drafted in Rome, ordering the King to cast off his concubine Anne within fifteen days, only the penalties being left blank. The shadow of Papal wrath hung over England. At Court Christmas was kept with great solemnity. "All men," states a chronicler, "said there was no music in that Christmas, because the Queen and ladies were absent." But, as in the dark days in the early part of the reign, after the failure of the Bordeaux expedition, the King pursued his inflexible course to the end. Opposition merely confirmed him in his plans. The Annates Bill of which he had boasted to the Imperial Ambassador was drafted as a fighting measure, in case the worst occurred. It armed the King for a greater struggle with the Papacy than had preceded Magna Carta. If the Court of Rome, its preamble ran, endeavoured to wield excommunication, interdict, or process compulsory in England, then all manner of sacraments and divine service should continue to be administered, and the interdict should not by any prelate or minister be executed or divulged. If any one named by the King to a bishopric were restrained by Bulls from Rome from accepting office he should be consecrated by the Archbishop, or any one named to an Archbishopric. And the Annates, a mainstay of the Papal finances, were limited to 5 per cent of their former amount.

This was the most difficult Bill which Henry ever had to steer through Parliament. He was obliged to go down to the House of Lords himself at least three times, and even then seemed likely to fail, until he thought of an entirely new expedient—the first public division of the House. "He thought of a plan that those among the Members who wished for the King's welfare and the prosperity of the kingdom (as they call it) should stand on one side of the House and those who opposed the measure on the other. For fear of the King's indignation a number of them went over," and with considerable amendment the Bill was passed.

The next step was to make the clergy submit to the royal

supremacy. Henry got the Commons to prepare a document called the Supplication against the Ordinaries, directed against the authority of Church courts. "Ordinaries" was the legal term for bishops and their deputies who enjoyed rights of jurisdiction. Although Convocation was truculent at first, making submission only in vague and ambiguous terms, Henry refused to compromise, and at the third attempt they agreed to articles of his own, making him effective master of the Church in England. On the very afternoon these articles were submitted for the royal consent, May 16, 1532, Sir Thomas More resigned the Lord Chancellorship as a protest against royal supremacy in spiritual affairs. He had tried to serve his sovereign faithfully in everything; now he saw that Henry's courses must inevitably conflict with his own conscientious beliefs.

Thus the English Reformation was a slow process. An opportunist King measured his steps as he went, until England was wholly independent of administration from Rome. Wolsey had done much to prepare the way. He had supported the Papacy during some of its most critical years, and in return had been allowed to exercise wide and sweeping powers which were usually reserved to the Pope himself or to one of his visiting legates. England therefore was more accustomed than any other province of Christendom to Papal jurisdiction being vested in one of its own priests, and this made it easier to transfer it to the Crown. Wolsey had also brought Papal authority in his own person nearer to men's lives than it had ever been, and this unsought familiarity bred dislike. The death in August of old Archbishop Warham, principal opponent of the King's divorce, opened further possibilities and problems. Henry did not hasten to appoint a successor. He had to consider how far he could go. If there were a struggle could any of his bishops be trusted to forget the oath which they had sworn to the Pope at their consecration? Would there be a rebellion? Would the Emperor, Queen Catherine's nephew, invade England from the Low Countries? Could the King rely on French neutrality?

In order to weigh these factors at first hand the King went over to Boulogne with only a few friends, including Anne Boleyn, for personal discussion with Francis I. He returned reassured. Confident that he could carry through even the most startling appointment to Canterbury, he recalled Cranmer from his embassy. Cranmer had been married twice, the second time in Germany after ordination, in the new German fashion for priests, to the niece of a well-known Lutheran. Since the marriage of priests was still illegal in England, Cranmer's wife went ahead in disguise. Cranmer himself took leave of the Emperor at Mantua on November 1st, 1532, and left the following day, arriving in London in the middle of December. A week later he was offered the Archbishopric of Canterbury. He accepted. Henceforward, until Henry died, Cranmer's wife was always hidden, and if she accompanied him was obliged, according to popular repute, to travel with the luggage in a vast chest specially constructed to conceal her.

A month later Henry secretly married Anne Boleyn. Historians have never discovered for certain who performed the ceremony, or where. Cranmer himself was not the priest. Both he and the Imperial Ambassador reported subsequently that the marriage had taken place in January 1533. Undoubtedly, in the eyes of the Roman Catholic world, Henry VIII committed bigamy, for he had been married nearly twenty-five years to Catherine of Aragon, and his marriage had not yet been annulled in Rome, or even in England, by any court or any public act. He simply assumed he had never been legally married at all, and left the lawyers and clergy to put the matter right afterwards.

Cranmer became Archbishop in the traditional manner. At the King's request Bulls had been obtained from Rome by threatening the Papacy with a rigorous application of the act of Annates. Cranmer swore to obey the Pope with the usual oath, though reservations were made before and afterwards, and he was consecrated with the full ceremonial. This was important: the man who was to carry through the ecclesiastical revolution had thus been accepted by the Pope and endowed with full authority. Two days afterwards however a Bill was introduced into Parliament vesting in the Archbishop of Canterbury the power, formerly possessed by the Pope, to hear and determine all appeals from the ecclesiastical courts in England. Future attempts to use any foreign process would involve the drastic penalties of Præmunire. The judgments of the English courts were not to be affected by any Papal verdict or by excommunication, and any priest who refused to celebrate divine service or administer the sacraments was made liable to imprisonment. This momentous Bill, the work of Thomas Cromwell, which abolished what still remained of Papal authority in England, passed through Parliament in due course, and became known as the Act of Appeals. The following month Henry himself wrote a letter describing his position as "King and Sovereign, recognising no superior in earth but only God, and not subject to the laws of any earthly creature." The breach between England and Rome was complete.

Having established his supremacy, Henry proceeded to exploit it. In March 1533 Convocation was asked two questions: Was it against the Law of God, and not open to dispensation by the Pope, for a man to marry his brother's wife, he being dead without issue, but having consummated the marriage? Answer by the prelates and clergy present: Yes. By Bishop Fisher of Rochester: No. Was Prince Arthur's marriage with Queen Catherine consummated? Answer by the clergy: Yes. By the Bishop: No. Thereupon the Bishop was arrested and committed to the Tower. About ten days later the Duke of Norfolk with royal commissioners waited on Queen Catherine at Ampthill. Every sort of reason was advanced why she should renounce her title voluntarily. She was blocking the succession. Her daughter would not be accepted by the country as Queen, and England might be plunged in chaos if she continued her unreasonable obstruction. If she resigned a great position would still be open to her. She refused to resign. Then she was informed of the decisions of Convocation. Steps would be taken to deprive her of the rank of Queen, to which she was no longer entitled. She declared her determination to resist. But the Commissioners had still another announcement to make. Catherine was in any case Queen no longer, for the King was already married to Anne Boleyn.

Thus Henry's secret marriage became known. A fortnight later Cranmer opened a court at Dunstable, and set a proctor to Ampthill citing Catherine to appear. She refused. In her absence the Archbishop pronounced judgment. Catherine's marriage with Henry had existed in fact but not in law; it was void from the beginning; and five days afterwards the marriage with Anne was declared valid. Queen Anne Boleyn was crowned on June 1 in Westminster Abbey.

The following month it became clear that the new Queen was expecting a child. As the confinement approached Henry remained with her at Greenwich, and took the greatest care she should not be disturbed. Much bad news came in from across the seas and frontiers, but on such occasions Henry rode out into the country and met the Council in the open, to prevent the Queen from conjecturing the gravity of the situation, or perhaps to avoid the plague. A magnificent and valuable bed, which had lain in the Treasury since it had formed part of a French nobleman's ransom, was brought forth, and in it on September 7, 1533, the future Queen Elizabeth was born.

Although bonfires were lighted there was no rejoicing in Henry's heart. A male heir had been his desire. After he had defied the whole world, perhaps committed bigamy, and risked deposition by the Pope and invasion, here was only a second daughter. "Do you wish to see your little daughter?" the old nurse asked, according to one account. "My daughter, my daughter!" replied the King in a passion. "You old devil, you witch, don't dare to speak to me!" He galloped at once away from Greenwich, away from Anne, and in three days had reached Wolf Hall, in Wiltshire, the residence of a worthy old courtier, Sir John Seymour, who had a clever son in the diplomatic service and a pretty daughter, a former Maid of Honour to Queen Catherine. Jane Seymour was about twenty-five, and although she was attractive no one considered her a great beauty. "Her skin," reported the Imperial Ambassador, "is so whitish that it may be called rather pale. She is not very clever, and is said to be rather arrogant." But she was gay, and generally liked, and Henry fell in love with her.

After the birth of Elizabeth criticism of the King and his ecclesiastical measures could no longer be stifled. If the choice was between two princesses, men said, then why not choose Mary, the legitimate one? But the King would have none of this argument. An Act was passed vesting the succession in Elizabeth. In March 1534 every person of legal age, male or female, throughout the kingdom was forced to swear allegiance to this Act and renounce allegiance to all foreign authority in England. The clergy were prohibited from preaching unless specially licensed; a Bidding prayer [1] was prescribed for use in all churches, containing the words, "Henry VIII being immediately next unto God, the only and supreme head of this Catholic Church of England, and Anne his wife, and Elizabeth daughter and heir to them both, our Princess." To publish or pronounce maliciously by express words that the King was a tyrant or heretic was made high treason. As the brutality of the reign increased many hundreds were to be hanged, disembowelled, and quartered on these grounds.

Fisher and Sir Thomas More, who both refused the oath, were confined in the Tower for many months. At his trial More offered a brilliant defence, but the King's former trust in him had now turned into vengeful dislike. Under royal pressure the judges pronounced him guilty of treason. While Fisher was in the Tower the Pope created seven cardinals, of whom one was "John, Bishop of Rochester, kept in prison by the King of England." Directly Henry heard the news he declared in anger several times that he would send Fisher's head to Rome for the Cardinal's hat. Fisher was executed in June 1535 and More in July. For their fate the King must bear the chief responsibility; it is a black stain on his record. Shortly afterwards Henry was excommunicated and in theory deprived of his throne by the Pope.

The resistance of More and Fisher to the royal supremacy in Church government was a noble and heroic stand. They realised the defects of the existing Catholic system, but they hated and feared the aggressive nationalism which was destroying the unity of Christendom. They saw that the break with Rome carried with it the threat of a despotism freed

[1] A Bidding prayer was one requested of the congregation in favour of certain persons or objects nominated by the King.

from every fetter. More stood forth as the defender of all that was finest in the medieval outlook. He represents to history its universality, its belief in spiritual values, and its instinctive sense of other-worldliness. Henry VIII with cruel axe decapitated not only a wise and gifted counsellor, but a system which, though it had failed to live up to its ideals in practice, had for long furnished mankind with its brightest dreams.

*   *   *   *   *

The King was still paying court to Jane Seymour when it became known that Anne was expecting another baby. But this time Henry refused to have anything to do with her. She was haggard and ill and had lost her freshness. Rumours were current at Court that he had only spoken to her ten times in three months, although formerly he could hardly bear to be separated from her for an hour. Anne became distracted with anxiety, and was obsessed with fears of a rising against her and the infant Elizabeth in favour of Catherine and Mary. Without consulting the King or his Council, she sent messages to Mary through her governess, making all sorts of promises if Mary would swear to the Act of Succession and renounce her claim to the throne. Promises were followed by threats; but Mary refused to give way. One day, after an unfavourable report from the governess, Anne was found in a tempest of tears. Soon afterwards her uncle, the Duke of Norfolk, strode into the room and told her that Henry had had a serious accident out hunting. In her grief and alarm she nearly fainted. Five days later she miscarried.

The King, instead of pitying her, gave way to an uncontrollable outburst of rage. He visited her, repeating over and over again, "I see that God does not mean me to have male children." As he turned to leave he added angrily that he would speak to her again as soon as she was better. Anne replied that it was not her fault she had failed to bear another child. She had been frightened when she heard of the King's fall; besides, she loved him so passionately, with so much more fervour than Catherine, that it broke her heart when she saw that he gave his love to others. At this allusion to Jane the King left the room in a towering passion, and refused for days to see her. Jane Seymour was installed at Greenwich. Through her serving-man, who had been taken into the pay of the Imperial Ambassador, we have a story of the royal courtship.

One day the King sent a page down from London with a purse full of gold and a letter in his own handwriting. Jane kissed the letter, but returned it to the page unopened. Then, falling on her knees, she said, "I pray you beseech the King to understand by my prudence that I am a gentlewoman of good and honourable family, without reproach, and have no greater treasure in the world than my honour, which I would not harm for a thousand deaths. If the King should wish to make me a present of money, I beg him to do so when God shall send me a husband to marry." The King was greatly pleased. She had, he said, displayed high virtue, and to prove that his intentions were wholly worthy of her he promised not to speak to her in future except in the presence of her relations.

In January 1536 Queen Catherine died. If the King was minded to marry again he could now repudiate Queen Anne without raising awkward questions about his earlier union. It was already rumoured by the Seymour party that in her intense desire for an heir Queen Anne had been unfaithful to the King soon after the birth of Elizabeth, with several lovers. If proved, this offence was capital. The Queen had accordingly been watched, and one Sunday two young courtiers, Henry Norris and Sir Francis Weston, were seen to enter the Queen's room, and were, it was said, overheard making love to her. Next day a parchment was laid before the King empowering a strong panel of counsellors and judges, headed by the Lord Chancellor, or any four of them, to investigate and try every kind of treason. The King signed. On Tuesday the Council sat all day and late into the night, but as yet there was not sufficient evidence. The following Sunday a certain Smeaton, a gentleman of the King's chamber, who played with great skill on the lute, was arrested as the Queen's lover. Smeaton subsequently under torture confessed to the charge. On Monday Norris was among the challengers at the May Day tournament at Greenwich, and as the King rode to London after the jousting he called Norris to his side and told him what was suspected. Although Norris denied everything he also was arrested and taken to the Tower.

That night Anne learned that Smeaton and Norris were in the Tower. The following morning she was requested to come before the Council. Although her uncle, the Duke of Norfolk, presided at the examination, no Queen of England, Anne complained afterwards, should have been treated with such brutality. At the conclusion of the proceedings she was placed under arrest, and kept under guard until the tide turned to take her up-river to the Tower. So quickly had the news spread that large crowds collected along the river-bank, and were in time to watch her barge rowing rapidly upstream with a detachment of the guard, her uncle Norfolk, and the two Chamberlains, Lord Oxford and Lord Sandys, on board. At the Traitor's Gate she was handed over to the Constable of the Tower, Sir William Kingston.

The same evening, at York Palace, when the Duke of Richmond, the King's bastard son, came as usual to say goodnight to his father, the King burst into tears. "By God's great mercy," he said, "you and your sister Mary have escaped the hands of that damned poisonous strumpet. She was plotting to poison you both." Henry tried to forget his shame and disgrace in a ceaseless round of feasting. "His Majesty," wrote the Imperial Ambassador, who however may well be suspected of malicious bias, "has been gayer since the arrest than ever before. He is going out to dinner here, there, and everywhere with the ladies. Sometimes he returns along the river after midnight to the sound of many instruments or the voices of the singers of his chamber, who do their utmost to interpret his delight at being rid of that thin old woman." (In fact she was aged twenty-nine.) "He went to dinner recently with the Bishop of Carlisle and some ladies, and next day the Bishop told me that he had behaved with almost desperate gaiety."

On Friday morning the special commissioners of treason appointed the previous week, including Anne Boleyn's father, the Earl of Wiltshire, and the entire bench of judges except one, formed the court for the trial of Anne's lovers. A special jury consisting of twelve knights had been summoned, and found the prisoners guilty. They were sentenced to be hanged, drawn, and quartered, but execution was deferred until after the trial of the Queen. This opened the following Monday in the Great Hall of the Tower. Twenty-six peers—half the existing peerage—sat on a raised dais under the presidency of the Duke of Norfolk, named Lord High Steward of England for the occasion. The Lord Chancellor, Sir Thomas Audley, who as a commoner by birth was not entitled to judge a Queen, sat next to the Duke to give legal advice. The Lord Mayor and a deputation of aldermen attended, with members of the public, by the King's command, in the well of the hall. The Queen was brought in by Sir Edmund Walsingham, the Lieutenant of the Tower, to listen to the indictment by the Attorney-General. She was charged with being unfaithful to the King; promising to marry Norris after the

King was dead; giving Norris poisoned lockets for the purpose of poisoning Catherine and Mary; and other offences, including incest with her brother. The Queen denied the charges vigorously, and replied to each one in detail. The peers retired, and soon returned with a verdict of guilty. Norfolk pronounced sentence: the Queen was to be burnt or beheaded, at the King's pleasure.

Anne received the sentence with calm and courage. She declared that if the King would allow it she would like to be beheaded like the French nobility, with a sword, and not, like the English nobility, with an axe. Her wish was granted; but no executioner could be found in the King's dominions to carry out the sentence with a sword, and it was found necessary to postpone the execution from Thursday to Friday while an expert was borrowed from St Omer, in the Emperor's dominions. During Thursday night she slept little. Distant hammering could be heard from the courtyard of the Tower, as a low scaffold, about five feet high, was erected for the execution. In the morning the public were admitted to the courtyard; and the Lord Chancellor entered soon afterwards with Henry's son, the Duke of Richmond, Cromwell, and the Lord Mayor and aldermen.

On May 19, 1536, the headsman was already waiting, leaning on his heavy two-handed sword, when the Constable of the Tower appeared, followed by Anne in a beautiful night robe of heavy grey damask trimmed with fur, showing a crimson kirtle beneath. She had chosen this garment in order to leave her neck bare. A large sum had been given to her to distribute in alms among the crowd. "I am not here," she said to them simply, "to preach to you, but to die. Pray for the King, for he is a good man and has treated me as well as could be. I do not accuse anyone of causing my death, neither the judges nor anyone else, for I am condemned by the law of the land and die willingly." Then she took off her pearl-covered headdress, revealing that her hair had been carefully bound up to avoid impeding the executioner.

"Pray for me," she said, and knelt down while one of the ladies-in-waiting bandaged her eyes. Before there was time to say a Paternoster she bowed her head, murmuring in a low voice, "God have pity on my soul." "God have mercy on my soul," she repeated, as the executioner stepped forward and slowly took his aim. Then the great blade hissed through the air, and with a single stroke his work was done.

As soon as the execution was known Henry appeared in yellow, with a feather in his cap, and ten days later was privately married to Jane Seymour at York Place. Jane proved to be the submissive wife for whom Henry had always longed. Anne had been too dominating and too impulsive. "When that woman desires anything," one of the ambassadors had written of Anne two years before her execution, "there is no one who dares oppose her, or could do so if he dared, not even the King himself. They say that he is incredibly subject to her, so that when he does not wish her to do what she wishes she does it in spite of him and pretends to fly into a terrible rage." Jane was the opposite, gentle though proud; and Henry spent a happy eighteen months with her. She was the only Queen whom Henry regretted and mourned, and when she died, still aged only twenty-two, immediately after the birth of her first child, the future Edward VI, Henry had her buried with royal honours in St George's Chapel at Windsor. He himself lies near her.

The End of the Monasteries

THOUGH all had been bliss at Court while Jane was Queen rural England was heavy with discontents. Henry was increasingly short of revenue and Church properties offered a tempting prize. Just before Anne's trial he had gone down to the House of Lords in person to recommend a Bill suppressing those smaller monasteries which contained fewer than twelve monks. There were nearly four hundred of them, and the combined rent of their lands amounted to a considerable sum. The religious orders had for some time been in decline, and parents were becoming more and more averse to handing over their sons to the cloisters. Monks turned to the land in search of recruits, and often waived the old social distinctions, taking the sons of poor tenant farmers. But the number of novices was rarely sufficient. At some houses the monks had given up all hope of carrying on, and squandered the endowments, cutting down woods, pawning the plate, and letting the buildings fall into disrepair or ruin. Grave irregularities had been discovered by the ecclesiastical Visitors over many years. The idea of suppression was not altogether new: Wolsey had suppressed several small houses to finance his college at Oxford, and the King had since suppressed over twenty more for his own benefit. Parliament made little difficulty about winding up the smaller houses, when satisfied that their inmates were either to be transferred to large houses or pensioned off. During the summer of 1536 royal commissioners toured the country, completing the dissolution as swiftly as possible.

The King had now a new chief adviser. Thomas Cromwell, in turn mercenary soldier in Italy, cloth agent, and money-lender, had served his apprenticeship in statecraft under Wolsey, but he had also learned the lessons of his master's downfall. Ruthless, cynical, Machiavellian, Cromwell was a man of the New Age. His ambition was matched by his energy and served by a penetrating intelligence. When he succeeded Wolsey as the King's principal Minister he made no effort to inherit the pomp and glory of the fallen Cardinal. Nevertheless his were more solid achievements in both State and Church. In the administration of the realm Cromwell devised new methods to replace the institutions he found at hand. Before his day Government policy had for centuries been both made and implemented in the royal household. Though Henry VII had improved the system he had remained in a sense a medieval king. Thomas Cromwell thoroughly reformed it during his ten years of power, and when he fell in 1540 policy was already carried out by Government departments, operating outside the Household. Perhaps his greatest accomplishment, though not so dramatic as his other work, was his inception of the Government service of modern England. Cromwell is the uncommemorated architect of our great departments of State.

As First Minister Cromwell handled the dissolution of the monasteries with conspicuous, cold-blooded efficiency. It was a step which appealed to the well-to-do. The high nobility and country gentry acquired on favourable terms all kinds of fine estates. Sometimes a neighbouring merchant, or a syndicate of City men and courtiers, bought or leased the confis-

cated lands. Many local squires had long been stewards of
monastic lands, and now bought properties which they had
managed for generations. Throughout the middle classes
there was great irritation at the privileges and wealth of the
Church. They resented the undue proportion of the national
income engrossed by those who rendered no economic service. The King was assured of the support of Parliament and
the prosperous classes. Most of the displaced monks, nearly
ten thousand in all, faced their lot with relief or fortitude, assisted by substantial pensions. Some even married nuns, and
many became respectable parish clergy. The dissolution
brought lands into the Crown's possession worth at the time
over £100,000 a year, and by the sale or lease of the rest
of the former monastic properties the Crown gained a million and a half—a huge sum for those days, though probably much less than the properties were worth. The main
result of this transaction was in effect, if not in intention, to
commit the landed and mercantile classes to the Reformation settlement and the Tudor dynasty.

The immediate impact on the masses is more difficult to
judge. There does not seem to have been any widespread unemployment or distress among the sturdy proletariat, but
many poor, weak, and ailing folk, especially in the North,
who had found their only succour in the good works of the
monastic orders, were left untended for a long time.

In the North also, where the old traditions died hard, the
new order aroused stiffer resistance than in the South, and
the new lay landlord could be harsher than his clerical predecessor. But laymen were not the only enclosing landlords, and
more than one pre-Reformation abbot had sought by one
means or another to improve farming and husbandry through
enclosure. English agriculture, to meet the demands of a

growing population and an expanding cloth industry, was turning from arable farming to pasture. Hence the broad acres on the ecclesiastical estates were now fertilised by the ideas and the money of their new owners, the country gentlemen and merchants. The Reformation is sometimes blamed for all the evils attributed to the modern economic system. Yet these evils, if such they were, had existed long before Henry VIII began to doubt the validity of his marriage to Catherine of Aragon. Thomas More, who did not live to see events run their course, had already in *Utopia* outlined to his contemporaries the sharp features of the new economy.

In the field of religious belief the Reformation brought profound change. The Bible now acquired a new and far-reaching authority. The older generation considered that Holy Writ was dangerous in the hands of the unlearned and should only be read by priests. "I never read the Scripture," said the Duke of Norfolk, "nor never will read it. It was merry in England afore the new learning came up: yea, I would all things were as hath been in time past." But complete printed Bibles, translated into English by Tyndal and Coverdale, had appeared for the first time late in the autumn of 1535, and were now running through several editions. The Government enjoined the clergy to encourage Bible-reading, and there were well-founded rumours that Thomas Cromwell, the King's vicegerent in spiritual affairs, had helped to promote the translation. Preaching, even by licensed preachers, was altogether suspended until Michaelmas, except in the presence of a bishop, and in August 1536 Cromwell ordered the Paternoster and Commandments to be taught in the mother tongue instead of in Latin. Next year *The Institution of a Christian Man,* prepared by Cranmer for popular edification, displayed a distinct leaning to the New Opinion. Here indeed was a change and a revelation. The country folk were deeply agitated, particularly in the fiercely Catholic and economically backward North.

*   *   *   *   *

In the autumn, when the new taxes came to be assessed after Michaelmas, farmers and yokels collected in large numbers throughout the North of England and Lincolnshire, swearing to resist the taxes and maintain the old order in the Church. The revolt, which took the name of "the Pilgrimage of Grace," was spontaneous. Its leader, a lawyer named Robert Aske, had his position thrust upon him. The nobles and higher clergy took no part. Although the rebels greatly outnumbered the loyal levies, and the King had no regular troops except the Yeomen of the Guard, Henry at once showed what Wolsey had called his "royal stomach." He refused to compromise with rebellion. When his Commissioners of Taxes were taken prisoners by the rebels in Lincolnshire he sent a terrifying message:

"This assembly is so heinous that unless you can persuade them to disperse and send a hundred of their ringleaders with halters round their necks to the Lieutenant to do with them as shall be thought best . . . we see no way to save them. For we have already sent . . . the Duke of Suffolk, our Lieutenant, . . . with a hundred thousand men, horse and foot, in harness, with munitions and artillery. . . . We have also appointed another great army to invade their territories as soon as they are out of them, and to burn, spoil, and destroy their goods, wives, and children with all extremity."

After this the Commissioners reported that the common people as a whole were prepared to recognise the King as Supreme Head of the Church and to allow him for this once to have the first-fruits and the tenths from the clergy together with the subsidy he was demanding. "But," they

· 75 ·

said, "he shall have no more money of the commons during his life, nor shall he suppress no more abbeys." They still protested against the King's choice of counsellors, and demanded the surrender of Cromwell, Cranmer, and four bishops who were suspected of heresy.

The King replied with vigour. "Concerning choosing of Counsellors, I never have read, heard, nor known that princes' counsellors and prelates should be appointed by rude and ignorant common people. . . . How presumptuous then are ye, the rude commons of one shire, and that one of the most brute and beastly of the whole realm, and of least experience, to find fault with your Prince. . . . As to the suppression of religious houses, know that this is granted us by all the nobles, spiritual and temporal, of this our realm, by Act of Parliament, and not set forth by any counsellors upon their mere will and phantasy as you full falsely would persuade our realm." If they did not submit, the King added, they with their wives and children would be utterly destroyed by the sword. The Yorkshire rebels had much the same aims, as their oath shows: "For the love I do bear unto Almighty God's faith I swear . . . to expulse all villein blood and evil counsels against the Commonwealth from His Grace and his Privy Council, to keep afore me the Cross of Christ, in my heart His faith, the restitution of the Church, the suppression of these heretics and their opinions."

In early 1537 the rebellion collapsed as quickly as it had arisen, but Henry determined to make examples of the ringleaders. Seventy were hanged as traitors at Carlisle Assizes alone, and when Norfolk, the victorious general, seemed inclined to clemency the King sent word that he desired a large number of executions. Altogether some two hundred and fifty of the insurgents were put to death.

The rebels had objected to the taxes and the suppression

of the monasteries. Henry now replied by tightening up the collection of taxes, and began suppressing the larger monasteries the moment the revolt was put down. As a further blow to the old school the Government commissioned in Paris a great printing of English Bibles, more sumptuous than any previous edition, and in September 1538 directed that every parish in the country should purchase a Bible of the largest volume in English, to be set up in each church, where the parishioners might most commodiously resort to the same and read it. Six copies were set up in St Paul's, in the City of London, and multitudes thronged the cathedral all day to read them, especially, we are told, when they could get any person that had an audible voice to read aloud. This Bible has remained the basis of all later editions, including the Authorised Version prepared in the reign of James I.

*　*　*　*　*

Up to this point Thomas Cromwell had consistently walked with success. But he now began to encounter the conservatism of the older nobility. They were more than content with the political revolution, but they wanted the Reformation to stop with the assertion of the royal supremacy, and they opposed the doctrinal changes of Cranmer and his following. The Duke of Norfolk headed the reaction, and the King, who was rigidly orthodox, except where his lusts or interests were stirred, agreed with it. Stephen Gardiner, Bishop of Winchester and later Queen Mary's adviser, was the brain behind the Norfolk party. Its leaders took pains to point out that France and the Emperor might invade England and execute the sentence of deposition which the Pope had pronounced. The King himself was anxious to avoid a total religious cleavage with the European Powers. The Catholic front seemed overwhelmingly strong, and the only allies which Cromwell could find abroad were minor

German princelings. With these large issues in their keeping, Norfolk's faction vigilantly awaited their chance. It came, like so much of the action of this memorable reign, as a result of the conjugal affairs of the King.

As Henry refused to compromise with the Continental Lutherans on matters of doctrine or modifications of the Church services, Cromwell could do no more than seek a political alliance with the Lutheran princes of Northern Germany, bring over learned Lutheran divines, and negotiate a German marriage for one of the English princesses, or even for Henry himself. The King was now a widower. One Continental house he considered marrying into was the Duchy of Cleves, which to some extent shared his own attitude in religion, hating the Papacy, yet restricting Lutheranism. Then news arrived of a startling diplomatic development. The French and Imperial Ambassadors waited together on the King to inform him that Francis I had invited the Emperor Charles V, who was in his Spanish dominions, to pass through Paris on his way to put down a revolt at Ghent, and the Emperor had accepted. The two sovereigns had resolved to forget old grudges and make common cause.

An alliance with the princes of Northern Germany against the two Catholic monarchs now seemed imperative, and negotiations for a marriage between Henry and Anne, the eldest Princess of Cleves, were hurried on. Anne's charms, Cromwell reported, were on everybody's lips. "Everyone," he announced, "praises her beauty both of face and body. One says she excels the Duchess of Milan as the golden sun does the silver moon." Holbein, the Court painter, and a masterly delineator of his age, had already been sent over to paint the portrait, which may now be seen in the Louvre. It does not flatter the Princess. "This," the English Ambassador at Cleves warned the King, "is a very lively image."

Anne, he added, spoke only German, spent her time chiefly in needlework, and could not sing or play any instrument. She was thirty years old, very tall and thin, with an assured and resolute countenance, slightly pockmarked, but was said to possess wit and animation, and did not over-indulge in beer.

Anne spent Christmas at Calais, waiting for storms to abate, and on the last day of the year 1539 arrived at Rochester. Henry had sailed down in his private barge, in disguise, bearing a fine sable fur among the presents. On New Year's Day he hurried to visit her. But on seeing her he was astonished and abashed. Embraces, presents, compliments, all carefully arranged on the voyage, were forgotten. He mumbled a few words and returned to the barge, where he remained silent for many minutes. At last he said very sadly and pensively, "I see nothing in this woman as men report of her, and I marvel that wise men should have made such report as they have done." "Say what they will," he told Cromwell on his return, "she is nothing fair. The personage is well and comely, but nothing else. . . . If I had known before as much as I know now she would not have come within this realm." Privately he dubbed her "the Flanders Mare."

But the threat from abroad compelled the King to fulfil his contract. "You had me pushed into a tight corner," he told the French Ambassador afterwards, "but, thank God, I am still alive, and not so little a King as I was thought." Since he now knew as much about the Canon Law on marriage as anyone in Europe, he turned himself into the perfect legal example of a man whose marriage might be annulled. The marriage was never consummated. He told his intimate counsellors that he had gone through the form of it from political necessity, against his true desire, and without inward consent, for fear of making a ruffle in the world and driving Anne's brother the Duke into the hands of the Emperor and the King of France. There was a pre-contract, not sufficiently cleared, in that she had been promised to the son of the Duke of Lorraine and not released. In fact he was merely waiting, watching the European situation, until it was safe to act.

Norfolk and Gardiner now saw their chance to break Cromwell, as Wolsey had been broken, with the help of a new lady. Yet another of Norfolk's nieces, Catherine Howard, was presented to Henry at Gardiner's house, and captured his affections at first sight. The Norfolk faction soon felt strong enough to challenge Cromwell's power. In June 1540 the King was persuaded to get rid of Cromwell and Anne together. Cromwell was condemned under a Bill of Attainder charging him principally with heresy and "broadcasting" erroneous books and implicitly with treason. Anne agreed to have her marriage annulled, and Convocation pronounced it invalid. She lived on in England, pensioned and in retirement, for another seventeen years. A few days after Cromwell was executed on July 28 Henry was privately married to his fifth wife, Catherine Howard.

Catherine, about twenty-two, with auburn hair and hazel eyes, was the prettiest of Henry's wives. His Majesty's spirits revived, his health returned, and he went down to Windsor to reduce weight. "The King," reported the French Ambassador in December, "has taken a new rule of living, to rise between five and six, hear Mass at seven, and then ride till dinnertime, which is at ten in the morning. He says that he feels much better in the country than when he lived all winter in his houses at the gates of London."

But wild, tempestuous Catherine was not long content with a husband nearly thirty years older than herself. Her

reckless love for her cousin, Thomas Culpeper, was discovered, and she was executed in the Tower in February
1542 on the same spot as Anne Boleyn. The night before
the execution she asked for the block so that she could practise laying her head upon it, and as she mounted the scaffold
said, "I die a Queen, but would rather die the wife of Culpeper. God have mercy on my soul. Good people, I beg you
to pray for me."

Henry's sixth wife, Catherine Parr, was a serious little
widow from the Lake District, thirty-one years of age,
learned, and interested in theological questions, who had had
two husbands before the King. She married Henry at Hampton Court on July 12, 1543, and until his death three years
later made him an admirable wife, nursing his ulcerated leg,
which grew steadily worse and in the end killed him. She
contrived to reconcile Henry with the future Queen Elizabeth;
both Mary and Elizabeth grew fond of her, and she had the
fortune to outlive her husband.

*　　*　　*　　*　　*

The brilliant young Renaissance prince had grown old and
wrathful. The pain from his leg made Henry ill-tempered;
he suffered fools and those who crossed him with equal lack
of patience. Suspicion dominated his mind and ruthlessness
marked his actions. At the time of his marriage with Catherine Parr he was engaged in preparing the last of his wars.
The roots of the conflict lay in Scotland. Hostility between
the two peoples still smouldered, ever and again flickering
into flame along the wild Border. Reviving the obsolete claim
to suzerainty, Henry denounced the Scots as rebels, and
pressed them to relinquish their alliance with France. The
Scots successfully defeated an English raid at Halidon Rig.
Then in the autumn of 1542 an expedition under Norfolk
had to turn back at Kelso, principally through the failure of

the commissariat, which, besides its other shortcomings, left the English army without its beer, and the Scots proceeded to carry the war into the enemy's country. Their decision proved disastrous. Badly led and imperfectly organised, they lost more than half their army of ten thousand men in Solway Moss and were utterly routed. The news of this second Flodden killed James V, who died leaving the kingdom to an infant of one week, Mary, the famous Queen of Scots.

At once the child became the focus of the struggle for Scotland. Henry claimed her for the bride of his own son and heir. But the Scots Queen-Mother was a French princess, Mary of Guise. The pro-French Catholic party, led by Cardinal Beaton, resisted, repudiated Henry's terms, and began negotiations for marrying Mary to a French prince. Such a marriage could never be accepted by England. The Imperial Ambassador, who sought Henry's aid in the Emperor's struggle with France, found himself eagerly welcomed at Court. Once again England and the Empire made common cause against the French, and in May 1543 a secret treaty was ratified between Charles V and Henry. Throughout the year, and well into the spring of 1544, the preparations continued. While Scotland was left to Edward Seymour, brother of Queen Jane, and now Earl of Hertford, the King himself was to cross the Channel and lead an army against Francis in co-operation with an Imperial force from the north-east.

The plan was excellent, but the execution failed. Henry and Charles distrusted each other; each suspected the other of seeking a separate peace. Wary of being drawn too deep into the Emperor's plans, Henry sat down to besiege Boulogne. The town fell on September 14, and Henry was able to congratulate himself on at least one tangible result from his campaign. Five days later the Emperor made his peace with Francis, and refused to listen to Henry's complaints and exhortations. Meanwhile the English in Scotland, after burning Edinburgh and laying waste much country, ceased to make headway, and in February 1545 were defeated at Ancrum Moor.

Henry's position was extremely grave. Without a single ally, the nation faced the possibility of invasion from both France and Scotland. The crisis called for unexampled sacrifices from the English people; never had they been called upon to pay so many loans, subsidies, and benevolences. To set an example Henry melted down his own plate and mortgaged his estates. At Portsmouth he prepared for the threatened invasion in person. A French fleet penetrated the Solent and landed troops in the Isle of Wight; but they were soon driven off, and the crisis gradually passed. Next year a peace treaty was signed, which left Boulogne in English hands for eight years, at the end of which time France was to buy it back at a heavy price. Scotland was not included in the settlement. The war in the North smouldered on, bursting into flame for a time at the assassination of Cardinal Beaton, but yielding no definite results. Henry completely failed in Scotland. He would make no generous settlement with his neighbours, yet he lacked the force to coerce them. For the next fifty years they were to tease and trouble the minds of his successors.

In 1546 Henry was as yet only fifty-five. In the autumn he made his usual progress through Surrey and Berkshire to Windsor, and early in November he came up to London. He was never to leave his capital alive again. In these last few months one question dominated all minds: the heir to the kingdom was known, a child of nine, but who would be the power behind the throne? Norfolk or Hertford? The party of reaction or the party of reform?

A sudden and unexpected answer was given. On December 12, 1546, Norfolk and his son Surrey, the poet, were arrested for treason and sent to the Tower. Surrey's foolish conduct had made trouble inevitable. He had talked wildly of the time when the King should be dead, and, inconveniently remembering his descent from Edward I, he had quartered the royal arms with his own, despite the heralds' prohibitions. The King remembered that years before Norfolk had been put forward as a possible heir to the throne, and Surrey had been suggested as a husband for Princess Mary. His suspicions aroused, he acted swiftly; in mid-January Surrey was executed.

Parliament assembled to pass a Bill of Attainder against Norfolk. On Thursday the 27th the royal assent was given and Norfolk was condemned to death. But that same evening the King himself was dying. The physicians dared not tell him so, for prophesying the King's death was treason by Act of Parliament. Then, as the long hours slowly passed, Sir Anthony Denny, "boldly coming to the King, told him what case he was in, to man's judgment not like to live; and therefore exhorted him to prepare himself for death." The King took the grim news with fortitude. Urged to summon the Archbishop, he replied that first he would "take a little sleep; and then, as I feel myself, I will advise upon the matter." While he slept Hertford and Paget walked the gallery outside, scheming and contriving how to secure their power. Shortly before midnight the King awoke. He sent for Cranmer. When he came Henry was too weak to speak; he could only stretch out his hand to Cranmer. In a few minutes the Supreme Head had ceased to breathe.

* * * * *

Henry's rule saw many advances in the growth and the character of the English state, but it is a hideous blot upon his record that the reign should be widely remembered for its executions. Two Queens, two of the King's chief Ministers, a saintly bishop, numerous abbots, monks and many ordinary folk who dared to resist the royal will were put to death. Almost every member of the nobility in whom royal blood ran perished on the scaffold at Henry's command. Roman Catholic and Calvinist alike were burnt for heresy and religious treason. These persecutions, inflicted in solemn manner by officers of the law, perhaps in the presence of the Council or even the King himself, form a brutal sequel to the bright promise of the Renaissance. The sufferings of devout men and women among the faggots, the use of torture, and the savage penalties imposed for even paltry crimes, stand in repellent contrast to the enlightened principles of humanism. Yet his subjects did not turn from Henry in loathing. He succeeded in maintaining order amid the turmoil of Europe without army or police, and he imposed on England a discipline which was not attained elsewhere. A century of religious wars went by without Englishmen taking up arms to fight their fellow-countrymen for their faith. We must credit Henry's reign with laying the basis of sea-power, with a revival of Parliamentary institutions, with giving the English Bible to the people, and above all with strengthening a popular monarchy under which succeeding generations worked together for the greatness of England while France and Germany were racked with internal strife.

The Protestant Struggle

THE English Reformation under Henry VIII had received its guiding impulse from the King's passions and his desire for power. He still deemed himself a good Catholic. However, none of his Catholic wives had borne him a son. Catherine of Aragon had given birth to the future Queen Mary, Anne Boleyn to the future Queen Elizabeth; but it was Jane, daughter of the Protestant house of Seymour, who had produced the future Edward VI. Fears of a disputed succession lay deeply engraved in Henry VIII and in his whole people, and it was chiefly the desire and the duty to safeguard the throne of England for his only legitimate son that had impelled him in his later years to break not only with Rome but with his inmost religious convictions. Nevertheless the Catholic Norfolks retained much of their power and influence. Their kinswoman Catherine Howard might be executed; their son, the poet Surrey, might follow her to the scaffold; monastery lands might be seized and the Bible printed in English; but while Henry lived they constituted a check and barrier to the Reforming party. Henry had restrained Cranmer's doctrinal innovations, and in the main upheld the whole Norfolk interest, represented in religion by Stephen Gardiner, Bishop of Winchester. Thus there was a working compromise. Henry wanted his own way on his throne and in his choice of consort, but he saw no need to change the faith or even the ritual to which his subjects had been born.

With the new reign a deeper and more powerful tide began to flow. The guardian and chief counsellor of the child-king was his uncle, Edward Seymour, now Duke of Somerset. He and Cranmer proceeded to transform the political reformation of Henry VIII into a religious revolution. Foreign scholars from Germany and Switzerland, and even from distant Poland, were given chairs in the Universities of Oxford and Cambridge to educate the new generation of clergy in the Reformed doctrines. The Book of Common Prayer, in shining English prose, was drawn up by Cranmer and accepted by Parliament in 1549. Then followed, after Somerset's fall, the Forty-two Articles of Religion, and a second Prayer Book, until, on paper at least, England became a Protestant State. Somerset and Cranmer were both men of sincerity; they believed in the religious ideas which they intended their countrymen to accept; but the mass of the people neither knew nor cared about theological warfare, and there were many who actively opposed the imported foreign creeds.

Somerset himself was merely one of the regents appointed under Henry's will, and his position as Protector, at once dazzling and dangerous, had little foundation in law or precedent. Rivals crowded jealously upon him. His brother, Thomas Seymour, Lord High Admiral, had his own ambitions. The pale child Edward VI, who was constitutionally consumptive, might not live long. The next Protestant heir was Princess Elizabeth. She was living with Lady Catherine Parr, last and most fortunate of Henry's wives, and Catherine Parr was now married to the Admiral. He thought fit to make advances to the young princess even before the death of his wife, and girlish romps took place in her bedroom that led to scandal. Proofs were discovered of Thomas Seymour's plots against his brother, and the Protector was forced in January 1549 to dispose of him by Act of Attainder and the block on Tower Hill. Thus Somerset surmounted the first crisis of the new reign.

*   *   *   *   *

Far more serious than such personal threats were the distresses and discontents in the countryside. The life and economy of medieval England were fast dissolving. Landlords saw that vast fortunes could be made from wool, and the village communal strips barred their profits. Warfare had been going on for decades between landowner and peasantry. Slowly and surely the rights and privileges of the village communities were infringed and removed. Common land was seized, enclosed, and turned to pasture for flocks. Dissolution of the monasteries removed the most powerful and conservative element in the old system, and for a time gave fresh impetus to a process already under way. The multiplication of enclosures caused distress throughout the realm. In some counties as much as one third of the arable land was turned over to grass, and the people looked in anger upon the new nobility, fat with sacrilegious spoil, but greedy still.

Somerset had thus to face one of the worst economic crises that England has endured. Not only was there widespread unemployment, but also hardship caused by Henry's debasement of the coinage. The popular preachers were loud in denunciation. The Sermon of the Plough, preached by Hugh Latimer at Paul's Cross in 1548, is a notable piece of Tudor invective. "In times past men were full of pity and compassion; but now there is no pity; for in London their brother shall die in the streets for cold; he shall lie sick at the door between stock and stock [that is, between the doorposts], and then perish for hunger. In times past, when any rich man died in London, they were wont to help the scholars at the universities with exhibition. When any man died they would

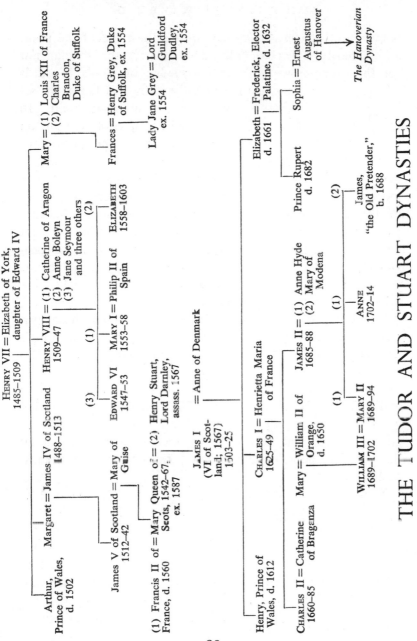

THE TUDOR AND STUART DYNASTIES

bequeath great sums of money toward the relief of the poor.
. . . Charity is waxen cold; none helpeth the scholar nor
yet the poor; now that the knowledge of God's Word is
brought to light, and many earnestly study and labour to set
it forth, now almost no man helpeth to maintain them." In
the spring of 1549 Latimer preached a course of sermons on
the evils of the age, upon "the monstrous and portentous
dearth made by man." "You landlords, you rent-raisers, I
may say you step-lords, you have for your possessions yearly
too much. . . . I tell you, my lords and masters, this is not
for the King's honour. It is to the King's honour that his subjects be led in the true religion. It is the King's honour that
the commonwealth be advanced, that the dearth be provided for, and the commodities of this realm so employed, as
it may be to the setting of his subjects on work and keeping
them from idleness. If the King's honour, as some men say,
standeth in the great multitude of people, then these gra-
ziers, enclosers, and rent-raisers are hinderers of the King's
honour; for whereas have been a great many householders
and inhabitants, there is now but a shepherd and his dog.
My lords and masters, such proceedings do intend plainly to
make of the yeomanry slavery. The enhancing and rearing
goe all to your private commodity and wealth. Ye had a single too much, and now ye have double too much; but let
the preacher preach till his tongue be worn to the stumps,
nothing is amended."

Somerset was surrounded by men who had made their
money by the methods which Latimer denounced. He himself sympathised with the yeomen and peasantry, and appointed commissions to inquire into the enclosures. But this
increased the discontent, and encouraged the oppressed to
take matters into their own hands. Two rebellions broke out.
The Catholic peasantry in the South-West rose against the
Prayer Book, and the yokels of the Eastern Counties against

the enclosing landlords. This gave a fine handle to Somerset's enemies. In Germany in 1524–26 the Reformation had been followed by the bloody Peasants' War, in which the poorer classes in the countryside and the towns rose with the blessing of the reformer Zwingli against their noble oppressors. The same thing seemed about to happen in the England of 1549. Foreign mercenaries suppressed the Western rebellion; but in Norfolk the trouble was more serious. A tannery-owner named Robert Ket took the lead. He established his headquarters outside Norwich on Mousehold Hill, where about sixteen thousand peasants gathered in a camp of turf huts roofed with boughs. Under a large oak tree Ket, day after day, tried country gentlemen charged with robbing the poor. No blood was shed, but property acquired by enclosing common land was restored to the public, and the rebels lived upon the flocks and herds of the landowners. The local authorities were powerless, and Somerset was known to recognise the justice of their grievances. The disorders spread to Yorkshire, and presently reverberated in the Midlands.

John Dudley, Earl of Warwick, son of the man who had been Henry VII's agent, now seized his opportunity. He had proved an able soldier in the French campaigns of Henry VIII, and had been careful to hide his real character and motives. He was a self-seeking, vigorous man, and the champion of wealth and property. Now he was given command of the troops to suppress the rising. The Government felt itself so militarily weak that followers of the rebels were offered a free pardon. Ket was not unmoved. The herald came to his camp, but a small incident brought disaster. While Ket was standing by the oak tree, meditating an interview with Warwick, a small urchin drew the attention of the herald's party "with words as unseemly as his gesture was filthy," and he was immediately shot with an arquebus. The murder enraged Ket's followers. Fighting began. Warwick's best troops were German mercenaries, whose precise fire-drill shattered the peasant array. Three thousand five hundred were killed. There were no wounded. A few made a stand for their lives behind a barricade of farm carts and surrendered. Ket was taken prisoner, and hanged at Norwich Castle. Warwick had by accident made his mark as a strong man.

Somerset's enemies claimed the credit for restoring order. They blamed the rising in the East on his enclosure commissions and his sympathy for the peasants, and the rebellion in the West on his religious reforms. His foreign policy had driven the Scots into alliance with France, and he had lost Henry's one conquest, Boulogne. Warwick became the leader of the Opposition. "The Lords in London," as Warwick's party were called, met to take measures against the Protector. No one moved to support him. They quietly took over the government. After a spell in the Tower, Somerset, now powerless, was for some months allowed to sit in the Council, but as conditions got worse so the danger grew of a reaction in his favour. In January 1552, splendidly garbed as for a state banquet, he was executed on Tower Hill. This handsome, well-meaning man had failed completely to heal the dislocation of Henry's reign and fell a victim to the fierce interests he had offended. Nevertheless the people of England remembered him for years as "the Good Duke."

His successors were less scrupulous, and even less successful. "Amidst the wreck of ancient institutions," says Froude, "the misery of the people, and the moral and social anarchy by which the nation was disintegrated, thoughtful persons in England could not fail by this time to be asking themselves what they had gained by the Reformation. . . . The Government was corrupt, the courts of law were venal. The trading classes cared only to grow rich. The multitude were mutinous from oppression. Among the good who remained unpolluted the best were still on the reforming side."

The nominal King of England, Edward VI, was a cold, prig-gish invalid of fifteen. In his diary he noted his uncle's death without a comment.

*　*　*　*　*

The Government of Warwick, now become Duke of Northumberland, was held together by class resistance to so-cial unrest. His three years of power displayed to the full the rapacity of the ruling classes. Doctrinal reformation was a pretence for confiscating yet more Church lands, and new bishops paid for their consecration with portions of the epis-copal estates. The so-called grammar schools of Edward VI were but the beginning of spacious plans carried out in Elizabeth's reign for endowing education out of the confis-cated lands of the monasteries. Thomas More's definition of government as "a conspiracy of rich men procuring their own commodities under the name and title of a commonwealth" fitted England very accurately during these years.

One gleam of enterprise distinguishes this period. It saw the opening of relations between England and a growing new Power in Eastern Europe, hitherto known as Muscovy, but soon to be called Russia. A small group of Englishmen con-ceived the idea of seeking a north-eastern passage to Asia through Arctic waters. Upon the northern coasts of Asia there might be people who would buy cloth and other Eng-lish products. As early as 1527 a small book had appeared prophesying such a discovery. One phrase rings out: "There is no land uninhabitable nor sea unnavigable." In 1553 an expedition was financed by the Muscovy Company of Mer-chant Adventurers with the backing of the Government. Sebastian Cabot, a wise old seaman who some fifty years earlier had accompanied his father on his voyage to New-foundland, was brought in as Governor of the company. In May three ships set sail under Hugh Willoughby and Richard Chancellor. Willoughby perished with his crew off Lapland, but Chancellor wintered in Archangel, and in the spring pushed overland to the Court of Ivan the Terrible at Moscow. The monopoly of the German Hansa towns, which had long blocked English merchants throughout Northern Europe, was now outflanked and trade began with Russia. On a second voyage Chancellor was drowned in a storm off Scotland. Another of his associates, Anthony Jenkinson, carried on his work. During the reign of Queen Elizabeth Jenkinson paid three visits to Russia and became a trusted friend of the Tsar. In the course of his travels he got as far as Bokhara, in Turkestan, on the old silk road of Marco Polo; he crossed into Persia, and was the first man to fly the English flag on the Caspian Sea. But these adventures belong to a greater age than that of Edward VI and his successor.

Under the Succession Act of 1543 the next heir to the throne was Princess Mary, the Catholic daughter of Catherine of Aragon. Northumberland might well tremble for the future. For a moment he thought of substituting Elizabeth for her half-sister; but Elizabeth, now aged nineteen and wise for her years, had no intention of committing herself to such an arrangement. A desperate scheme was evolved. The younger daughter of Henry VII had married the Duke of Suffolk, and their heirs had been named in Henry VIII's will as next in line of succession after his own children. The eldest grandchild in this Suffolk line was Lady Jane Grey, a girl of sixteen. Northumberland married this girl to his son, Guildford Dudley. Nothing remained but to effect a military *coup* when the young King died. But Princess Mary, now aged thirty-six, took care to avoid Northumberland's advances. When Edward fell ill she took refuge on the estates of the Duke of Norfolk, ignoring a summons to appear at her brother's deathbed. On July 6, 1553, Edward VI expired, and Lady Jane Grey was proclaimed Queen in London. The only response to this announcement was gathering resistance:

Northumberland was too much hated throughout the land. The common people flocked to Mary's support. The Privy Counsellors and the City authorities swam with the tide. Northumberland was left without an ally. In August Mary entered London with Elizabeth at her side. Lady Jane and her husband were consigned to the Tower. In vain Northumberland grovelled. He asserted that he had always been a Catholic, with shattering effect on the Protestant Party. But nothing could save him from an ignominious death. To one of his former associates he wrote, "An old proverb there is, and that most true—a living dog is better than a dead lion. Oh that it would please her good Grace to give me life—yea, the life of a dog." This may serve as his epitaph.

*   *   *   *   *

The woman who now became Queen was probably the most unhappy and unsuccessful of England's sovereigns. Mary Tudor, the only surviving child of Catherine of Aragon and Henry VIII, had been brought up in the early years of her father's reign with all the ceremony due to the heiress to the throne. She had been betrothed at different times to the heirs both of France and the Empire. As with her mother, religion dominated her being, and Catherine's divorce and the break with Rome brought tragic and catastrophic change. Mary had been declared illegitimate by Act of Parliament; she was pressed to forsake her religion, and endured bitter conflicts between her duty to her father and her conscience. Her half-sister and half-brother overshadowed her at Court. She had clung to her confessors and her chapel throughout the reign of Edward VI, and was naturally feared by the ruling group of Protestant politicians in London. The Spanish blood in her was strong. She entered into close and confidential relations with Renard, the Imperial Ambassador. Her accession portended a renewal of the Roman connection and a political alliance with the Empire.

We are assured that, except in matters of religion, Mary was by nature merciful. She certainly accepted the allegiance of the counsellors who came meekly to her. The most adroit among them, William Cecil, was to keep close to Government circles throughout her reign, and great was to be his future under her successor. Princess Elizabeth smoothly ordered Mass to be said in her household, and avoided communications with men under suspicion.

Secure upon the throne, Mary proceeded to realise the wish of her life—the restoration of the Roman communion. In Stephen Gardiner, Bishop of Winchester, one of Norfolk's circle in the later years of Henry VIII, she found an able and ardent servant. The religious legislation of the Reformation Parliament was repealed. But one thing Mary could not do. She could not restore to the Church the lands parcelled out among the nobility. The Tudor magnates were willing to go to Mass, but not to lose their new property. Even so there was trouble. Mary never realised that the common people, particularly in London, coupled Catholicism with foreign influence. They had indeed been taught to do so under Henry VIII, but the feeling was older than that. The English Bible and the English Prayer Book were in their hands, and there was a wide, if superficial, attachment to the Reformed Faith. Protestant leaders fled to Geneva and the German Rhineland towns. There was rioting in the capital. Gardiner's life was threatened. He wore a mail shirt throughout the day and was guarded by a hundred men at night. A dead dog was flung through the window of the Queen's chamber, a halter round its neck, its ears cropped, and bearing a label saying that all the priests in England should be hanged.

The most urgent question was whom Mary should marry. The Commons supported an English candidate, Edward Courtenay, Earl of Devon, a descendant of the house of York. But Mary's eyes were fixed overseas. Renard, envoy of the Emperor Charles V, worked fast, and she promised to wed the Emperor's son, the future Philip II of Spain. Sir Thomas Wyatt, son of the poet of Henry VIII's reign, formed a plot to prevent the marriage by force, and Courtenay gathered a conspiracy against her in the West. News of the Spanish betrothal filtered through the Court and reached the people. Ugly stories of the Inquisition and the coming of Spanish troops passed from mouth to mouth. The Commons came in deputation to beg the Queen not to violate the feelings of the nation. But Mary had all the obstinacy of the Tudors and none of their political sense. She was now on the threshold of her dreams—a Catholic England united in intimate alliance with the Catholic Empire of the Habsburgs.

All eyes turned to Princess Elizabeth, in watchful retirement at Hatfield. The English succession was vital to the Courts of Europe. The French Ambassador, Noailles, began to be active. The stakes were high. In the rivalry of Valois and Habsburg which tormented Europe England's support might mean victory or defeat. Elizabeth was suspected of turning for advice to the Frenchman. It was suggested that she might marry Courtenay. But events began to move fast. In the West Courtenay precipitated a rising. Soon after the Spanish match was proclaimed rebellion broke out yet again in Southern England. Sir Thomas Wyatt raised his standard in Kent and marched slowly towards London, gathering men as he came. The capital was in alarm. The citizens went in fear of the sack of their houses. But Mary, bitter and disappointed with her people, and knowing she had failed to win their hearts, showed she was not afraid. If Wyatt entered the capital her ambitions as a Catholic Queen were doomed. In a stirring speech at Guildhall she summoned the Londoners to her defence. There was division among the rebels. Wyatt was disappointed by Courtenay, whose rising was a pitiable failure. The Kentish rebels hoped to force terms from the

Queen, not to depose her. Straggled fighting took place in the streets, and the Queen's men cut up the intruders. Wyatt was executed. This sealed the fate of Lady Jane Grey and her husband. In February 1554 the two walked calmly to their death on Tower Hill.

Elizabeth's life was now in great danger. Though Wyatt had exonerated her she was the only rival claimant to the throne, and the Spaniards demanded her execution before their prince was committed to marrying the Queen. But Mary had shed blood enough and Renard could not persuade her to sign away the life of her half-sister. Every argument was used. He wrote to his master, "Madam Elizabeth goes to-day to the Tower, pregnant, they say, for she is a light woman, as her mother was. With her dead and Courtenay, there will be none left in this kingdom to dispute the crown or trouble the Queen." Elizabeth indeed had very little hope, and had determined to ask, like her mother, that she might be beheaded with the sword. But, fearlessly and passionately, she denied all disloyal dealings with Courtenay or Wyatt. Perhaps Mary believed her. At any rate, after some months she was released and sent to Woodstock, where, in quiet and pious seclusion, she awaited the turn of fortune.

As summer came Philip sailed northwards across the seas. Mary journeyed to Winchester to greet her bridegroom. With all the pomp of sixteenth-century royalty the marriage was solemnised in July 1554 according to the rites of the Catholic Church. Gardiner was now dead; but a successor was found in the English cardinal Reginald Pole. Pole had been in exile throughout the reign of Henry VIII, his family having been lopped and shorn in Henry's judicial murders. This representative of the Pope was not only a Prince of the Church, but practically a Prince of the Blood, a second cousin of the Queen and a grandson of "false, fleeting, per-jured Clarence." He was a zealous and austere Catholic, and now came as Legate to take his place with Renard in the intimate counsels of the Queen and enforce the conversion of the whole land.

Mary had been for ever odious in the minds of a Protestant nation as the Bloody Queen who martyred her noblest subjects. Generations of Englishmen in childhood learnt the sombre tale of their sacrifice from Foxe's *Book of Martyrs,* with its gruesome illustrations. These stories have become part of the common memory of the people—the famous scenes at Oxford in 1555, the faggots which consumed the Protestant bishops, Latimer and Ridley, the pitiful recantation and final heroic end in March 1556 of the frail, aged Archbishop, Cranmer. Their martyrdom rallied to the Protestant faith many who till now had shown indifference.

These martyrs saw in vision that their deaths were not in vain, and, standing at the stake, pronounced immortal words. "Be of good comfort, Master Ridley," Latimer cried at the crackling of the flames. "Play the man. We shall this day light such a candle, by God's grace, in England as I trust shall never be put out."

In vain the Queen strove to join English interests to those of the Spanish state. She had married to make England safe for Catholicism, and she had sacrificed what little personal happiness she could hope for to this dream. As the wife of the King of Spain, against the interests of her kingdom, and against the advice of prudent counsellors, among them Cardinal Pole, she allowed herself to be dragged into war with France, and Calais, the last possession of the English upon the Continent, fell without resistance. This national disgrace, this loss of the symbol of the power and glory of medieval England, bit deep into the hearts of the people and into the conscience of the Queen. Hope of a child to secure the Catholic succession was unfulfilled. Her unhappiness was hardly redeemed by one vision of accomplishment. Yet, unchronicled and without praise, her reign witnessed one modest achievement, which has rarely received the attention of historians. Mary's Ministers, during her brief reign, embarked upon a major task of retrenchment and reform; by the time of her death they had done much to purge the government of the corrupt extravagance of Northumberland's régime.

Philip retired to the Netherlands and then to Spain, aloof and disappointed at the barrenness of the whole political scheme. Surrounded by disloyalty and discontent, Mary's health gave way. In November 1558 she died, and a few hours later, in Lambeth Palace, her coadjutor, Cardinal Pole, followed her. The tragic interlude of her reign was over. It had sealed the conversion of the English people to the Reformed faith.

*　*　*　*　*

In its beginning the Protestant Reformation in Europe had been a local revolt against the abuses of an organisation. But this motive was removed when after some years the Catholic Church set its house in order. What remained was the insurgence of the Northern races against the entire apparatus of the Roman Church in so far as this seemed to conflict with the forward movement of the human mind. The Christian revelation could now be borne forward into ages that no longer required the moulds into which the barbaric conquerors of the ancient world had, necessarily and beneficently, been constrained after the collapse of the Roman Empire. Until the reign of Henry VIII there lay beneath the quarrels of the nobility, the conflicts between King and Church, between the ruling classes and the people, a certain broad unity of acceptance. The evils and sorrows of the medieval ages had lasted so long that they seemed to be the inseparable conditions of existence in a world of woe. No one had novel remedies or even consolations to propose. With the

Reformation there came a new influence, cutting to the very roots of English life, stirring the souls of all classes to action or resistance, and raising standards for which great and small alike were prepared to suffer or inflict the worst extremities. The old framework, which, in spite of its many jars, had held together for centuries, was now torn by a division in which all other antagonisms of class and interest were henceforward to be ranged and ruled. Hitherto, amid their quarrels and tribulations, there had been one people and one system. Henceforward, for many generations to come, not only England but all the countries of Europe were to range themselves for or against the Protestant Reformation.

The violence of this convulsion can hardly be measured by us to-day, and it followed in England a less destructive course than in Germany or France. This was because the issue came to a head at a comparatively early stage, and under the strong government of the Tudors. Nevertheless the doctrinal revolution enforced by Cranmer under Edward VI, and the Counter-Revolution of Gardiner, Pole, and their assistants under Mary, exposed our agitated Islanders in one single decade to a frightful oscillation. Here were the citizens, the peasants, the whole mass of living beings who composed the nation, ordered in the name of King Edward VI to march along one path to salvation, and under Queen Mary to march back again in the opposite direction; and all who would not move on the first order or turn about on the second must prove their convictions, if necessary, at the gibbet or the stake. Thus was New England imposed on Old England; thus did Old England in terrible counter-stroke resume a fleeting sway; and from all this agony there was to emerge under Queen Elizabeth a compromise between Old and New which, though it did not abate their warfare, so far confined its fury that it could not prove mortal to the unity and continuity of national society.

Good Queen Bess

ELIZABETH was twenty-five years old when, untried in the affairs of State, she succeeded her half-sister on November 17, 1558. It was England's good fortune that the new Queen was endowed by inheritance and upbringing with a combination of very remarkable qualities. There could be no doubt who her father was. A commanding carriage, auburn hair, eloquence of speech, and natural dignity proclaimed her King Henry's daughter. Other similarities were soon observed: high courage in moments of crisis, a fiery and imperious resolution when defied, and an almost inexhaustible fund of physical energy. She enjoyed many of the same pastimes and accomplishments as the King had done—a passion for the chase, skill in archery and hawking, and in dancing and music. She could speak six languages, and was well read in Latin and Greek. As with her father and grandfather, a restless vitality led her hither and thither from mansion to mansion, so that often none could tell where in a week's time she might be sleeping.

A difficult childhood and a perilous adolescence had been Elizabeth's portion. At one stage in her father's lifetime she had been declared illegitimate and banished from Court. During Mary's reign, when her life might have been forfeited by a false step, she had proved the value of caution and dissemblance. When to keep silence, how to bide her time and husband her resources, were the lessons she learnt from her youth. Many historians have accused her of vacillation and parsimony. Certainly these elements in her character were justly the despair of her advisers. The royal treasury however was never rich enough to finance all the adventurous projects urged upon her. Nor was it always unwise amid the turbulent currents of the age to put off making irrevocable decisions. The times demanded a politic, calculating, devious spirit at the head of the state, and this Elizabeth possessed. She had, too, a high gift for picking able men to do the country's work. It came naturally to her to take the credit for their successes, while blaming them for all that went wrong.

In quickness of mind the Queen was surpassed by few of her contemporaries, and many envoys to her Court had good reason to acknowledge her liveliness of repartee. In temperament she was subject to fits of melancholy, which alternated with flamboyant merriment and convulsive rage. Always subtle of intellect, she was often brazen and even coarse in manners and expression. When angered she could box her Treasurer's ears and throw her slipper in her Secretary's face. She was outwardly very free in her more tender relations with the opposite sex, so that, in the words of an illustrious counsellor, "one day she was greater than man, and the next less than woman." Nevertheless she had a capacity for inspiring devotion that is perhaps unparalleled among British sovereigns. There may be something grotesque to modern eyes in the flattery paid her by the Court, but with her people she never went wrong. By instinct she knew how to earn popular acclaim. In a sense her relationship with her subjects was one long flirtation. She gave to her country the love that she never entirely reposed in any one man, and her people responded with a loyalty that almost amounted to worship. It is not for nothing that she has come down to history as Good Queen Bess.

Few sovereigns ever succeeded to a more hazardous inheritance than she. England's link with Spain had brought the loss of Calais and the hostility of France. Tudor policy in Scotland had broken down. The old military danger of the Middle Ages, a Franco-Scottish alliance, again threatened. In the eyes of Catholic Europe Mary, the Queen of Scots, and wife of the Dauphin of France, who became King Francis II in 1559, had a better claim to the English throne than Elizabeth, and with the power of France behind her she stood a good chance of gaining it. Mary of Guise, the Regent and Queen-Mother of Scotland, pursued a pro-French and pro-Catholic policy, and in Edinburgh and Paris the Guises held the keys of power. Even before the death of Henry VIII England's finances had been growing desperate. English credit at Antwerp, the centre of the European money market, was so weak that the Government had to pay 14 per cent for its loans. The coinage, which had been debased yet further under Edward VI, was now chaotic. England's only official ally, Spain suspected the new régime for religious reasons. This is how a former Clerk of the Council under Edward VI surveyed the scene when Elizabeth ascended the throne: "The Queen poor, the realm exhausted, the nobility poor and decayed. Want of good captains and soldiers. The people out of order. Justice not executed. All things dear. Excess in meat, drink, and apparel. Divisions among ourselves. Wars with France and Scotland. The French King bestriding the realm, having one foot in Calais and the other in Scotland. Steadfast enmity but no steadfast friendship abroad."

Elizabeth had been brought up a Protestant. She was a paragon of the New Learning. Around her had gathered some of the ablest Protestant minds: Matthew Parker, who was to be her Archbishop of Canterbury; Nicholas Bacon, whom she appointed Lord Keeper of the Great Seal; Roger Ascham, the foremost scholar of the day; and, most important of all, William Cecil, the adaptable civil servant who had already held office as Secretary under Somerset and Northumberland. Of sixteenth-century English statesmen Cecil was undoubtedly the greatest. He possessed a consuming thirst for information about the affairs of the realm, and was to display immense industry in the business of office. Cautious good judgment marked all his actions. Elizabeth, with sure instinct, summoned him to her service. "This judgment I have of you," she charged him, "that you will not be corrupted by any manner of gifts, that you will be faithful to the State, and that, without respect to any private will, you will give me that counsel that you think best." It was a tremendous burden which the young Queen imposed upon her First Minister, then aged thirty-eight. Their close and daily collaboration was to last, in spite of shocks and jars, until Cecil's death, forty years later.

Religious peace at home and safety from Scotland were the foremost needs of the realm. England became Protestant by law, Queen Mary's Catholic legislation was repealed, and the sovereign was declared supreme Governor of the English Church. But this was not the end of Elizabeth's difficulties. New ideas were in debate, not only on religious doctrine and Church government, but on the very nature and foundations of political power. Ever since the days of Wyclif in the 1380's there had been, running in secret veins under the surface of society in England, a movement of resistance to the Church order. With the Reformation the notion that it might be a duty to disobey the established order on the grounds of private conviction became for the first time since the conversion to Christianity of the Roman Empire the belief of great numbers. But so closely were Church and State involved that disobedience to the one was a challenge to the other. The idea that a man should pick and choose for himself what doctrines he should adhere to was almost as alien to the mind of the age as the idea that he should select what laws he should obey and what magistrates he should respect. The most that could be allowed was that he should outwardly conform and think what he liked in silence. But in the great turmoil of Europe silence was impossible. Men talked: secretly to one another, openly in their writings, which were now printed in a thousand copies, kindling excitement and curiosity wherever they were carried. Even if it were granted that Affairs of State could only be lawfully debated by those called thereto, common men could still search the Scriptures, and try the doctrines of the Church, its government, its rites and ceremonies, by the words of the Evangelist and Apostles.

It is at this point that the party known as the Puritans, who were to play so great a rôle in the next hundred years, first enter English history. Democratic in theory and organisation, intolerant in practice of all who differed from their views, the Puritans challenged the Queen's authority in Church and State, and although she sought for freedom of conscience and could maintain with sincerity that she "made no windows into men's souls," she dared not let them organise cells in the body religious or the body politic. A discordant and vigorous minority could rupture the delicate harmony that she was patiently weaving. Protestantism must be saved from its friends. She saw in practical terms what her successor, James I, expounded in theory, "No Bishop, no King," and she realised that unless the Government controlled the Church it would be too weak to survive the Counter-Reformation now gathering head in Catholic Europe. So Elizabeth had soon to confront not only the Catholic danger from abroad, but Puritan attack at home, led by fanatical exiles of Mary's reign who now streamed back from Geneva and from the Rhineland towns.

Nevertheless the Reformation in Europe took on a new aspect when it came to England. All the novel questions agi-

tating the world—the relation of the National Church to
Rome on one side and to the national sovereign on the other;
its future organisation; its articles of religion; the disposal of
its property, and the property of its monasteries—could only
be determined in Parliament, where the Puritans soon
formed a growing and outspoken opposition. The gentry in
Parliament were themselves divided. On two points alone
perhaps were they heartily in accord: once they had got their
share of abbey lands they did not mean to part with them, and
anything was better than having the Wars of the Roses over
again. Otherwise they fell into two great divisions, those who
thought things had gone far enough, and those who wanted
to go a step farther. It was the future distinction of Cavalier
and Puritan, Churchman and Dissenter, Tory and Whig. But
for a long time it was subdued by common horror of a disputed succession and a civil war, and by the rule that only
the crown could initiate policy and public legislation.

*   *   *   *   *

The immediate threat lay north of the Border. French
troops supported the French Queen-Mother in Scotland. A
powerful Puritan party among the Scottish nobility, abetted
by the persecuted preachers, were in arms against them,
while John Knox raised his harsh voice against foreign rule
and from exile in Geneva poured forth his denunciations of
"the monstrous regiment of women." He meant of course
that rule by women seemed to him unnatural. Elizabeth
watched these doings with interest and anxiety. If the French
party got control of Scotland their next move would be
against her throne. Want of money forbade a major military
effort, but the Fleet was sent to blockade the Scottish ports
and prevent reinforcements arriving from France. Arms and
supplies were smuggled across the Border to the Protestant
party. Knox was permitted to return to his native land by

way of England, and his preachings had a powerful effect. A small English army intervened on the Scottish Protestant side, and at this moment Mary of Guise died. Elizabeth's efforts had been modest, but they prevailed. By the Treaty of Leith in 1560 the Protestant cause in Scotland was assured for ever. France herself now plunged into religious strife, and was obliged at the same time to concentrate her forces against the Habsburg Empire. Elizabeth gained a respite and could look squarely to the future.

One thing seemed certain to all contemporaries. The security of the English State depended in the last resort on an assured succession. The delicate question of the Queen's marriage began to throw its shadow across the political scene, and it is in her attitude to this challenge that the strength and subtleties of Elizabeth's character are revealed. The country was well aware of the responsibility which lay upon her. If she married an Englishman her authority might be weakened, and there would be fighting among the suitors. The perils of such a course were borne in on her as she watched the reactions of her Court to her long and deep affection for the handsome, ambitious Robert Dudley, a younger son of Northumberland, whom she made Earl of Leicester. This was no way out. During the first months of her reign she had also to consider the claims of her brother-in-law, Philip II of Spain. A Spanish marriage had brought disaster to her sister, but marriage to Philip might buy a powerful friend; refusal might drive his religious animosity into the open. But by 1560 she had achieved a temporary security and could wait her time. Marriage into one of the reigning houses of Europe would mean entangling herself in its European policy and facing the hostility of her husband's rivals. In vain the Houses of Parliament begged their Virgin Queen to marry and produce an heir. Elizabeth was angry. She would admit no discussion. Her policy was to spend her life in saving her people from such a commitment, and using her potential value as a match to divide a European Combination against her.

*　　*　　*　　*　　*

Meanwhile there was Mary Stuart, Queen of Scots. Her young husband, King Francis II, had died shortly after his accession, and in December 1560 she returned to her own kingdom. Her mother's uncles, the Guises, soon lost their influence at the French Court, and her mother-in-law, Catherine de Médicis, replaced them as Regent for King Charles IX. Thus in the last half of the sixteenth century women for a time controlled three countries—France, England, and Scotland. But of the three only the grip of Elizabeth held firm.

Mary Stuart was a very different personality from Elizabeth, though in some ways her position was similar. She was a descendant of Henry VII; she held a throne; she lived in an age when it was a novelty for a woman to be the head of a state; and she was now unmarried. Her presence in Scotland disturbed the delicate balance which Elizabeth had achieved by the Treaty of Leith. The Catholic English nobility, particularly in the North, were not indifferent to Mary's claims. Some of them dreamed of winning her hand. But Elizabeth knew her rival. She knew that Mary was incapable of separating her emotions from her politics. The Queen of Scots lacked the vigilant self-control which Elizabeth had learnt in the bitter years of childhood. Mary's marriage points the contrast between the two sovereigns. Elizabeth had seen and avoided the danger of choosing a husband from her Court. Mary had only been a few years in Scotland when she married her cousin, Henry Stuart, Lord Darnley, a weak, conceited youth who had both Tudor and Stuart blood in his veins. The result was disaster. The old feudal factions, now sharpened by religious conflict, seized Scotland in their grip. Mary's power melted slowly and steadily away. Favourites brought from the cultured French Court to cheer her in this grim land were unpopular, and one of them, David Riccio, was killed before her eyes. Her husband became a tool of her opponents. In desperation she connived at his murder, and in 1567 married his murderer, a warlike Border lord, James Hepburn, Earl of Bothwell, whose unruly sword might yet save her throne and her happiness. But defeat and imprisonment followed, and in 1568 she escaped into England and threw herself upon the mercy of the waiting Elizabeth.

Mary in England proved even more dangerous than Mary in Scotland. She became the focus of plots and conspiracies against Elizabeth's life. The survival of Protestant England was menaced by her existence. Secret emissaries of Spain crept into the country to nourish rebellion and claim the allegiance of Elizabeth's Catholic subjects. The whole force of the Counter-Reformation was unloosed against the one united Protestant country in Europe. If England were destroyed it seemed that Protestantism could be stamped out in every other land. Assassination was to be the first step. But Elizabeth was well served. Francis Walsingham, Cecil's assistant and later his rival in the Government, tracked down Spanish agents and English traitors. This subtle intellectual and ardent Protestant, who had remained abroad throughout the reign of Mary Tudor, and whose knowledge of European politics surpassed that of anyone else in Elizabeth's counsel, created the best secret service of any Government of the time. But there was always a chance that someone would slip through; there was always a danger so long as Mary lived that public discontent or private ambition would use her and her claims to destroy Elizabeth. In 1569 the threat became a reality.

In the North of England society was much more primitive than in the fertile South. Proud, independent, semi-feudal nobles now felt themselves threatened not only by Elizabeth's authority but by a host of new gentry like the Cecils and the Bacons, enriched by the dissolution of the monasteries and hungry for political power. Moreover, there was a deep religious division between North and South. The South was largely Protestant; the North remained dominantly Catholic. In the bleak, barren dales the monasteries had been the centre of communal life and charity. Their destruction had provoked the Pilgrimage of Grace against Henry VIII, and still incited a stubborn and passive resistance to the religious changes of Elizabeth. The idea was now advanced that Mary should marry the Duke of Norfolk, senior of the pre-Tudor nobility, and his somewhat feeble head was turned at the prospect of gambling for a throne. He repented in time. But in 1569 the Earls of Northumberland and Westmorland led a rising in the North. Mary was confined at Tutbury in the care of Lord Hunsdon, Elizabeth's soldier cousin on the Boleyn side, a trustworthy servant throughout her reign, and one of her few relations. Before the rebels could seize many she was conveyed hurriedly southwards. Elizabeth was slow to realise the danger. "The Earls," she said, "were old in blood but poor in force." The rebels planned to hold the North of England and wait to be attacked. They were far from sure of each other. In the South the Catholic lords made no move. There seems to have been no common plan of action, and the rebel force scattered into small parties in the northern hills. Ignominiously they dribbled across the Border to safety, and the first act of the widespread Catholic conspiracy against Elizabeth was over. After twelve years of very patient rule she was unchallenged Queen of all England.

* * * * *

Rome was prompt to retaliate. In February 1570 Pope Pius V, a former Inquisitor-General, issued a Bull of excommunication against Elizabeth. From this moment Spain, as head of Catholic Europe, was supplied with a spiritual weapon should the need for attack arise. Elizabeth's position was weakened. Parliament became increasingly agitated at the spinsterhood of their Queen, and their constant petitioning irritated her into action. She entered into negotiations with Catherine de Médicis, and a political alliance was concluded at Blois in April 1572. Both women distrusted the Spanish power, since Catherine realised that Catholic France had as much to fear from Spain as Protestant England. For a short time events ran with Elizabeth. Spain's weakness centred in the Netherlands, where a robust population with immense taxable resources had long fretted under Philip's rule. The whole territory was on the edge of rebellion, and the treaty was hardly signed when the famous Dutch resisters of tyranny, who were known as the "Sea Beggars," seized the town of Brill, and the Low Countries blazed into revolt. Elizabeth now had a potential new ally on the Continent. She even thought of marrying one of Queen Catherine's younger sons, on condition that France did not take advantage of the turmoil to expand into the Netherlands. But a terrible event in Paris dashed such prospects. By a sudden massacre of the Huguenots on the eve of the feast of St Bartholomew, August 23, 1572, the Guises, pro-Spanish and ultra-Catholic, recaptured the political power they had lost ten years earlier. Feeling ran high in London. The English Ambassador, Francis Walsingham, was recalled. When the French Ambassador came to explain away the event

Elizabeth and her Court, clothed all in black, received him in silence. Having thus done her duty as a Protestant Queen, Elizabeth stood godmother to the French King's baby and continued her matrimonial negotiations with his brother.

Her alliance with the French Court however had clearly failed and Elizabeth was now driven to giving secret subsidies and support to the French Huguenots and the Dutch. Success depended on the most accurate timing, as her funds were very limited and she could seldom afford to help except when the rebels were on the edge of disaster. Walsingham, now Secretary of State, and second only to Cecil in the Queen's Council, was far from content. Exile in Mary's reign and service as Ambassador in Paris had convinced him that Protestantism would only survive in Europe if England gave it unlimited encouragement and aid. In the long run there could be no compromise with the Catholics. Sooner or later war would come, and he urged that everything should be done to preserve and secure potential allies before the final clash.

Opposed to all this was Cecil, now Lord Burghley. Friendship with Spain, symbolised in the marriage of Catherine of Aragon and nourished by commercial interests, had been a Tudor tradition since the days of Henry VII, and good relations with the Power that still controlled a large part of the Netherlands could alone preserve the great market for English wool and cloth. Queen Mary's marriage with Philip had been widely unpopular in England; but in Burghley's view this was no time to go to the opposite extreme and intervene in the Netherlands on the side of Philip's rebels. Such a step would inflame the Puritan extremists and inject a dangerous fanaticism into foreign policy. When Burghley became Lord Treasurer in 1572 his attitude hardened. Aware of the slender resources of the State, deeply concerned for the loss of trade with Spain and the Netherlands, he maintained that Walsingham's policy would founder in bankruptcy and disaster.

Elizabeth was inclined to agree. She did not much like assisting other people's rebels—"you and your brethren in Christ," she once said mockingly to Walsingham. She was unsympathetic to irreconcilable Puritanism. But Walsingham's case had been violently strengthened by the Massacre of St Bartholomew, and she was compelled to move into a cold war in the Netherlands, and an undeclared war at sea, until she was confronted with the massive onslaught of an Armada.

* * * * *

These happenings had their effect on politics in England. Most of the Puritans had at first been willing to conform to Elizabeth's Church settlement in the hope of transforming it from within, but they now strove to drive the Government into an aggressive Protestant foreign policy, and at the same time secure their own freedom of religious organisation. Their position in the country was strong. They had allies at Court and Council, like Walsingham, with whom the Queen's favourite, Leicester, was now closely associated. In the towns and counties of South-Eastern England they were vociferous. In defiance of the Church Settlement they began to form their own religious communities, with their own ministers and forms of worship. Their aim and object was nothing less than the establishment of a theocratic despotism. Like the Catholics they held that Church and State were separate and independent. Unlike them, they believed the seat of Church authority lay in the council of elders, the Presbytery, freely chosen by the flock, but, once chosen, ruling with unlimited scope and supplanting the secular power over a large area of human life.

To such men the Elizabethan Settlement, the Anglican Church, with its historic liturgy and ceremonial, its comprehensive articles and its episcopal government, were abhorrent because unscriptural, as Calvin interpreted Scripture. It had indeed some of the weaknesses of a compromise. Moreover, outside London, the universities, and a few great towns, the average parson in the early years of Elizabeth's reign was not an impressive figure. Sometimes he had kept his benefice by conforming under Edward VI, changing his creed under Mary, and finally accepting what a rural bench once described as "the religion set forth by Her Majesty" as the only way of earning a living. With barely enough Latin to read the old service books, and scarcely literate enough to deliver a decent sermon, he was no match for the controversialists and disputants charged with enthusiasm and new ideas, eloquent preachers, scurrilous pamphleteers, who were stealing his flock from him, and implanting in them novel and alarming notions about the rights of congregations to organise themselves, to worship in their own way, and to settle their own Church order. And why not, some day, their own political order? If not in England, perhaps in another land? A crack was opening in the surface of English society, a crack which would widen into a gulf. The Lutheran Church fitted well enough with monarchy, even with absolutism, but Calvinism, as it spread out over Europe, was a dissolving agency, a violent interruption of historic continuity, and with the return and resurgence of the exiles who had fled from Mary Tudor an explosive element was lodged in the English Church and State which ultimately was to shatter both. Elizabeth knew that the Puritans were perhaps her most loyal subjects, but she feared that their violent impulse might not only provoke the European conflict she dreaded, but imperil the very unity of the realm. Neither she nor her Government dared yield a fraction of their authority. This was no time for religious war or upheaval at home.

Elizabeth's Council therefore struck back. The censorship of the Press was entrusted to a body of ecclesiastical commissioners, known as the Court of High Commission, which had been constituted in 1559 to deal with offences against the Church Settlement. This combining of the functions of bishop and censor infuriated the Puritan party. They set up a secret, itinerant Press which poured forth over the years a stream of virulent and anonymous pamphlets, culminating in 1588 with those issued under the name of "Martin Marprelate," attacking the persons and office of "the wainscot-faced bishops." Their sturdy and youthful invective shows a robust and relishing consciousness of the possibilities of English prose. The pamphlets are loaded with coarse, effective adjectives, and the sentences lumber along like the hay-cart in which the press itself was at one time concealed. For months the agents of High Commission hunted the originators of this secret propaganda. In the end an accident precipitated the press out of the hay-cart in a village street and led to the arrest of the printers. The authors were never traced.

* * * * *

The Catholic onslaught also gathered force. Throughout the 1570's numbers of Catholic priests were arriving in England from the English seminaries at Douai and St Omer, charged with the task of nourishing Catholic sentiment and maintaining connection between the English Catholics and Rome. Their presence at first aroused little apprehension in Government circles. Elizabeth was slow to believe that any of her Catholic subjects were traitors, and the failure of the 1569 rising had strengthened her confidence in their loyalty. But about the year 1579 missionaries of a new and formidable type began to slip into the country. These were the Jesuits, the heralds and missionaries of the Counter-Reformation. Their lives were dedicated to re-establishing the Catholic faith throughout Christendom. They were fanatics, indifferent to personal danger, and carefully chosen for their work. By their enemies they were accused of using assassination to achieve their aims. Foremost among them were Edmund Campion and Robert Parsons. Their movements were carefully watched by Walsingham's spies, and a number of plots against Elizabeth's life were uncovered. The Government was forced to take more drastic measures. Queen Mary had burnt some three hundred Protestant martyrs in the last three years of her reign. In the last thirty years of Elizabeth's reign about the same number of Catholics were executed for treason.

The conspiracies naturally focused upon the person of Mary Queen of Scots, long captive. She was the heir to the English throne in the event of Elizabeth's removal from the world. Elizabeth herself was reluctant to recognise the danger to her life, yet the plots sharpened the question of who should succeed to the English throne. The death of Mary would make her son James the heir to the crown of England, and James was in safe Calvinist hands in Scotland. To avoid having another Catholic Queen it was only necessary to dispose of Mary before the Jesuits, or their allies, disposed of Elizabeth. Walsingham and his party in the Council now concentrated their efforts on persuading the Queen that Mary must die. Plying her with evidence of Mary's complicity in the numerous conspiracies, they pressed hard on Elizabeth's conscience; but she shrank from the calculated shedding of royal blood.

There were signs that the Jesuit missions were not entirely

without result. But Elizabeth would not be hurried. She would wait upon events. They were soon decisive. In the midsummer of 1584 William the Silent, leader of the Dutch Protestant revolt against Spain, was fatally wounded by a Spanish agent in his house at Delft. Walsingham's arguments against Mary were overwhelmingly strengthened by this assassination, and English opinion reacted vehemently. At the same time Spanish feeling against England, already embittered by the raids conducted with Elizabeth's connivance of the English privateers, blazed into startling hostility. The Netherlands, once Spanish order had been restored, were to be a base for a final attack upon the Island, and Elizabeth was compelled to send Leicester with an English army to Holland to prevent the complete destruction of the Dutch.

* * * * *

A voluntary association of Protestant gentry was formed in 1585 for the defence of Elizabeth's life. In the following year evidence of a conspiracy, engineered by one Anthony Babington, an English Catholic, was laid before the Council by Walsingham. One of his agents had mingled with the conspirators for over a year. Mary's connivance was undeniable. Elizabeth was at last persuaded that her death was a political necessity. After a formal trial Mary was pronounced guilty of treason. Parliament petitioned for her execution, and Elizabeth at last signed the death warrant. Within twenty-four hours she regretted it and tried, too late, to stop the execution. She had a natural horror of being responsible for the judicial murder of a fellow sovereign, although she knew it was essential for the safety of her country. She was anxious that the supreme and final decision should not rest upon her.

The scene of Mary's death has caught the imagination of history. In the early morning of February 8, 1587, she was summoned to the great hall of Fotheringay Castle. Accompanied by six of her attendants, she awaited the servants of the English Queen. From the neighbouring countryside the gentry gathered to witness the sentence. Mary appeared at the appointed hour soberly clad in black satin. In the quietness of the hall she walked with stately movements to the cloth-covered scaffold erected by the fireplace. The solemn formalities were smoothly completed. But the zealous Dean of Peterborough attempted to force upon the Queen a last-minute conversion. With splendid dignity she brushed aside his loud exhortations. "Mr Dean," she said, "I am a Catholic, and must die a Catholic. It is useless to attempt to move me, and your prayers will avail me but little."

Mary had arrayed herself superbly for the final scene. As she disrobed for the headsman's act, her garments of black satin, removed by the weeping handmaids, revealed a bodice and petticoat of crimson velvet. One of her ladies handed her a pair of crimson sleeves, which she put on. Thus the unhappy Queen halted, for one last moment, standing blood-red from head to foot against the black background of the scaffold. There was a deathly hush throughout the hall. She knelt, and at the second stroke the final blow was delivered. The awed assembly had fulfilled its task. In death the majestic illusion was shattered. The head of an ageing woman with false hair was held up by the executioner. A lapdog crept out from beneath the clothes of the bleeding trunk.

As the news reached London bonfires were lit in the streets. Elizabeth sat alone in her room, weeping more for the fate of a Queen than a woman. The responsibility for this deed she shifted with an effort on to the shoulders of her masculine advisers.

The Spanish Armada

WAR was now certain. The chances were heavily weighted in favour of Spain. From the mines of Mexico and Peru there came a stream of silver and gold which so fortified the material power of the Spanish Empire that King Philip could equip his forces beyond all known scales. The position was well understood in the ruling circles of England. So long as Spain controlled the wealth of the New World she could launch and equip a multitude of Armadas; the treasure must therefore be arrested at its source or captured from the ships which conveyed it across the oceans. In the hope of strengthening her own finances and harassing the enemy's preparations against the Netherlands and ultimately against herself, Elizabeth had accordingly sanctioned a number of unofficial expeditions against the Spanish coasts and colonies in South America. These had continued for some time, and as yet without open declaration of war, but she had come to realise that scattered raids of which she professed no prior knowledge could do no lasting harm to the Spanish Empire beyond the seas or the Spanish power in Northern Europe. Gradually therefore these expeditions had assumed an official character, and the Royal Navy surviving from the days of Henry VIII was rebuilt and reorganised by John Hawkins, son of a Plymouth merchant, who had formerly traded with the Portuguese possessions in Brazil. Hawkins had learnt his seamanship in slave-running on the West African coast and in shipping Negroes to the Spanish colonies. In 1573 he was appointed Treasurer and Controller of the Navy. He had moreover educated an apt pupil, a young adventurer from Devon, Francis Drake.

This "Master Thief of the unknown world," as his Spanish contemporaries called Drake, became the terror of their ports and crews. His avowed object was to force England into open conflict with Spain, and his attacks on the Spanish treasure ships, his plundering of Spanish possessions on the western coast of the South American continent on his voyage round the world in 1577, and raids on Spanish harbours in Europe, all played their part in driving Spain to war. From their experiences on the Spanish Main the English seamen knew they could meet the challenge so long as reasonable equality was maintained. With the ships that Hawkins had built they could fight and sink anything the Spaniards might send against them.

Meanwhile Elizabeth's seamen had been gaining experience in unexplored waters. Spain was deliberately blocking the commercial enterprise of other nations in the New World so far as it was then known. A Devon gentleman, Humphrey Gilbert, began to look elsewhere, and was the first to interest the Queen in finding a route to China, or Cathay as it was called, by the North-West. He was a well-read man who had studied the achievements of contemporary explorers. He knew there were plenty of adventurers schooled in the straggling fighting in France and in the Netherlands on whose services he could call. In 1576 he wrote *A Discourse to prove a Passage by the North-West to Cathaia and the East Indies*. His book closed with a notable challenge: "He is not worthy to live at all, that for fear or danger of death shunneth his country's service and his own honour; seeing death is inevitable and the fame of virtue is immortal." His ideas inspired the voyages of Martin Frobisher, to whom the Queen granted a licence to explore. The Court and the City financed the expedition, and two small ships of twenty-five tons sailed in search of gold. Having charted the bleak coasts round Hudson Straits Frobisher came back. High hopes were entertained that the samples of black ore he brought with him might contain gold. There was disappointment when the ore was assayed and proved worthless. No quick riches were to be gained from adventures in the North-West.

Gilbert however was undaunted. He was the first Englishman who realised that the value of these voyages did not lie only in finding precious metals. There were too many people in England. Perhaps they could settle in the new lands. The idea of planting colonies in America now began to take hold of men's imaginations. A few bold spirits were already dreaming of New Englands that would arise across the ocean. At first they had strictly practical aims in mind. In the hope of transporting the needy unemployed to the New World, and of finding new markets among the natives for English cloth, Gilbert himself obtained a charter from Elizabeth in 1578, "to inhabit and possess at his choice all armed and heathen lands not in the actual possession of any Christian peoples." With eleven ships manned by many gentlemen adventurers, including his own stepbrother, Walter Raleigh, of whom more hereafter, he made several hopeful voyages, but none met with success.

In 1583 Gilbert took possession of Newfoundland in the Queen's name, but no permanent settlement was made. Resolved to try again in the following year, he set out for home. The little convoy encountered terrible seas, "breaking short and high pyramid-wise." A narrative written by one Edward

Hays survives. "Monday the 9th September in the afternoon, the frigate was near cast away, oppressed by waves, yet at that time recovered: and giving forth signs of joy, the General, sitting abaft with a book in his hand, cried out to us in the *Hind* so oft as we approached within hearing, 'We are as near to heaven by sea as by land.' " That night at twelve o'clock the lights of Gilbert's ship, the *Squirrel*, suddenly disappeared. The first great English pioneer of the West had gone to his death. Walter Raleigh tried to continue Gilbert's work. In 1585 a small colony was established on Roanoke Island, off the American continent, and christened Virginia in honour of the Queen. It was a vague term which came to include both the modern state and North Carolina. This venture also foundered, as did a second attempt two years later. But by now the threat from Spain was looming large, and to meet it all endeavour was concentrated at home. Colonial efforts were postponed for another twenty years by the Spanish War. In national resources the struggle that broke out was desperately unequal, but the Queen's seamen had received an unrivalled training which was to prove England's salvation.

*   *   *   *   *

The Spaniards had long contemplated an enterprise against England. They realised that English intervention threatened their attempts to reconquer the Netherlands and that unless England was overwhelmed the turmoil might continue indefinitely. Since the year 1585 they had been gathering information from many sources. English exiles sent lengthy reports to Madrid. Numerous agents supplied Philip with maps and statistics. The Spanish archives contain several draft plans for the invasion of England.

Troops were not the difficulty. If order were maintained for a while in the Netherlands an expeditionary force could be detached from the Spanish army. A corps was deemed sufficient. The building and assembly of a fleet was a more formidable undertaking. Most of the King of Spain's ships came from his Italian possessions and were built for use in the Mediterranean. They were unsuited to a voyage round the western coasts of Europe and up the Channel. The galleons constructed for the trade routes to the Spanish colonies in South America were too unwieldy. But in the year 1580 Philip II had annexed Portugal, and the Portuguese naval constructors had not been dominated by the Mediterranean. They had experimented with classes of ships for action in the South Atlantic, and Portuguese galleons therefore formed the basis of the fleet which was now concentrated in the harbour of Lisbon. Every available vessel was summoned into Western Spanish waters, including even the privately owned galleons of the convoying force named the Indian Guard. Preparations were delayed for a year by Drake's famous raid on Cadiz in 1587. In this "singeing of the King of Spain's beard" a large quantity of stores and ships was destroyed. Nevertheless in May 1588 the Armada was ready. A hundred and thirty ships were assembled, carrying 2,500 guns and more than 30,000 men, two thirds of them soldiers. Twenty were galleons, forty-four were armed merchantmen, and eight were Mediterranean galleys. The rest were either small craft or unarmed transports. Their aim was to sail up the Channel, embark the expeditionary corps of 16,000 veterans from the Netherlands under Alexander of Parma, and land it on the south coast of England.

The renowned Spanish Admiral Santa Cruz was now dead, and the command was entrusted to the Duke of Medina-Sidonia, who had many misgivings about the enterprise. His tactics followed the Mediterranean model of grappling with the enemy ships and gaining victory by boarding. His fleet was admirably equipped for carrying large numbers of men; it was strong in heavy short-range cannon, but weak in long-distance culverins—this was why the English kept out of range until the last battle. The seamen were few in proportion to the soldiers. These were recruited from the dregs of the Spanish population and commanded by army officers of noble families who had no experience of naval warfare. Many of the vessels were in bad repair; the provisions supplied under a corrupt system of private contract were insufficient and rotten; the drinking water leaked from butts of unseasoned wood. Their commander had no experience of war at sea, and had begged the King to excuse him from so novel an adventure.

The English plan was to gather a fleet in one of the south-western ports, intercept the enemy at the western entrance to the Channel, and concentrate troops in the south-east to meet Parma's army from the Flemish shore. It was uncertain where the attack would fall, but the prevailing westerly winds made it likely that the Armada would sail up the Channel, join Parma, and force a landing on the Essex coast.

The nation was united in the face of the Spanish preparations. Leading Catholics were interned in the Isle of Ely, but as a body their loyalty to the Crown was unshaken. An army was assembled at Tilbury which reached twenty thousand men, under the command of Lord Leicester. This, with the muster in the adjacent counties, constituted a force which should not be underrated. While the Armada was still off the coasts of England Queen Elizabeth reviewed the army at Tilbury and addressed them in these stirring words:

My loving people, who have been persuaded by some that are careful for our safety to take heed how we commit ourselves to armed multitudes, for fear of treachery. But I assure you I do not desire to live to distrust my faithful and loving people. Let tyrants fear. I have always so behaved myself that, under God, I have placed my chiefest strength and safeguard in the loyal hearts and goodwill of my subjects; and therefore I am come amongst you, as you see, resolved, in the midst and heat of the battle, to live or die amongst you all, to lay down for my God, and for my kingdom, and for my people, my honour and my blood, even in the dust. I know I have the body of a weak and feeble woman, but I have the heart and stomach of a king, and of a king of England too, and think foul scorn that Parmá or Spain or any prince of Europe should dare to invade the borders of my realm; to which, rather than any dishonour shall grow by me, I myself will take up arms, I myself will be your general, judge and re-warder of every one of your virtues in the field. I know already for your forwardness you have deserved rewards and crowns; and we do assure you, in the word of a prince, they shall be duly paid you.

*   *   *   *   *

Hawkins's work for the Navy was now to be tested. He had begun over the years to revise the design of English ships from his experience of buccaneering raids in colonial waters. The castles which towered above the galleon decks had been cut down; keels were deepened, and design was concen-trated on seaworthiness and speed. Most notable of all, heavier long-range guns were mounted. Cannon were tradi-tionally deemed "an ignoble arm," fit only for an opening salvo to a grappling fight, but Hawkins, with ships built to weather any seas, opposed hand-to-hand fighting and advo-cated battering the enemy from a distance with the new guns. The English sea-captains were eager to try these novel tactics against the huge overmasted enemy galleons, with their flat bottoms and a tendency to drift in a high wind. In spite of Hawkins's efforts only thirty-four of the Queen's ships, carrying six thousand men, could put to sea in 1588. As was the custom however all available privately owned vessels were hastily collected and armed for the service of the Government, and a total of a hundred and ninety-seven ships was mustered; but at least half of them were too small to be of much service.

The Queen had urged her seamen to "keep an eye upon Parma," and she was nervous of sending the main fleet as far west as Plymouth. Drake was for bolder measures. In a dispatch of March 30, 1588, he proposed sending the main body to attack a port on the Spanish coast—not Lisbon, which was well fortified, but somewhere near by, so as to force the Armada to sea in defence of the coastline. Thus, it was argued, the English would be certain of engaging the Spanish fleet and there would be no danger of its slipping past them on a favourable wind into the Channel.

The Government preferred the much more perilous idea of stationing isolated squadrons at intervals along the south coast to meet all possible lines of attack. They insisted on concentrating a small squadron of the Queen's ships at the eastern end of the Channel to keep watch on Parma. Drake and his superior, Lord Howard of Effingham, the commander of the English fleet, were alarmed and impatient, and with the greatest difficulty prevented a further dispersion of their forces. A southerly gale stopped their attacking the Spanish coast, and they were driven into Plymouth with their supplies exhausted and scurvy raging through the ships.

In the event they had plenty of time to consider their strategy. The Armada left the Tagus on May 20, but was smitten by the same storms which had repulsed Howard and Drake. Two of their 1,000-ton ships were dismasted. They put in to refit at Corunna, and did not set sail again until

July 12. News of their approach off the Lizard was brought into Plymouth harbour on the evening of July 19. The English fleet had to put out of the Sound the same night against light adverse winds which freshened the following day. A sober nautical account of the operation is preserved in Howard's letter to Walsingham of July 21.

> Although the wind was very scant we first warped out of harbour that night, and upon Saturday turned out very hardly, the wind being at south-west; and about three o'clock of the afternoon descried the Spanish fleet, and did what we could to work for the wind, which [by this] morning we had recovered, descrying their fleet to consist of 120 sail, whereof there are four galleases [galleys] and many ships of great burden. At nine of the clock we gave them fight, which continued until one.[1]

If Medina-Sidonia had attacked the English vessels to leeward of his ships as they struggled to clear the land on the Saturday there would have been a disaster for the English. But his instructions bound him to sail up the Channel, unite with Parma, and help transport to England the veteran troops assembled near Dunkirk. His report to Madrid shows how little he realised his opportunity. By difficult, patient, precarious tacking the English fleet got to windward of him, and for nine days hung upon the Armada as it ran before the westerly wind up the Channel, pounding away with their long-range guns at the lumbering galleons. They had gained the weather gauge. On July 23 the wind sank and both fleets lay becalmed off Portland Bill. The Spaniards attempted a counter-attack with Neapolitan galleys, rowed by hundreds of slaves, but Drake, followed by Howard, swept in upon the main

---

[1] Laughton, *Defeat of the Spanish Armada* (Navy Records Society, 1894), vol. i, p. 273.

body, and, as Howard reported, "the Spaniards were forced to give way and flocked together like sheep."

A further engagement followed on the 25th off the Isle of Wight. It looked as if the Spaniards planned to seize the island as a base. But as the westerly breeze blew stronger the English still lay to windward and drove them once more to sea in the direction of Calais, where Medina, ignorant of Parma's movements, hoped to collect news. The Channel passage was a torment to the Spaniards. The guns of the English ships raked the decks of the galleons, killing the crews and demoralising the soldiers. The English suffered hardly any loss.

Medina then made a fatal mistake. He anchored in Calais Roads. The Queen's ships which had been stationed in the eastern end of the Channel joined the main fleet in the straits, and the whole sea-power of England was now combined. A council of war held in the English flagship during the evening of July 28 resolved to attack. The decisive engagement opened. After darkness had fallen eight ships from the eastern squadron which had been filled with explosives and prepared as fire-ships—the torpedoes of those days—were sent against the crowded Spanish fleet at anchor in the roads. Lying on their decks, the Spanish crews must have seen unusual lights creeping along the decks of strange vessels moving towards them. Suddenly a series of explosions shook the air, and flaming hulks drifted towards the anchored Armada. The Spanish captains cut their cables and made for the open sea. Collisions without number followed. One of the largest galleys, the *San Lorenzo*, lost its rudder and drifted aground in Calais harbour, where the Governor interned the crew. The rest of the fleet, with a south-south-west wind behind it, made eastwards to Gravelines.

Medina now sent messengers to Parma announcing his arrival, and by dawn on July 29 he was off the sandbanks of

Gravelines expecting to find Parma's troops ready shipped in their transports. But there was no sail to be seen. The tides in Dunkirk harbour were at the neap. It was only possible to sail out with a favourable wind upon a spring tide. Neither condition was present. The army and the transports were not at their rendezvous. The Spaniards turned to face their pursuers. A desperate fight raged for eight hours, a confused conflict of ships engaging at close quarters. The official report sent to the English Government was brief: "Howard in fight spoiled a great number of the Spaniards, sank three and drove four or five on the banks." The English had completely exhausted their ammunition, and but for this hardly a Spanish ship would have got away. Yet Howard himself scarcely realised the magnitude of his victory. "Their force is wonderful great and strong," he wrote on the evening after the battle, "yet we pluck their feathers by little and little."

The tormented Armada now sailed northwards out of the fight. Their one aim was to make for home. The horrors of the long voyage round the north of Scotland began. Not once did they turn upon the small, silent ships which followed them in their course. Neither side had enough ammunition.

The homeward voyage of the Armada proved the qualities of the Spanish seamen. Facing mountainous seas and racing tides, they escaped from their pursuers. The English ships, short of food and shot, their crews grumbling at their wretched outfits, were compelled to turn southwards to the Channel ports. The weather helped the Spaniards. The westerly wind drove two of the galleons as wrecks upon the coast of Norway; but then it shifted. As Medina recorded, "We passed the isles at the north of Scotland, and we are now sailing towards Spain with the wind at north-east." Sailing southwards, they were forced to make for the western coast of Ireland to replenish their supplies of water. They had already cast their horses and mules into the sea. The decision to put in on the Irish coast was disastrous. Their ships had been shattered by the English cannonades and now were struck by the autumn gales. Seventeen went ashore. The search for water cost more than five thousand Spanish lives. Nevertheless over sixty-five ships, about half of the fleet that had put to sea, reached Spanish ports during the month of October.

The English had not lost a single ship, and scarcely a hundred men. But their captains were disappointed. For the last thirty years they had believed themselves superior to their opponents. They had now found themselves fighting a much bigger fleet than they had imagined the Spaniards could put to sea. Their own ships had been sparingly equipped. Their ammunition had run short at a crucial moment. The gunnery of the merchant vessels had proved poor and half the enemy's fleet had got away. There were no boastings; they recorded their dissatisfactions.

But to the English people as a whole the defeat of the Armada came as a miracle. For thirty years the shadow of Spanish power had darkened the political scene. A wave of religious emotion filled men's minds. One of the medals struck to commemorate the victory bears the inscription *"Afflavit Deus et dissipantur"*—"God blew and they were scattered."

Elizabeth and her seamen knew how true this was. The Armada had indeed been bruised in battle, but it was demoralised and set on the run by the weather. Yet the event was decisive. The English seamen might well have triumphed. Though limited in supplies and ships the new tactics of Hawkins had brought success. The nation was transported with relief and pride. Shakespeare was writing *King John* a few years later. His words struck into the hearts of his audiences:

> Come the three corners of the world in arms,
> And we shall shock them. Nought shall make us rue
> If England to itself do rest but true.

Gloriana

WITH 1588 the crisis of the reign was past. England had emerged from the Armada year as a first-class Power. She had resisted the weight of the mightiest empire that had been seen since Roman times. Her people awoke to a consciousness of their greatness, and the last years of Elizabeth's reign saw a welling up of national energy and enthusiasm focusing upon the person of the Queen. In the year following the Armada the first three books were published of Spenser's *Faerie Queene,* in which Elizabeth is hymned as Gloriana. Poets and courtiers alike paid their homage to the sovereign who symbolised the great achievement. Elizabeth had schooled a generation of Englishmen.

The success of the seamen pointed the way to wide opportunities of winning wealth and fame in daring expeditions. In 1589 Richard Hakluyt first published his magnificent book, *The Principal Navigations, Traffics and Discoveries of the English Nation.* Here in their own words the audacious navigators tell their story. Hakluyt speaks for the thrusting spirit of the age when he proclaims that the English nation, "in searching the most opposite corners and quarters of the world, and, to speak plainly, in compassing the vast globe of the earth more than once, have excelled all the nations and peoples of the earth." Before the reign came to a close another significant enterprise took its beginning. For years past Englishmen had been probing their way through to the East, round the Cape of Good Hope and overland across the expanses of the Middle East. Their venturies led to the founding of the East India Company. At the start it was a small and struggling affair, with a capital of only £72,000. Dazzling dividends were to be won from this investment. The British Empire in India, which was to be painfully built up in the course of the next three centuries, owes its origins to the charter granted by Queen Elizabeth to a group of London merchants and financiers in the year 1600.

The young men who now rose to prominence in the Court of the ageing Queen plagued their mistress to allow them to try their hand in many enterprises. The coming years resound with attacks upon the forces and allies of Spain throughout the world—expeditions to Cadiz, to the Azores, into the Caribbean Sea, to the Low Countries, and, in support of the Huguenots, to the northern coasts of France. The story is one of confused running fights, conducted with slender re- sources and culminating in a few great moments. The war against Spain, which had never been officially declared, ex- tended its heavy burden into the first year of the reign of Elizabeth's successor. The policy of the English Government was to distract the enemy in every quarter of the world, and by subsidising the Protestant elements in the Low Countries and in France to prevent any concentration of force against them- selves. At the same time England intervened to prevent the Spaniards from seizing ports on the Norman and Breton coasts which might be used as bases for another invasion. As a result of these continued though rather meagre efforts the slow victory of the Dutch in Holland and the Huguenots in France brought its reward. The eventual triumph of Henry of Navarre, the Protestant champion and heir to the French throne, was due as much to his acceptance of the Catholic faith as to victories in the field. Paris, as he is supposed to have said, was worth a Mass. His decision put an end to the French religious wars and removed the danger to England of a

Spanish-backed monarch in Paris. The Dutch too were beginning to hold their own. The Island was at last secure.

But there was no way of delivering a decisive stroke against Spain. The English Government had no money for further efforts. The total revenues of the Crown hardly exceeded £300,000 a year, including the fruits of taxation granted by Parliament. Out of this sum all expenses of Court and Government had to be met. The cost of defeating the Armada is reckoned to have amounted to £160,000, and the Netherlands expeditionary force at one stage was calling for £126,000 a year. The lights of enthusiasm slowly faded out. In 1595 Raleigh again tried his hand, this time in search of Eldorado in Guiana. But his expedition brought no profits home. At the same time Drake and the veteran Hawkins, now in his sixties, set out on a last voyage. Hawkins fell ill, and as his fleet was anchoring off Porto Rico he died in his cabin. Drake, cast down by the death of his old patron, sailed on to attack the rich city of Panama. With a dash of his former spirit he swept into the bay of Nombre de Dios. But conditions were now very different. The early days had gone for ever. Spanish government in the New World was now well equipped and well armed. The raid was beaten off. The English fleet put out to sea, and in January 1596 Francis Drake, having assumed his armour to meet death like a soldier, expired in his ship. John Stow, a contemporary English chronicler, writes of him, "He was as famous in Europe and America as Tamburlaine in Asia and Africa."

As the conflict with Spain drew inconclusively on, and both sides struck at each other in ever-growing, offensive exhaustion, the heroic age of sea fights passed away. One epic moment has survived in the annals of the English race—the last fight of the *Revenge* at Flores, in the Azores. "In the year 1591," says Bacon, "was that memorable fight of an

English ship called the *Revenge,* under the command of Sir
Richard Grenville, memorable (I say) even beyond credit and
to the height of some heroical fable: and though it were a
defeat, yet it exceeded a victory; being like the act of Samson,
that killed more men at his death, than he had done in the
time of all his life. This ship, for the space of fifteen hours,
sate like a stag amongst hounds at bay, and was sieged and
fought with, in turn, by fifteen great ships of Spain, part of a
navy of fifty-five ships in all; the rest like abettors looking on
afar off. And amongst the fifteen ships that fought, the great
San Philippo was one; a ship of fifteen hundred ton, prince
of the twelve *Sea Apostles,* which was right glad when she
was shifted off from the *Revenge.* This brave ship the *Revenge,* being manned only with two hundred soldiers and
marines, whereof eighty lay sick, yet nevertheless after a fight
maintained (as was said) of fifteen hours, and two ships of
the enemy sunk by her side, besides many more torn and bat-
tered and great slaughter of men, never came to be entered,
but was taken by composition; the enemies themselves having
in admiration the virtue of the commander and the whole
tragedy of that ship."

It is well to remember the ordinary seamen who sailed in
ships sometimes as small as twenty tons into the wastes of the
North and South Atlantic, ill-fed and badly paid, on risky adventures backed by inadequate capital. These men faced
death in many forms—death by disease, death by drowning,
death from Spanish pikes and guns, death by starvation and
cold on uninhabited coasts, death in the Spanish prisons. The
Admiral of the English fleet, Lord Howard of Effingham,
spoke their epitaph: "God send us to sea in such a company
together again, when need is."

*   *   *   *   *

Victory over Spain was the most shining achievement of Elizabeth's reign, but by no means the only one. The repulse of the Armada had subdued religious dissension at home. Events which had swung England towards Puritanism while the Catholic danger was impending swung her back to the Anglican settlement when the peril vanished in the smoke of the burning Armada at Gravelines. A few months later, in a sermon at St Paul's Cross, Richard Bancroft, who was later to be Archbishop of Canterbury, attacked the Puritan theme with the confidence of a man who was convinced that the Anglican Church was not a political contrivance, but a divine institution. He took the only line on which the defence of the Church could be sustained with an enthusiasm equal to that of its assailants: it was not "the religion set forth by Her Majesty," but the Church of the Apostles still subsisting by virtue of the episcopal succession. But Bancroft saw also that to maintain the cause a better type of clergy was needed, men of "solid learning," and such he set himself to provide. "If he had lived," Clarendon wrote a century later, "he would quickly have extinguished all that fire in England which had been kindled at Geneva." But the fire was still dangerously smouldering when Elizabeth died.

Nevertheless the Church she had nursed to strength was a very different body from the half-hearted and distracted community of her early years: more confident, more learned, far less inclined to compromise with dissidents within or separatists without; strong in the attachment of thousands to whom its liturgy had become dear by habit and who thought of it as the Church into which they had been baptised. Their devotion to the Church of England as a sacred institution was as profound and sincere as the attachment of the Calvinist to his presbytery or the Independent to his congregation. And, bitter as the coming divisions were to be, England united in prizing Elizabeth's service to her people and to religion. "Queen Elizabeth of famous memory," Oliver Cromwell called her, and added, "we need not be ashamed to call her so." And those whose memories went back to the dark years of disaster and persecution, who had seen the Spanish peril growing till it broke in ruins, could hardly fail to re-echo in their hearts the majestic utterance of Richard Hooker, author of the classic justification of the Elizabethan Church, *Of the Laws of Ecclesiastical Polity*. "As, by the sword of God and Gideon, was sometime the cry of the people of Israel," he wrote, "so it might deservedly be at this day the joyful song of innumerable multitudes, and the true inscription, style, or title of all churches yet standing within this realm: by the goodness of Almighty God and his servant Elizabeth, we are."

*   *   *   *   *

By now the men who had governed England since the 1550's were passing from power and success to their graves. Leicester had died in the last days of 1588, Walsingham in 1590, and Burghley in 1598. The fifteen years which followed the Armada are dominated by other figures. War with Spain had set a premium on martial virtues. Young and eager men like Walter Raleigh and Robert Devereux, Earl of Essex, quarrelled for permission to lead enterprises against the Spaniards. The Queen hesitated. She knew that the security she had striven for all her life was very fragile. She knew the danger of provoking the might of Spain, backed as it was by all the wealth of the Indies. She was growing old and out of touch with the younger generation, and her quarrel with Essex marked and revealed her changing mood.

Essex was Leicester's stepson, and Leicester brought him into the circle of the Court. He found the Government in the hands of the cautious Cecils, William, Lord Burghley, and his son Robert. The Queen's favour had lighted upon the hard, handsome, and ambitious Captain of the Guard, Sir Walter Raleigh. Essex was the younger and the more fiery, and he soon displaced the Captain in the affections of Elizabeth. He too was ambitious, and set out to create his own party in Court and Council and subdue the influence of the Cecils. He found support in the Bacon brothers, Anthony and Francis, sons of the Lord Keeper, Nicholas Bacon, who had earlier in the reign been a colleague and brother-in-law of Burghley's. The young nephews were discontented with Burghley's lack of attention. They were dangerous enemies, and Essex was a convenient figurehead for thrusting a more forward policy upon the Queen. They had both served in the Embassy in Paris, and, like Walsingham, had built up an admirable intelligence service. It was with their help that Essex became an expert on foreign affairs and showed the Queen that he had ability as well as charm. In 1593 he was made a Privy Counsellor. Relations with Spain were again becoming tense. Essex soon headed the war party in the Council; and once the old Lord Treasurer pulled a Prayer Book out of his pocket and, shaking a finger at his young opponent, read out the verse, "Bloodthirsty and deceitful men shall not live out half their days." In 1596 an expedition was sent against Cadiz under the joint command of Essex and Raleigh. In the sea fight for the harbour Raleigh was the outstanding leader. The Spanish fleet was burned and the town lay open to the English crews. Essex was the hero of the shore fight. It was a brilliant combined operation, and Cadiz was held by the English for a fortnight. The fleet returned home triumphant, but, to Elizabeth's regret, little the richer. During its absence Robert Cecil had become Secretary of State.

Victory at Cadiz heightened the popularity of Essex among

the younger members of the Court and throughout the country. The Queen received him graciously, but with secret misgiving. Was he the incarnation of the spirit of this new generation, whose rash eagerness she feared? Would the younger men look to him rather than to her as their leader? For the moment all went well. Essex was made Master of the Ordnance. He was given command of an expedition to intercept a further Armada now gathering in the ports of Western Spain. In the summer of 1597 it seemed that another "Enterprise of England" was about to sail. The English ships headed south-west and made for the Azores. There was no sign of the great fleet whose passage they were to bar, but the islands made a convenient base where they could await the treasure ships from the New World. Raleigh too was in the expedition. The English failed to take any of the island ports; the Spanish Treasure Fleet eluded them; the Armada put out into the Bay of Biscay with the seas clear of defending ships to the north. Once again the winds saved the Island. The badly manned galleons tottered into a northern gale scattered and sinking. The disorganised fleet crept back into its ports. King Philip was kneeling in his chapel in the Escorial praying for his ships. Before the news of their return could reach him he was seized with a paralytic stroke, and the tale of their failure was brought to him on his deathbed.

Essex came home to find a sovereign still vigorous and dominating. The muddle and quarrelling which had marred the Azores expedition enraged Elizabeth. She declared she would never send the Fleet out of the Channel again, and this time she kept her word. Essex retired from Court, and thunderous days followed. Essex was sure he was misunderstood. There was a plaintive correspondence. Wild thoughts went surging through his mind. A little group gathered round him and schemed to force the sun of the royal favour into the heavens again.

Troubles in Ireland, which now came to a head, seemed to offer him the chance of recovering both the Queen's goodwill and his own prestige. Throughout the reign Ireland had presented an intractable problem. Henry VIII had assumed the title of King of Ireland, but this involved no real extension of his authority. Though Irish chiefs were given English titles, in the hope of converting them into magnates on the English pattern, they still clung to their ancient feuding clan-life, and largely ignored the commands of the Lord Lieutenants in Dublin. The Counter-Reformation revived and reanimated opposition to Protestant England. For the Queen's Government in London this meant strategic anxieties, since any power hostile to England could readily take advantage of Irish discontents. Able Viceroys with small forces tried hard to impose order and respect for English law, and efforts were made to plant and colonise the country with reliable settlers. But these measures met with no striking success. In the first thirty years of Elizabeth's reign Ireland was shaken by three major rebellions. Now in the 1590's a fourth rising had erupted into a wearing and expensive war.

With Spanish backing, Hugh O'Neill, Earl of Tyrone, was threatening the whole English dominance of Ireland. If Essex became Lord Deputy and destroyed the rebellion he might recover his power in England. It was a perilous gamble. In April 1599 Essex was allowed to go to Ireland, at the head of the largest army that England had ever sent there. He accomplished nothing and was on the verge of ruin. But he planned a dramatic stroke. Disobeying the express orders of the Queen, he deserted his command and rode in haste to London unannounced. Robert Cecil had quietly waited for his rival to overreach himself. Angry scenes followed between Essex and the Queen, and the Earl was confined to his house. Weeks dragged by, and a desperate plot was made by Essex and his younger companions, including Shake-speare's patron, the Earl of Southampton. There was to be a rising in the City, a concentration upon Whitehall, and a seizure of the Queen's person. To symbolise the result a new play, which culminated in a royal dethronement, was to be produced at Southwark—Shakespeare's *Richard II*.

The scheme failed, and the end came in February 1601 with Essex's death on Tower Hill. Among the witnesses of the execution was Walter Raleigh. Silently Raleigh walked across to the door of the White Tower and climbed the stair-way through the armoury, to look down upon the block where he too, last of the Elizabethans, was to meet the same end. The young Earl of Southampton was spared.

Elizabeth well understood the issues at stake. Essex had been not simply a courtier soliciting, and even fighting for, the affections of his Queen. He was the leader of a bid for power by a faction of her Court. Acutely aware of the Queen's ad-vancing years, he aimed to control the succession and to dominate the next sovereign. This was not yet an age of party politics, but of patronage and clientage. No fundamental prin-ciple divided Essex from Raleigh or the Bacons from Cecil. The spoils of office, power, and influence were at stake, and victorious Essex would have dispensed appointments through-out England, and perhaps even have dictated terms to the Queen. But long years of statesmanship served Elizabeth better than the driving ambition of a courtier half her age. She struck back; and in destroying Essex she saved England from the consumption of civil war.

For the English cause in Ireland the flight of Essex proved a blessing. He was succeeded by Lord Mountjoy, a tenacious and energetic commander, who soon had the rebellion under control. When a Spanish force, some four thousand strong, landed at Kinsale in 1601 they were too late. Mountjoy

routed their Irish allies and compelled the Spaniards to surrender. Even Tyrone finally made his submission. Ireland
had at last, though only temporarily, been conquered by English arms.

* * * * *

If Essex challenged the political power of Elizabeth, more
significant for the future was the challenge to her constitutional power in the Parliament of 1601. Throughout the
reign the weight and authority of Parliament had been steadily growing. Now the issue turned on monopolies. For some
time the Crown had eked out its slender income by various
devices, including the granting of patents of monopolies to
courtiers and others in return for payment. Some of these
grants could be justified as protecting and encouraging inven-
tions, but frequently they amounted merely to unjustified
privileges, involving high prices that placed a burden upon
every citizen. In 1601 grievances flared up into a full-dress
debate in the House of Commons. An angry Member read
out a list extending from a patent for iron manufacture to a
patent for drying pilchards. "Is not bread there?" shouted
another back-bencher. The uproar in the House brought a
stinging rebuke from Mr Secretary Cecil. "What an indignity
then is it," he exclaimed, "that when any is discussing this
point he should be cried and coughed down. This is more
fit for a grammar-school than a Parliament." But the Queen
preferred subtler methods. If the Commons pushed their proposals to a division the whole basis of her constitutional
authority would be under fire. She acted swiftly now. Some
monopolies were abolished forthwith. All, she promised,
would be investigated. So she forestalled the direct challenge,
and in a golden speech to a large gathering of her Commons
summoned to her chamber she told them, "Though God
hath raised me high, yet this I account the glory of my crown,

that I have reigned with your loves." It was to be her last appearance in their midst.

The immense vitality displayed by the Queen throughout the troublous years of her rule in England ebbed slowly and relentlessly away. She lay for days upon a heap of cushions in her room. For hours the soundless agony was prolonged. The corridors without echoed with the hurrying of agitated feet. At last Robert Cecil dared to speak. "Your Majesty, to content the people you must go to bed." "Little man," came the answer, "is 'must' a word to use to princes?" The old Archbishop of Canterbury, Whitgift, her "little black husband," as she had once called him, knelt praying at her side. In the early hours of the morning of March 24, 1603, Queen Elizabeth died.

* * * * *

Thus ended the Tudor dynasty. For over a hundred years, with a handful of bodyguards, they had maintained their sovereignty, kept the peace, baffled the diplomacy and onslaughts of Europe, and guided the country through changes which might well have wrecked it. Parliament was becoming a solid affair based on a working harmony between Sovereign, Lords and Commons, and the traditions of English monarchical government had been restored and gloriously enhanced. But these achievements carried no guarantee of their perpetuation. The monarchy could only govern if it was popular. The Crown was now to pass to an alien Scottish line, hostile in political instincts to the class which administered England. The good understanding with Parliament which the Tudors had nourished came to a fretful close. The new kings soon clashed with the forces of a growing nation, and out of this conflict came the Civil War, the Republican interlude, the Restoration and the Revolution settlement.

BOOK FIVE

THE
CIVIL WAR

The United Crowns

KING JAMES OF SCOTLAND was the only son of
Mary Queen of Scots. He had been subjected from his
youth to a rigid Calvinist upbringing which was not much
to his taste. With little money and strict tutors he had long
coveted the throne of England, but till the last moment the
prize had seemed elusive. The struggle for power and favour
between Essex and Robert Cecil might always have provoked
Elizabeth, whom he knew only by intermittent correspondence, into some swift decision which would lose him the
crown. But now all appeared settled. Cecil was his ally and
skilful manager in the tense days after the Queen died. James
was proclaimed King James I of England without opposition,
and in April 1603 began a leisurely journey from Holyrood
to London.

He was a stranger and an alien, and his qualifications for
governing England were yet to be tested. "So ignorant," says
Trevelyan, was James "of England and her laws that at
Newark he ordered a cut-purse caught in the act to be hanged
without a trial at a word from his royal mouth." The execution did not take place. James detested the political ideas of
his Calvinist mentors. He had fixed ideas about kingship and
the divine right of monarchs to rule. He was a scholar with
pretensions to being a philosopher, and in the course of his
life published numerous tracts and treatises, ranging from
denunciations of witchcraft and tobacco to abstract political
theory. He came to England with a closed mind, and a weakness for lecturing. But England was changing. The habit of

obedience to a dynasty had died with the last of the Tudors. Spain was no longer a threat, and the Union of the Crowns deprived foreign enemies of an ally, or even a foothold, in the Island. The country gentlemen on whom the Tudors relied to maintain a balance against the old nobility, and on whom they had devolved the whole business of local government, were beginning to feel their strength. England was secure, free to attend to her own concerns, and a powerful class was now eager to take a hand in their management. On the other hand, James's title to the crown was not impeccable, and the doctrine of Divine Right, originally devised to justify the existence of national sovereignties against a universal Church or Empire, was called in to fortify his position. But how to reconcile a king claiming to rule by Divine Right and a Parliament with no other basis than ancient custom?

Over these deep-cutting issues there loomed a fiscal crisis of the first magnitude. The importation of precious metals from the New World had swelled the rise in prices, and throughout Europe inflation reigned; every year the fixed revenues of the Crown were worth less and less. By extreme frugality Elizabeth had postponed a conflict. But it could not be averted, and bound up with it was a formidable constitutional problem. Who was to have the last word in the matter of taxation? Hitherto everyone had accepted the medieval doctrine that "The King may not rule his people by other laws than they assent unto, and therefore he may set upon them no imposition, i.e. tax, without their assent." But no one had analysed it, or traced out its implications in any detail. If this were the fundamental law of England, did it come from the mists of antiquity or from the indulgence of former kings? Was it the inalienable birthright of Englishmen, or a concession which might be revoked? Was the King beneath the law or was he not? And who was to say what the law was? The greater part of the seventeenth century was to be spent in trying to find answers, historical, legal, theoretical, and practical, to such questions. Lawyers, scholars, statesmen, soldiers, all joined in this great debate. Relief at an undisputed succession gave the new sovereign a loyal, and even enthusiastic, reception. But James and his subjects were soon at odds about this and other topics.

His first Parliament at once raised the question of Parliamentary privilege and Royal Prerogative. In dutiful but firm language the Commons drew up an Apology reminding the King that their liberties included free elections, free speech, and freedom from arrest during Parliamentary sessions. "The prerogative of princes," they protested, "may easily and daily grow, while the privileges of the subject are for the most part at an everlasting stand. . . . The voice of the people . . . in the things of their knowledge is said to be as the voice of God." James, like his son after him, treated these expressions of national grievance contemptuously, brushing them aside as personal insults to himself and mere breaches of good manners.

Hitherto James had been straitened; now he thought he was rich. The "beggarly Scotsmen" who had come South with him also enriched themselves. The expenses of the Court increased at an alarming rate. To his surprise James very soon found himself pressed for money. This meant frequent Parliaments. Frequent Parliaments gave Members the opportunity to organise themselves, and James neglected to control Parliamentary sessions through his Privy Counsellors, as Elizabeth had done. Robert Cecil, now Earl of Salisbury, had no direct contact with the Commons. The King indulged his taste for lecturing, and frequently reminded them of his Divine Right to rule and their solemn duty to supply his needs.

It was an ancient and obstinate belief that the King should "live of his own," and that the traditional revenues from the Crown lands and from the customs should suffice for the upkeep of the public services. Parliament normally voted customs duties to each monarch for life, and did not expect to have to provide more money except in emergencies. To meet his needs James had to stress and revive the prerogative rights of taxation of the medieval kings, and he soon irritated a House which remembered its recent victory over Elizabeth upon monopolies. Fortunately the judges ruled that the ports were under the King's exclusive jurisdiction and that he could issue a "book of rates"—that is, impose extra customs duties —as he thought fit. This gave James a revenue that, unlike the old feudal grants, rose with the increasing national wealth and the higher prices. The Commons questioned the judges' ruling, and James made matters worse by turning the argument into a technical one about Royal Prerogative. Here, but only for a time, the matter rested.

The King had decided views on religion. He was greeted upon his accession with a petition from the Puritans, whose organisation Elizabeth had broken in the 1590's. The opponents of the episcopal State Church now hoped that the new King from Calvinist Scotland would listen to their case; a milder party would have been satisfied with some modification of ceremony. But James had had enough of the Kirk. He realised that Calvinism and monarchy would quarrel in the long run and that if men could decide for themselves about religion they could also decide for themselves on politics. In 1604 he held a conference at Hampton Court between the Puritan leaders and those who accepted the Elizabethan system. His prejudice was soon manifest. In the middle of the debate he accused the Puritans of aiming "at a Scottish presbytery which agreeth as well with the monarch as

God and the Devil. . . . Then Jack and Tom and Will and Dick shall meet and at their pleasure censor me and my Council and all our proceedings. Then Will shall stand up and say, 'It must be thus'; then Dick shall reply and say, 'Nay, marry, but we will have it thus.' . . . Stay, I pray you, for one seven years before you demand that from me, and if then you find me pursy and fat, and my windpipes stuffed, I will perhaps hearken to you; for let that Government be once up, I am sure I shall be kept in breath; then shall we all of us have work enough, both our hands full." James made it clear there would be no changes in the Elizabethan Church Settlement. His slogan was "No Bishop, no King."

The Catholics were also anxious and hopeful. After all, the King's mother had been their champion. Their position was delicate. If the Pope would allow them to give their secular allegiance to the King, James might let them practise their own religion. But the Pope would not yield. He forbade allegiance to a heretical sovereign. Upon this there could be no compromise. A European controversy was raging about the nature of obedience and James plunged into the argument. The Jesuits who had assailed Elizabeth were all-powerful at Rome, and replied with many volumes attacking his right to the throne. The air seemed charged with plots. James, although inclined to toleration, was forced to act. Catholics were fined for refusing to attend the services of the Established Church and their priests were banished.

Disappointment and despair led a small group of Catholic gentry to an infernal design for blowing up James and his whole Parliament by gunpowder while they were in session at Westminster. They hoped that this would be followed by a Catholic rising and that in the confusion a Catholic régime might be re-established with Spanish help. The chief plotter was Robert Catesby, assisted by Guy Fawkes, a veteran of the Spanish wars against the Dutch. One of their followers warned a relative who was a Catholic peer. The story reached Cecil, and the cellars of Parliament were searched. Fawkes was taken on the spot, and there was a storm of excitement in the City. James went down to open Parliament, and made an emotional speech upon what an honourable end it would have been to die with his faithful Commons. Kings, he said, were exposed to perils beyond those of ordinary mortals; only his own cleverness had saved them all from destruction. The House displayed an incomprehensible indifference, and, turning to the business of the day, discussed the petition of a Member who had asked to be relieved of his Parliamentary duties owing to an attack of gout. The conspirators were hunted down, tortured and executed. So novel and so wholesale a treason exposed the Catholic community to immediate and severe persecution and a more persistent and widespread detestation. The Thanksgiving Service for the deliverance of November 5 was not removed from the Prayer Book till 1854; and the anniversary, which even now is celebrated by bonfires and fireworks, was marred and enlivened until modern times by anti-Popery demonstrations.

*   *   *   *   *

At this time a splendid and lasting monument was created to the genius of the English-speaking peoples. All the Puritan demands had been rejected, but towards the end of the Hampton Court conference a Puritan divine, Dr John Reynolds, President of the Oxford College of Corpus Christi, had asked, seemingly on the spur of the moment, if a new version of the Bible could be produced. The idea appealed to James. Till now the clergy and laity had relied on a number of different translations—Tyndal's, Coverdale's, the Geneva Bible, the "Bishop's Bible" of Queen Elizabeth. Their texts varied. Some were disfigured by marginal notes and glosses upholding and advocating partisan interpretations of Scripture and extremist theories of ecclesiastical organisation. Each party and sect used the version which best suited its own views and doctrines. Here, thought James, was the chance to rid the Scriptures of propaganda and produce a uniform version which could be entrusted to all. Within a few months committees or "companies" were set up, two each in Oxford, Cambridge, and Westminster, comprising in all about fifty scholars and divines. They were selected for this work without regard to their theological or ecclesiastical bias. Directions were issued with speed. Each committee was assigned a portion of the text, and their draft was to be scrutinised by all the other committees and finally revised by a committee of twelve. Tendentious renderings were forbidden, and marginal notes or glosses were prohibited except for cross-references or to explain the meaning of Greek or Hebrew words which were difficult to translate. About three years passed in preliminary research, and the main work did not get under way till 1607, but it was then accomplished with remarkable swiftness. In an age without an efficient postal service or mechanical methods of copying and duplicating texts, the committees, though separated by considerable distances, finished their task in 1609. Nine months sufficed for the scrutiny of the supervisory committee, and in 1611 the Authorised Version of the Bible was produced by the King's Printer.

It won an immediate and lasting triumph. Copies could be bought for as little as five shillings, and even with the inflated prices of to-day can still be purchased for this sum. It superseded all other versions. No new revision was deemed necessary for nearly three hundred years. In the crowded emigrant ships which sailed to the New World of America there was little room for baggage. If the adventurers took books with them they took the Bible, Shakespeare, and later *The Pil-*

grim's Progress, and the Bible they mostly took was the Authorised Version of King James I. About ninety million complete copies are thought to have been published in the English language alone. It has been translated into more than seven hundred and sixty tongues. The Authorised Version is still the most popular in England and the United States. This may be deemed James's greatest achievement, for the impulse was largely his. The Scottish pedant built better than he knew. The scholars who produced this masterpiece are mostly unknown and unremembered. But they forged an enduring link, literary and religious, between the English-speaking peoples of the world.

* * * * *

James and his Parliaments grew more and more out of sympathy as the years went by. The Tudors had been discreet in their use of the Royal Prerogative and had never put forward any general theory of government, but James saw himself as the schoolmaster of the whole island. In theory there was a good case for absolute monarchy. The whole political development of the sixteenth century was on his side. He found a brilliant supporter in the person of Francis Bacon, the ambitious lawyer who had dabbled in politics with Essex and crept back to obedience when his patron fell. Bacon held a succession of high legal offices, culminating in the Lord Chancellorship. He maintained that the absolute and enlightened rule of the King with the help of his judges was justified by its efficiency, but his theories were unreal and widely unpopular.

The subsequent conflict centred on the nature of the Royal Prerogative and the powers of an Act of Parliament. The modern view had not yet emerged that an Act of Parliament was supreme and unalterable unless repealed or amended, and that the sovereign power of the State could be exercised in no other way. The Tudor statutes had indeed been the instruments of profound changes in Church and State, and there seemed little they could not do. But statutes required both the assent of Parliament and the approval of the King. No Parliament could meet without the summons of the King, or sit after he had dismissed it. Little else but financial necessity could compel the King to call a Parliament. If money could be raised elsewhere he might govern for years at a time without one. Moreover, a certain undefined prerogative power the King assuredly had; the exigencies of government required it. Who was to say what he could and could not do? If the King chose, on grounds of public interest, to make an ordinance dispensing with a statute, who could say he was acting illegally?

At this point the Common Lawyers, headed by Chief Justice Coke, stepped to the forefront of English history. Coke, one of the most learned of English judges, gave a blunt answer to these controversies. He declared that conflicts between Prerogative and statute should be resolved not by the Crown but by the judges. It was a tremendous assertion, for if the judges were to decide which laws were valid and which were not they would become the ultimate lawgivers in the State. They would form a Supreme Court, assessing the legality of both royal and Parliamentary enactments. Coke's high claims were not without foundation. They rested on the ancient tradition that law declared in the courts was superior to law published by the central authority. Coke himself was reluctant to admit that law could be made, or even changed. It existed already, merely awaiting revelation and exposition. If Acts of Parliament conflicted with it they were invalid. Thus at the beginning of his career Coke was not fighting on the same side as Parliament. In England his main assertions on behalf of fundamental law were overruled. It was to be otherwise in the United States.

James had a very different view of the function of judges. They might have the duty of deciding between the conflicting claims of statute and Prerogative, but if so they were bound to decide in the Crown's favour. Their business, as Bacon put it, was to be "lions under the throne." As judges were appointed by the King and held office during his good pleasure, they should obey him like other royal servants. The controversy was embittered by personal rivalry between Bacon and Coke, who now found himself in an untenable position. No judge could be impartial about the King's Prerogative if he were liable to instant dismissal on the King's command. James first tried to muzzle Coke by promoting him from the Court of Common Pleas to the King's Bench. Unsuccessful in this, he dismissed him in 1616. The remaining members of the Bench sided with James.

Five years later Coke entered the House of Commons and found that the most active lawyers of the day were in agreement with him. Their leadership was readily accepted. Few of the country gentlemen sitting in the Commons had any deep knowledge of Parliamentary history, or could produce any coherent theory to justify the claims of Parliament. They simply felt a smouldering injustice at the arbitrary conduct and jarring theories of the King. For all its stirring movements, this was an age of profound respect for precedents and constitutional forms. If the lawyers had remained solid for the Crown and the whole weight of legal opinion had been thrown into the royal scale the Commons' task would have been much harder. With all the force of interpreted precedent against them, they would have had to break with the past and admit they were revolutionaries; but the adherence of the lawyers freed them from an agonising choice. Coke, Selden, and others, including Pym, who had read law at the Middle Temple even if he had not practised, formed a group of able leaders, who took and held the initiative. Learned in the law, and not always too scrupulous in the interpretations they twisted from it, they gradually built up a case on which Parliament could claim with conviction that it was fighting, not for something new, but for the traditional and lawful heritage of the English people. Thus were laid the foundations of the united and disciplined opposition which Pym was to lead against King Charles.

James had no sympathy with these agitations. He did not care for compromise; but, shrewder than his son, he saw when compromise would suit him best. It was only the need of money that forced him to deal with Parliament at all. "The House of Commons," he once told the Spanish Ambassador, "is a body without a head. The Members give their opinions in a disorderly manner. At their meetings nothing is heard but cries, shouts, and confusion. I am surprised that my ancestors should ever have permitted such an institution to come into existence. I am a stranger, and found it here when I arrived, so that I am obliged to put up with what I cannot get rid of."

*   *   *   *   *

James's foreign policy perhaps met the needs of the age for peace, but often clashed with its temper. When he came to the throne England was still technically at war with Spain. With Cecil's support hostilities were concluded and diplomatic relations renewed. In all the circumstances this may be deemed to have been a wise and prudent step. The main struggle had already shifted from the high seas to Europe. The house of Habsburg, at the head of the Holy Roman Empire, still dominated the Continent from Vienna. The territories of the Em-

peror and of his cousin the King of Spain now stretched from
Portugal to Poland, and their power was backed by the pros-
elytising fervour of the Jesuits. The Commons and the country remained vehemently hostile to Spain, and viewed with
alarm and anxiety the march of the Counter-Reformation.
But James was unmoved. He regarded the Dutch as rebels
against the Divine Right of Kings. The Spanish Ambassador,
Count Gondomar, financed a pro-Spanish party at the new
Court; learning nothing from Tudor experience, James proposed not merely an alliance with Spain, but a Spanish match
for his son.

His daughter however was already in the opposite camp.
The Princess Elizabeth had married one of the Protestant
champions of Europe, Frederick, the Elector Palatine of the
Rhine, and Frederick was soon projected into violent revolt
against the Habsburg Emperor Ferdinand. Habsburg attempts
to recover for the Catholic faith those areas in Germany which
the law of the Empire had recognised as Protestant provoked
the vehement opposition of the Protestant princes. The storm
centre was Bohemia, where a haughty, resolute Czech nobility obstructed the centralising policy of Vienna both in
religion and politics. In the fifteenth-century days of John
Huss they had set up their own Church and fought both
Pope and Emperor. Now they defied Ferdinand. In 1618
their leaders flung the Imperial envoys from the windows
of the royal palace in Prague. This action, later known as the
Defenestration, started a war which was to ravage Germany
for thirty years. The Czechs offered Frederick the throne of
Bohemia. Frederick accepted, and became the recognised
leader of the Protestant revolt.

Although his daughter was now Queen of Bohemia, James
showed no wish to intervene on her behalf. He was resolved
to keep out of the conflict in Europe at all costs, and judged

he could best help his son-in-law's cause through friendship with Spain. Parliament was indignant and alarmed. He reminded them that these matters were beyond their scope. No taunts of personal timidity moved him. He stuck to his convictions and kept the peace. Whether this was wise and far-sighted is not easy to measure; it was certainly unpopular.

The Elector Frederick was soon driven out of Bohemia, and his hereditary lands were occupied by Habsburg troops. So short had been his reign that he is known to history as "the Winter King." The House of Commons clamoured for war. Private subscriptions and bands of volunteers were raised for the defence of the Protestants. James contented himself with academic discussions upon Bohemian rights with the Spanish Ambassador. He clung to the belief that a matrimonial alliance between the royal families of England and Spain would ensure peace with the strongest Power. No convulsions on the Continent must impede this scheme. To pose as Protestant champion in the great war now begun might gain a fleeting popularity with his subjects, but would also deliver him into the hands of the House of Commons. Parliament would assuredly demand some control over the expenditure of the money it voted for arms, and was unlikely to be generous. Puritan forces in the country would make themselves heard in louder tones. Besides, the fortunes of war were notoriously uncertain. James seems genuinely to have believed in his mission as the Peacemaker of Europe, and also to have had a deep-rooted nervous dislike of fighting, founded in the tumultuous experiences of his youth in Scotland. He ignored the demand for intervention, and continued his negotiations for the Spanish match.

*   *   *   *   *

In the midst of these turmoils Sir Walter Raleigh was executed on Tower Hill to please the Spanish Government. Raleigh had been imprisoned at the beginning of the reign for conspiring to supplant James by his cousin, Arabella Stuart. This charge was probably unjust, and the trial was certainly so. Raleigh's dream of finding gold on the Orinoco River, which had cheered his long confinement, ended in disaster in 1617. This last expedition of his, for which he was specially released from the Tower, had merely affronted the Spanish governors of South America. The old capital sentence was now revived against him. His death on October 29, 1618, was intended to mark the new policy of appeasement and prepare the way for good relations with Spain. This deed of shame sets a barrier for ever between King James and the English people. There are others.

James was much addicted to favourites, and his attention to handsome young men resulted in a noticeable loss of respect for the monarchy. After the death of his wise counsellor, Robert Cecil, the Court had been afflicted by a number of odious scandals. One of his favourites, Robert Carr, created Earl of Somerset by the King's caprice, was implicated in a murder by poison, of which his wife was undoubtedly guilty. James, who could deny Carr nothing, at first paid little attention to the storm raised by this crime; but even he found it impossible to maintain him in high office. Carr was succeeded in the King's regard by a good-looking, quick-witted, extravagant youth, George Villiers, soon ennobled as Duke of Buckingham. This young man quickly became all-powerful at Court, and in the affections of James. He formed a deep and honourable friendship with Charles, Prince of Wales. He accepted unhesitatingly the royal policy of a Spanish marriage, and in 1623 staged a romantic journey to Madrid for the Prince and himself to view the bride. Their unorthodox behaviour failed to impress the formal and ceremonious Court of Spain. Moreover, the Spaniards demanded concessions for the English Catholics, which James knew Parliament would never grant. They refused to intercede with the Emperor for the restoration of the Palatinate lands to Frederick. In the end the King's better feelings triumphed. "I like not," he declared, "to marry my son with a portion of my daughter's tears." The negotiations with Spain foundered. Contrary winds delayed the return of the Prince of Wales and his companion, now disenchanted with all things Spanish. The English fleet which was to escort him remained weather-bound at Santander. England waited in a tremor; and when the news spread through the country that he was safely back at Portsmouth, unwedded to the Infanta, unseduced from the Protestant faith, a surge of joy arose among all classes. The overpowering wish and potent will of England was to resist, and if necessary to fight, Spain and all that Spain meant. Memories of the Armada and Good Queen Bess cheered men's minds. The deadly sin of Papist idolatry, as they conceived it, terrified their souls. Foxe's *Book of Martyrs*, first published in 1563, and still widely read, taught them the duty and the splendour of rising above all physical danger or suffering. The streets were crowded with wagons carrying faggots for the bonfires. The red glow of rejoicing was reflected in the London sky.

But the King and his Council had gone too far on this path not to be smitten and shaken by its sudden closing. The Council, deeply committed, told the King that Buckingham had spoiled the affair by his impatience and conceit. They made heavy case against Buckingham's behaviour. They cleared the Spanish Court from the charge of discourtesy and justified the Spanish attitude towards the Palatinate. But Buckingham and Charles were now eager for war. James at first wavered. He was, he said, an old man who once knew something about politics. Now the two beings he loved best in the world urged him upon a course directly contrary to his judgment and past action.

In this sharp pinch Buckingham with remarkable agility turned himself from a royal favourite into a national, if short-lived, statesman. While using all his personal address to over-persuade the sovereign, he sought and obtained the support of Parliament and people. He took a number of steps which recognised, in a manner unknown since the days of the house of Lancaster, Parliamentary rights and power. Whereas all interference by Parliament in foreign affairs had been repelled by the Tudors, and hitherto by James, the Minister-Favourite now invited Lords and Commons to give their opinion. The answer of both Houses was prompt and plain. It was contrary, they said, to the honour of the King, to the welfare of his people, to the interest of his children, and to the terms of his former alliances to continue the negotiations with Spain. Upon this Buckingham did not conceal that he differed somewhat from his master. He said bluntly and publicly that he wished to tread only one path, whereas the King thought he could walk in two different paths at once. He would not be a mere flatterer; he must express his convictions or be a traitor.

At these developments Parliament was delighted. But now came the question of raising funds for the war that was to follow. James and Prince Charles had in mind campaigns in Europe that would seek to regain the Palatinate. Parliament urged a purely naval war with Spain, in which great profits from the Indies might be won. Suspicious of the King's intentions, the Commons voted less than half the sum for which he asked, and laid down stringent conditions as to how it should be spent.

Buckingham trimmed his sails and for the moment preserved his new Parliamentary prestige. This he used to break his rival, Lord Treasurer Cranfield. The Treasurer, now Earl of Middlesex, was one of the outstanding "new men" in the kingdom. He was a merchant who had risen to great wealth and high office. He was now dismissed and imprisoned by the Parliamentary engine of impeachment. This weapon had already been used against Bacon, who was found guilty of corruption in 1621, dismissed from the Chancellorship, fined and banished. It was never to be laid aside until many great issues, already alive, but little comprehended by Buckingham or by his dear friend Charles, had been settled once and for all.

No sooner was the Spanish match broken off than Buckingham turned to France for a bride for Charles. When he and the Prince of Wales had passed through Paris on their way to Madrid Charles had been struck by the charm of Marie de Médicis' daughter, Henrietta Maria, sister of Louis XIII and then in her fourteenth year. Buckingham found the negotiations agreeable to the French Court, and especially to Queen Marie. A marriage with a Protestant princess would have united Crown and Parliament. But this was never the intention of the governing circle. A daughter of France seemed to them the only alternative to the Infanta. How could England face Spain alone? If we could not lean on Spain, it seemed that we must have France. The old King wanted to see his son married. He said he lived only for him. He ratified the marriage treaty in December 1624. Three months later the first King of Great Britain was dead.

The Mayflower

THE struggle with Spain had long absorbed the energies of Englishmen, and in the last years of Queen Elizabeth few fresh enterprises had been carried out upon the oceans. For a while little was heard of the New World. Hawkins and Drake in their early voyages had opened up broad prospects for England in the Caribbean. Frobisher and others had penetrated deeply into the Arctic recesses of Canada in search of a north-west passage to Asia. But the lure of exploration and trade had given way to the demands of war. The novel idea of founding colonies also received a setback. Gilbert, Raleigh, and Grenville had been its pioneers. Their bold plans had come to nothing, but they left behind them an inspiring tradition. Now after a lapse of time their endeavours were taken up by new figures, less glittering, more practical and luckier. Piecemeal and from many motives the English-speaking communities in North America were founded. The change came in 1604, when James I made his treaty of peace with Spain. Discussion that had been stimulated by Richard Hakluyt's *Discourse on Western Planting* was revived. Serious argument by a group of writers of which he was the head gained a new hearing and a new pertinence. For there were troubles in England. People reduced to beggary and vagabondage were many, and new outlets were wanted for the nation's energies and resources.

* * * * *

The steady rise in prices had caused much hardship to wage earners. Though the general standard of living improved during the sixteenth century, a wide range of prices rose sixfold, and wages only twofold. Industry was oppressed by excessive Government regulation. The medieval system of craftsmen's guilds, which was still enforced, made the entry of young apprentices harsh and difficult. The squirearchy, strong in its political alliance with the Crown, owned most of the land and ran all the local government. The march of enclosures, which they pursued, drove many English peasants off the land. The whole scheme of life seemed to have contracted and the framework of social organisation had hardened. There were many without advantage, hope, or livelihood under the new conditions. Colonies, it was thought, might help to solve these distressing problems.

The Government was not uninterested. Trade with lively colonies promised an increase in the customs revenue on which the Crown heavily depended. Merchants and the richer landed gentry saw new opportunities across the Atlantic for profitable investment, and an escape from cramping restrictions on industry and the general decline of European trade during the religious wars. Capital was available for overseas experiments. Raleigh's attempts had demonstrated the ill success of individual effort, but a new method of financing large-scale trading enterprises was evolving in the shape of the joint stock company. In 1606 a group of speculators acquired a royal charter creating the Virginia company. It is interesting to see how early speculation in its broadest sense begins to play its part in the American field.

A plan was carefully drawn up in consultation with experts such as Hakluyt, but they had little practical experience and underestimated the difficulties of the profoundly novel departure they were making. After all, it is not given to many to start a nation. It was a few hundred people who now took the first step. A settlement was made at Jamestown, in the

Chesapeake Bay, on the Virginian coast, in May 1607. By the following spring half the population was dead from malaria, cold, and famine. After a long and heroic struggle the survivors became self-supporting, but profits to the promoters at home were very small. Captain John Smith, a military adventurer from the Turkish wars, became the dictator of the tiny colony, and enforced harsh discipline. The marriage of his lieutenant John Rolfe with Pocahontas, the daughter of an Indian chief, caused a sensation in the English capital. But the London company had little control and the administration of the colony was rough-and-ready. The objects of the directors were mixed and ill defined. Some thought that colonisation would reduce poverty and crime in England. Others looked for profit to the fisheries of the North American coast, or hoped for raw materials to reduce their dependence on the exports from the Spanish colonies. All were wrong, and Virginia's fortune sprang from a novel and unexpected cause. By chance a crop of tobacco was planted, and the soil proved benevolent. Tobacco had been introduced into Europe by the Spaniards and the habit of smoking was spreading fast. Demand for tobacco was great and growing, and the profits on the Virginia crop were high. Small-holders were bought out, big estates were formed, and the colony began to stand on its own feet. As it grew and prospered its society came to resemble the Mother Country, with rich planters in the place of squires. They were not long in developing independence of mind and a sturdy capacity for self-government. Distance from the authorities in London greatly aided them in this.

*   *   *   *   *

Beneath the drab exterior of Jacobean England, with favouritism at Court and humiliation in Europe, other and more vital forces were at work. The Elizabethan bishops had driven the nobler and tougher Puritan spirits out of the Established Church. But though they destroyed the organisation of the party small illegal gatherings of religious extremists continued to meet. There was no systematic persecution, but petty restrictions and spyings obstructed their peaceful worship. A congregation at Scrooby, in Nottinghamshire, led by one of their pastors, John Robinson, and by William Brewster, the Puritan bailiff of the manor of the Archbishop of York, resolved to seek freedom of worship abroad. In 1607 they left England and settled at Leyden, hoping to find asylum among the tolerant and industrious Dutch. For ten years these Puritan parishioners struggled for a decent existence. They were small farmers and agricultural workers, out of place in a maritime industrial community, barred by their nationality from the guilds of craftsmen, without capital and without training. The only work they could get was rough manual labour. They were persistent and persevering, but a bleak future faced them in Holland. They were too proud of their birthright to be absorbed by the Dutch. The authorities had been sympathetic, but in practice unhelpful. The Puritans began to look elsewhere.

Emigration to the New World presented itself as an escape from a sinful generation. There they might gain a livelihood unhampered by Dutch guilds, and practise their creed unharassed by English clerics. As one of their number records, "The place they had thoughts on was some of those vast and unpeopled countries of America, which are fruitful and fit for habitation; being devoid of all civil inhabitants; where there are only savage and brutish men, which range up and down little otherwise than the wild beasts of the same."

Throughout the winter of 1616–17, when Holland was threatened with a renewal of war with Spain, there were many discussions among the anxious community. A mortal risk and high adventure lay before them. To the perils of the unknown, to famine, and the record of past failures were added gruesome tales of the Indians; how they flayed men with the shells of fishes and cut off steaks which they broiled upon the coals before the eyes of the victims. But William Bradford, who was to become Governor of the new colony, pleaded the argument of the majority. In his *History of the Plymouth Plantation* he has expressed the views they held at the time. "All great and honourable actions are accompanied with great difficulties, and must be both enterprised and overcome with answerable courages. The dangers were great, but not desperate; the difficulties were many, but not invincible. For though there were many of them likely, yet they were not certain; it might be sundry of the things feared might never befall; others by provident care and the use of good means might in a great measure be prevented; and all of them, through the help of God, by fortitude and patience, might either be borne or overcome. Such attempts were not to be made and undertaken without good ground and reason; not rashly or lightly as many have done for curiosity or hope of gain. But their condition was not ordinary; their ends were good and honourable, their calling lawful, and urgent; and therefore they might expect the blessing of God in their proceeding. Yea, though they should lose their lives in this action, yet might they have comfort in the same, and their endeavours would be honourable. They lived here but as men in exile, and in a poor condition; and as great miseries might possibly befall them in this place, for the twelve years of truce were now out, and there was nothing but beating of drums, and preparing for war, the events whereof are always uncertain. The Spaniard might prove as cruel as the savages of America, and the famine and pestilence as sore here as there, and their liberty less to look out for remedy."

Their first plan was to settle in Guiana, but then they

realised it was impossible to venture out upon their own. Help must come from England. They accordingly sent agents to London to negotiate with the only body interested in emigration, the Virginia company. One of the members of its council was an influential Parliamentarian, Sir Edwin Sandys. Supported by the London merchant backers of the company, he furthered the project. Here were ideal settlers, sober, hardworking, and skilled in agriculture. They insisted upon freedom of worship, and it would be necessary to placate the Anglican bishops. Sandys and the emissaries from Holland went to see the King. James was sceptical. He asked how the little band proposed to support itself in the company's territory in America. "By fishing," they replied. This appealed to James. "So God have my soul," he exclaimed in one of his more agreeable remarks, " 'tis an honest trade! It was the Apostles' own calling."

The Leyden community was granted a licence to settle in America, and arrangements for their departure were hastened on. Thirty-five members of the Leyden congregation left Holland and joined sixty-six West Country adventurers at Plymouth, and in September 1620 they set sail in the *Mayflower,* a vessel of 180 tons.

After two and a half months of voyaging across the winter ocean they reached the shores of Cape Cod, and thus, by an accident, landed outside the jurisdiction of the Virginia company. This invalidated their patent from London. Before they landed there was trouble among the group about who was to enforce discipline. Those who had joined the ship at Plymouth were no picked band of saints, and had no intention of submitting to the Leyden set. There was no possibility of appealing to England. Yet, if they were not all to starve, some agreement must be reached.

Forty-one of the more responsible members thereupon drew

up a solemn compact which is one of the remarkable documents in history, a spontaneous covenant for political organisation. "In the name of God, Amen. We whose names are under-written, the loyal subjects of our dread sovereign Lord, King James, by the grace of God, of Great Britain, France, and Ireland king, defender of the faith, etc. Having undertaken, for the glory of God, and advancement of the Christian faith, and honour of our king and country, a voyage to plant the first colony in the Northern parts of Virginia, do by these presents solemnly and mutually in the presence of God, and one of another, covenant and combine ourselves together into a civil body politic, for our better ordering and preservation and furtherance of the ends aforesaid; and by virtue hereof to enact, constitute, and frame such just and equal laws, ordinances, acts, constitutions, and offices, from time to time, as shall be thought most meet and convenient for the general good of the colony, unto which we promise all due submission and obedience."

In December on the American coast in Cape Cod Bay these men founded the town of Plymouth. The same bitter struggle with nature that had taken place in Virginia now began. There was no staple crop. But by toil and faith they survived. The financial supporters in London reaped no profits. In 1627 they sold out and the Plymouth colony was left to its own resources. Such was the founding of New England.

*　　*　　*　　*　　*

For ten years afterwards there was no more planned emigration to America; but the tiny colony of Plymouth pointed a path to freedom. In 1629 Charles I dissolved Parliament and the period of so-called Personal Rule began. As friction grew between Crown and subjects, so opposition to the Anglican Church strengthened in the countryside. Absolutism was commanding the Continent, and England seemed to be going the same way. Many people of independent mind began to consider leaving home to find freedom and justice in the wilds.

Just as the congregation from Scrooby had emigrated in a body to Holland, so another Puritan group in Dorset, inspired by the Reverend John White, now resolved to move to the New World. After an unhappy start this venture won support in London and the Eastern Counties among backers interested in trade and fishing as well as in emigration. Influential Opposition peers lent their aid. After the precedent of Virginia a chartered company was formed, eventually named "The Company of the Massachusetts Bay in New England." News spread rapidly and there was no lack of colonists. An advance party founded the settlement of Salem, to the north of Plymouth. In 1630 the Governor of the company, John Winthrop, followed with a thousand settlers. He was the leading personality in the enterprise. The uneasiness of the time is reflected in his letters, which reveal the reasons why his family went. "I am verily persuaded," he wrote about England, "God will bring some heavy affliction upon this land, and that speedily; but be of good comfort. . . . If the Lord seeth it will be good for us, He will provide a shelter and a hiding place for us and others. . . . Evil times are coming when the Church must fly into the wilderness." The wilderness that Winthrop chose lay on the Charles River, and to this swampish site the capital of the colony was transferred. Here from modest beginnings arose the city of Boston, which was to become in the next century the heart of resistance to British rule, and long remain the intellectual capital of America.

The Massachusetts Bay company was by its constitution a joint stock corporation, organised entirely for trading purposes, and the Salem settlement was for the first year controlled from London. But by accident or intent there was no mention in the charter where the company was to hold its meetings. Some of the Puritan stockholders realised that there was no obstacle to transferring the company, directors and all, to New England. A general court of the company was held, and this momentous decision taken. From the joint stock company was born the self-governing colony of Massachusetts. The Puritan landed gentry who led the enterprise introduced a representative system, such as they had known in the days before King Charles's Personal Rule. John Winthrop guided the colony through this early phase, and it soon expanded. Between 1629 and 1640 the colonists rose in numbers from three hundred to fourteen thousand. The resources of the company offered favourable prospects to small emigrants. In England life for farm labourers was often hard. Here in the New World there was land for every newcomer and freedom from all restrictions upon the movement of labour and such other medieval regulations as oppressed and embittered the peasantry at home.

The leaders and ministers who ruled in Massachusetts however had views of their own about freedom. It must be the rule of the godly. They understood toleration as little as the Anglicans, and disputes broke out about religion. By no means all were rigid Calvinists, and recalcitrant bodies split off from the parent colony when such quarrels became strident. Outside of the settlement were boundless beckoning lands. In 1635 and 1636 some colonists moved to the valley of the Connecticut River, and founded the town of Hartford near its banks. They were joined by many emigrants direct from England. This formed the nucleus of the settlement of the River Towns, later to become the colony of Connecticut. There, three thousand miles from home, enlightened rules of government were drawn up. A "Fundamental Order" or constitution was proclaimed, similar to the Mayflower compact

RUPERT'S LAND

HUDSON BAY

Hudson Bay Company

CANADA
(French)

L. Ontario

L. Erie

Appalachian Mountains

(French) (English)
NEWFOUNDLAND

ACADIA
(French)

MAINE 1622
(to Mass.)

NEW HAMPSHIRE 1622

MASSACHUSETTS 1628

NEW YORK 1664

Plymouth 1620

RHODE ISLAND 1647

CONNECTICUT 1633

NEW JERSEY 1664

MARY-LAND 1634

DELAWARE 1664

VIRGINIA 1607

ROANOKE ISLAND 1587

ATLANTIC

OCEAN

NORTH CAROLINA 1663

SOUTH CAROLINA c 1670

BERMUDA 1609

FLORIDA
(Spanish)

THE AMERICAN COLONIES
IN THE
SEVENTEENTH CENTURY

BAHAMAS

about fifteen years before. A popular Government, shared in by all the freemen of the colony, was set up, and maintained itself in a modest way until its position was formally regularised after the Restoration of the Stuart monarchy.

The founders of Connecticut had gone out from Massachusetts to find new and larger lands in which to settle. Religious strife drove others beyond the bounds of the parent colony. A scholar from Cambridge, Roger Williams, had been forced to leave the university by Archbishop Laud. He followed the now known way to the New World, and settled in Massachusetts. The godly there seemed to him almost as oppressive as the Anglican Church in England. Williams soon clashed with the authorities, and became the leader of those idealists and humbler folk who sought escape from persecution in their new home overseas. The magistrates considered him a promoter of disorder, and resolved to send him back to England. Warned in time, he fled beyond their reach, and, followed at intervals by others, founded the town of Providence, to the south of Massachusetts. Other exiles from Massachusetts, some of them forcibly banished, joined his settlement in 1636, which became the colony of Rhode Island. Roger Williams was the first political thinker of America, and his ideas influenced not only his fellow colonists, but the revolutionary party in England. In many ways he foreshadowed the political conceptions of John Milton. He was the first to put into practice the complete separation of Church from lay government, and Rhode Island was the only centre in the world at that time where there was complete religious toleration. This noble cause was sustained by the distilling and sale of spirits, on which the colony thrived.

By 1640 five main English settlements had thus been established in North America: Virginia, technically under the direct rule of the Crown, and administered, somewhat ineffectually, by a standing committee of the Privy Council since the company's charter was abrogated in 1624; the original Pilgrim settlement at Plymouth, which, for want of capital, had not expanded; the flourishing Massachusetts Bay colony, and its two offshoots, Connecticut and Rhode Island.

The last four were the New England colonies. In spite of religious divergences they were much alike. All were coastal settlements, bound together by trade, fisheries, and shipping, and soon forced to make common cause against their neighbours. For the French were already reaching out from their earlier bases in Canada, having ousted an adventurous band of Scotsmen who had been ensconced for a time on the upper reaches of the St Lawrence. By 1630 the river was entirely in French hands. The only other waterway, the Hudson, was ruled by the Dutch, who had established at its mouth in 1621 the colony of New Netherland, later to become New York. By moving their company to the New World the English in Massachusetts had shelved relations with the home Government. The Plymouth colony was practically autonomous after the shareholders sold out in 1627. There was however no question of their demanding independence from England. That would have exposed them to attack and conquest by the French or the Dutch. But these dangers still lay in the future. England meanwhile was busy with her own affairs. For a moment in 1635 Charles I and his Council had considered sending an expedition to assert his authority in America. The colonists built forts and blockhouses and prepared to fight. But the Civil War in England suspended such designs, and they were left to themselves to grow for nearly a quarter of a century.

*   *   *   *   *

Two other ventures, both essentially commercial, established the English-speaking peoples in the New World. Since

· 175 ·

Elizabethan days they had often tried to get a foothold in the Spanish West Indies. In 1623, on his way back from a fruitless expedition to Guiana, a Suffolk gentleman named Thomas Warner explored one of the less inhabited West Indian islands. He deposited a few colonists on St Christopher, and hurried home to get a royal patent for a more extensive enterprise. This achieved, he returned to the Caribbean, and, though much harassed by Spanish raids, he established the English in this disputed sea. By the 1640's Barbados, St Christopher, Nevis, Montserrat, and Antigua were in English hands and several thousand colonists had arrived. Sugar assured their prosperity, and the Spanish grip on the West Indies was shaken. There was much competition and warfare in the succeeding years, but for a long time these island settlements were commercially much more valuable to England than the colonies in North America.

Another settlement of this period was sponsored by the monarchy. In theory all land settled by Englishmen belonged to the King. He had the right to grant such portions as he chose either to recognised companies or to individuals. Just as Elizabeth and James had granted industrial and commercial monopolies to courtiers, so now Charles I attempted to regulate colonial settlement. In 1632 George Calvert, Lord Baltimore, a Roman Catholic courtier who had long been interested in colonisation, applied for a patent for settling in the neighbourhood of Virginia. It was granted after his death to his son. The terms of the patent resembled the conditions under which land was already held in Virginia. It conferred complete proprietary rights over the new area, and tried to transport the manorial system to the New World. The government of the colony was vested in the Baltimore family, who had supreme power of appointment and regulation. Courtiers and merchants subscribed to the venture, and the new colony was named Maryland in honour of Charles's Queen, Henrietta Maria. Although the proprietor was a Roman Catholic there was a tolerant flavour about its government from the beginning, because Baltimore had only obtained his patent by proclaiming the religion of the Established Church as the official creed of the new settlement. The aristocratic nature of the régime was much modified in practice, and the powers of the local administration set up by Baltimore increased at the expense of his paper rights.

In these first decades of the great emigration over eighty thousand English-speaking people crossed the Atlantic. Never since the days of the Germanic invasions of Britain had such a national movement been seen. Saxon and Viking had colonised England. Now, one thousand years later, their descendants were taking possession of America. Many different streams of migrants were to make their confluence in the New World and contribute to the manifold character of the future United States. But the British stream flowed first and remained foremost. From the beginning its leaders were out of sympathy with the Government at home. The creation of towns and settlements from the wilderness, warfare with the Indians, and the remoteness and novelty of the scene widened the breach with the Old World. During the critical years of settlement and consolidation in New England the Mother Country was paralysed by civil war. When the English State again achieved stability it was confronted with self-supporting, self-reliant communities which had evolved traditions and ideas of their own.

Charles I and Buckingham

O F the many descriptions of Charles I at the beginning of his reign none is more attractive than the cameo which we owe to the profound studies of the German historian, Ranke. He was, he says, "in the bloom of life: he had just completed his twenty-fifth year. He looked well on horseback: men saw him govern with safety horses that were hard to manage: he was expert in knightly exercises: he was a good shot with the cross-bow, as well as with the gun, and even learned how to load a cannon. He was hardly less unweariedly devoted to the chase than his father. He could not vie with him in intelligence and knowledge, nor with his deceased brother Henry in vivacious energy and in popularity of disposition. . . . In moral qualities he was superior to both. He was one of those young men of whom it is said that they have no fault. His strict propriety of demeanour bordered on maiden bashfulness: a serious and temperate soul spoke from his calm eyes. He had a natural gift for apprehending even the most complicated questions, and he was a good writer. From his youth he showed himself economical; not profuse, but at the same time not niggardly; in all matters precise." [1] He had however suffered from infantile paralysis and spoke with a stammer.

A great political and religious crisis was overhanging

[1] Ranke, *History of England* (1875), vol. i, p. 537.

England. Already in King James's time Parliament had begun to take the lead, not only in levying taxes but increasingly in the conduct of affairs, and especially in foreign policy. It is remarkable to see how far-reaching was the interest shown by the educated part of the English nation in Europe; and as they thought and moved so did the great mass of the people behind them. Events in Prague or Ratisbon seemed as important to Englishmen as what happened in York or Bristol. The frontiers of Bohemia, the conditions in the Palatinate, ranked as high as many domestic questions. This wide outlook was no longer due, as in the days of the Plantagenets, to dynastic claims of Continental sway. The furious winds of religious strife carried men's thoughts afar. The English people felt that their survival and their salvation were bound up for ever with the victory of the Reformed Faith, and they watched with straining, vigilant eyes every episode which marked its advance or misfortune. An intense desire for England to lead and champion the Protestant cause wherever it was assailed drove forward the Parliamentary movement with a force far greater than would ever have sprung merely from the issues which were now opening at home. Lord Acton declares that "the progress of the world towards self-government would have been arrested but for the strength afforded by the religious motive in the seventeenth century."

The secular issues were nevertheless themselves of enormous weight. Tudor authority had been accepted as a relief from the anarchy of the Wars of the Roses, and had now ceased to fit either the needs or the temper of a continually growing society. Men looked back to earlier times. Great lawyers like Coke and Selden had directed their gaze to the rights which they thought Parliament had possessed under the Lancastrian kings. Ranging farther, they spoke with pride of the work of Simon de Montfort, of Magna Carta, and even of still more ancient rights in the mists of Anglo-Saxon monarchy. From these studies they derived the conviction that they were the heirs of a whole structure of fundamental law inherent in the customs of the Island, and now most apt and vital to their immediate problems. The past seemed to them to provide almost a written Constitution, from which the Crown was now threatening to depart. But the Crown also looked back, and found many precedents of a contrary character, especially in the last hundred years, for the most thorough exercise of the Royal Prerogative. Both King and Parliament had a body of doctrine upon which they dwelt with sincere conviction. This brought pathos and grandeur to the coming struggle.

A society more complex than that of Tudor England was coming into existence. Trade, both foreign and internal, was expanding. Coal mining and other industries were rapidly developing. Larger vested interests were in being. In the van stood London, ever-glorious champion of freedom and progress; London, with its thousands of lusty, free-spoken prentices and its wealthy City guilds and companies. Outside London many of the landed gentry, who supplied numerous Members to Parliament, were acquiring close connections with new industry and trade. In these years the Commons were not so much seeking to legislate as trying to wring from the Crown admissions of ancient custom which would prevent before it was too late all this recent growth from falling under an autocratic grip.

The men at the head of this strenuous and, to our time, invaluable movement were notable figures. Coke had taught the later Parliaments of James I the arguments upon which they could rest and the methods by which they might prevail. His knowledge of the Common Law was unique. He unearthed an armoury of precedents, and set many to work upon their furbishing and sharpening. Two country gentlemen stand with him: one from the West, Sir John Eliot, a Cornishman; the other, Thomas Wentworth, a Yorkshire squire. Both these men possessed the highest qualities of force and temper. For a time they worked together; for a time they were rivals; for a time they were foes. By opposite paths both reached the extremity of sacrifice. Behind them at this time, lacking nothing in grit, were leaders of the Puritan gentry, Denzil Holles, Arthur Hazelrigg, John Pym—Pym was eventually to go far and to carry the cause still farther. He was a Somerset man, a lawyer, strongly anti-High-Church, and with an interest in colonial ventures. Here was a man who understood every move in the political game, and would play it out remorselessly.

*   *   *   *   *

The Parliaments of James, and now those of Charles, were for war and intervention in Europe. They sought to use the money-power, of which they were the masters, to induce the King and his Ministers to tread these dangerous paths. They knew well, among other things, that the stresses of war would force the Crown to come to them. They saw that their power would grow with the adoption of their policy, which was also their faith. The pacifism of James I, often ignominious, had upon the whole avoided this trap. But King Charles and Buckingham were high-spirited men in the ardour of youth. The King was affronted by the manner in which his father's overtures for a Spanish match, and he himself, had been slighted in Madrid. He was for war with Spain. He even wished to call Parliament together without issuing writs for the new election consequent upon a demise of the Crown. He at once carried through his marriage with the French princess, Henrietta Maria. Her arrival at Dover surrounded by a throng of French Papists and priests was the first serious shock to

· 181 ·

Charles's popularity. The new Parliament granted supplies against Spain; but their purpose to review the whole question of indirect taxation was plain when they resolved that the customs duties of tonnage and poundage without which the King could not live, even in peace, should for the first time for many reigns be voted, not for the King's life, but only for one year. This restriction galled and wounded Charles, but did not deter him from the war. Thus at the very outset of his reign he placed himself in a position of exceptional dependence upon Parliament, while resenting its increasing claims.

The war with Spain went badly. Buckingham led an expedition to Cadiz in an attempt to emulate the feats of Queen Elizabeth's days, but it accomplished nothing. On his return Parliament resolved to unseat the glittering, profuse, incompetent Minister. "We protest," the Commons told Charles, "that until this great person be removed from intermeddling with the great affairs of State any money we shall or can give will through his misemployment be turned rather to the hurt and prejudice of this your kingdom than otherwise." Buckingham was impeached, and to save his friend the King hastily dissolved Parliament.

A new complication was now added to the scene. Charles had hoped to conclude an alliance with France against the Habsburg rulers of Spain and the Empire. But France showed no desire to fight for the recovery of the Palatinate on England's behalf. Disputes also arose over the fulfilment of Charles's treaty of marriage with Queen Henrietta Maria, and the breach was widened by the cause of the Huguenots. The new, powerful French Minister, Cardinal Richelieu, was determined to curb the independence of the Huguenots in France, and in particular to reduce their maritime stronghold of La Rochelle. English sympathies naturally lay with these French Protestants whom they had helped to sustain in the days of Henry of Navarre, and the two countries drifted into war. In 1627 a considerable force was despatched under Buckingham to help the Rochelais. It landed off the coast in the Île de Ré, failed to storm the citadel, and withdrew in disorder. Thus Buckingham's military efforts were once more marked by waste and failure. At home the billeting of soldiers brought an acute grievance into thousands of cottage homes. This was aggravated by the arbitrary decisions of martial law, which was used to settle all disputes between soldiers and civilians.

The King was torn between the grinding need of finding money for the war and the danger that Parliament would again impeach his friend. In his vexation, and having the war on his hands, he resorted to dubious methods of raising money. He demanded a forced loan; and when many important persons refused to pay he threw them into prison. Five of these prisoners, known as the Five Knights, appealed against these proceedings. But King's Bench ruled that *habeas corpus* could not be used against imprisonments "by special command of the King." From the agitation this aroused sprang the famous Petition of Right.

Forced loans could not suffice to replenish the Treasury, and having secured a promise that the impeachment of Buckingham would not be pursued the King agreed to summon Parliament. The country was now in a ferment. The election returned men pledged to resist arbitrary exactions. The Parliament which assembled in March 1628 embodied the will of the natural leaders of the nation. It wished to support the war, but it would not grant money to a King and Minister it distrusted. The nobility and gentry, Lords and Commons alike, were resolute in defence of property, and also of its twin cause at this time, liberty. The King used the threat of despotic action. He must have "such supply as to secure our-

selves and save our friends from imminent ruin. . . .
Every man must now do according to his conscience, wherefore if you (which God forbid) should not do your duties in
contributing what this State at this time needs I must . . .
use those other means which God hath put into my hands
to save that which the follies of other men may otherwise
hazard to lose. Take not this as threatening, for I scorn to
threaten any but my equals, . . . but as an admonition."

It must not be supposed that all the wrongdoing was on
one side. Parliament, which had approved the wars, was
playing a hard game with the King, confronting him with the
shame to his princely honour of deserting the Huguenots, or
else yielding the Prerogative his predecessors had so long
enjoyed. Their tactics were artful, and yet justified by their
convictions and by the facts. They offered no fewer than five
subsidies, amounting to £300,000, all to be paid within
twelve months. Here was enough to carry on the war; but
before they would confirm this in a Bill they demanded their
price.

The following four resolutions were passed unanimously:
that no freeman ought to be restrained or imprisoned unless some lawful cause was expressed; that the writ of *habeas
corpus* ought to be granted to every man imprisoned or restrained, even though it might be at the command of the
King or of the Privy Council; that if no legal cause for imprisonment were shown the party ought to be set free or
bailed; that it was the ancient and undoubted right of every
freeman to have a full and absolute property in his goods and
estate, and that no tax, loan, or benevolence ought to be levied by the King or his Ministers without common consent
by Act of Parliament.

At Coke's prompting the Commons now went on to

frame the Petition of Right. Its object was to curtail the King's Prerogative. The Petition complained against forced loans, imprisonment without trial, billeting, and martial law. These and others of the King's proceedings were condemned "as being contrary to the rights and liberties of the subject, and the laws and statutes of the nation." Unless the King accepted the Petition he would have no subsidies, and must face the wars to which Parliament had incited him as best he could. Charles, resorting to manœuvre, secretly consulted the judges, who assured him that even his consent to these liberties would not affect his ultimate Prerogative. He was none too sure of this; and when his first evasive answer was delivered in the House of Lords a howl went up, not only from the Commons, but from the great majority of all assembled. He therefore fell back upon the opinion of the judges and gave full consent *que droict soit fait comme il est désiré,* while making mental reservation. "Now," said the King, "I have performed my part. If this Parliament have not a happy conclusion the sin is yours. I am free of it." On this there was general rejoicing. The Commons voted all the subsidies, and believed that a definite bargain had been struck.

We reach here, amid much confusion, the main foundation of English freedom. The right of the Executive Government to imprison a man, high or low, for reasons of State was denied; and that denial, made good in painful struggles, constitutes the charter of every self-respecting man at any time in any land. Trial by jury of equals, only for offences known to the law, if maintained, makes the difference between bond and free. But the King felt this would hamper him, and no doubt a plausible case can be advanced that in times of emergency dangerous persons must be confined. The terms "protective arrest" and "shot while trying to escape" had not yet occurred to the mind of authority. We owe them to the genius of a later age.

At the back of the Parliamentary movement in all its expressions lay a deep fear. Everywhere in Europe they saw the monarchies becoming more autocratic. The States-General, which had met in Paris in 1614, had not been summoned again; it was not indeed to be summoned until the clash of 1789. The rise of standing armies, composed of men drilled in firearms and supported by trains of artillery, had stripped alike the nobles and the common people of their means of independent resistance. Rough as the times had been in the earlier centuries, "bills and bows" were a final resource which few kings had cared to challenge. But now on the Parliamentary side force as yet was lacking.

* * * * *

Both sides pressed farther along their paths. The King, having got his money, dwelt unduly upon the assurances he had received from the judges that his Prerogative was intact. The Commons came forward with further complaints against the growth of Popery and Arminianism (the form of High Church doctrine most directly opposed to Calvinism), about the mismanagement of the war, and about injury to trade and commerce from naval weakness in the Narrow Seas. They renewed their attack on Buckingham, asking the King whether it was consistent with his safety, or the safety of the realm, that the author of so many calamities should continue to hold office or remain near his sacred person. But now the King and Buckingham hoped that a second and successful expedition would relieve the Huguenots in La Rochelle. Charles dismissed the Houses. Before he had need of them again he and his cherished Minister would present them with a military or diplomatic result in which all could rejoice. Far better to rescue Protestants abroad than to persecute Catholics at home. A King who had delivered La Rochelle could surely claim the right to exercise indulgence even to Papists in his own land. This was not a discreditable position to take up; but Fate moved differently.

Buckingham himself was deeply conscious of the hatreds of which he was the object, and it is clear that in putting himself at the head of a new expedition to La Rochelle he hoped to win again for himself some national backing, which would at least divide his pursuers. But at the moment when his resolves were at their highest, as he was about to embark at Portsmouth, commander-in-chief of a formidable armament, with new engines for breaking the boom which Richelieu had built across the beleaguered harbour, he was stabbed to death by a fanatical naval lieutenant.

The murderer, John Felton, seems to have been impaled by nature upon all those prongs of dark resolve which make such deeds possible. He had the private sting of being passed over for promotion. He was embittered by the favouritism shown to officers who had never fought. But the documents which he left behind him proved him a slave of larger thoughts. Parliament's remonstrations to the King against Buckingham's lush splendour and corrupt methods had sunk into his soul. He held that the welfare of the people is the highest law, and that "God Himself has enacted this law, that whatsoever is for the profit or benefit of the Commonwealth should be accounted to be lawful." After the deed he mingled in the crowd, but when he heard men denouncing the villain who had slain the noble Duke he came forward, saying, "No villain did it, but an honourable man. I am the man." A lean man he was, with red hair and dark, melancholy features. He flung at the crowd who shouted at him, "In your hearts you rejoice in my deed." On some of the ships the sailors cheered his name. Afterwards, in the grey approach of doom, he became convinced that he had been wrong. He accepted the view "that the common good could no way be a pretence to a particular mischief." He asked to be allowed to testify to this before his execution.

The death of Buckingham was a devastating blow to the young King. He never forgave Eliot, to whose accusing speeches he ascribed Felton's act. At the same time it immensely relieved his public difficulties, for much of the anger of the Parliament died with the favourite; and it brought for the first time a unity into his married life. Hitherto he had been morally and mentally dominated by "Steenie," the beloved friend of his boyhood and youth, to whom he confided his inmost thoughts. For three years he had lived in cold estrangement from the Queen. It was even said that the marriage had never been consummated; and he had distressed her by dismissing all her French attendants. The death of Buckingham was the birth of his love for his wife. Little but storm lay before them, but henceforth they faced it together.

*　　*　　*　　*　　*

Though the Commons had granted the five subsidies they held tonnage and poundage in reserve. When the year lapsed for which this had been voted the Parliamentary party throughout the country were angered to find that the King continued to collect the tax by his officers, as had been the custom for so many reigns. Distraint and imprisonment were used against those who refused to pay. In all this was seen the King's contempt for the Petition of Right, and his intention to escape from the assent he had given to it. When copies of the Petition were printed it was found that the King's first evasive answer was appended, and not his later plain acceptance in the ancient form. The expedition to La Rochelle, which had sailed under another commander, miscarried. Cardinal Richelieu succeeded in maintaining his boom against the English ships and appliances, and eventually the Huguenots in despair surrendered the city to the King of France. This collapse caused shock and grief throughout England.

Thus when Parliament met again at the beginning of 1629 there was no lack of grievances both in foreign and domestic policy. Yet it was upon questions of religion that the attack began. The Commons showed themselves to be in a most aggressive mood, and worked themselves into passion by long debates upon the indulgence and laxity with which the laws against Popery were enforced. This brought the great majority of them together; and the zealots, who, however intolerant, were ardent to purify what they deemed a corrupt Church, joined with the patriots who were laying the foundations of English freedom. Just as the Moslem, defending his native soil, fortifies himself with the Koran, just as the rhinoceros trusts to his horn or the tiger to his claws, so these harassed Parliamentarians found in the religious prejudices of England a bond of union and eventually a means of war.

In a comprehensive resolution the Commons declared that whoever furthered Popery or Arminianism, whoever collected or helped to collect tonnage and poundage before it was granted, or even paid it, was a public enemy. The personal censures formerly heaped on Buckingham were now transferred to the Lord Treasurer, Richard Weston, who was denounced as a Papist, if not indeed a Jesuit, engaged in exacting taxes illegally. All this was embodied in a single Remonstrance. The Speaker, who had been gained to the King's side, announced on March 2 that the King adjourned the House till the 10th, thus frustrating the carrying of the Remonstrance. A wave of wrath swept through the assembly. When the Speaker rose to leave he was forced back and held down on his chair by two resolute and muscular Members,

Holles and Valentine. The doors were barred against Black Rod, and the Remonstrance, recited from memory by Holles, was declared carried by acclamation. The doors were then opened and the Members poured forth tumultuously. It was a long time before any of them met in their Chamber again. It had become plain to all that King and Commons could not work together on any terms. The next week Parliament was dissolved and the period of King Charles's Personal Rule began.

The Personal Rule

T HE Personal Rule of the King was not set up covertly or by degrees. Charles openly proclaimed his intention. "We have showed," he said, "by our frequent meeting our people, our love to the use of Parliaments; yet, the late abuse having for the present driven us unwillingly out of that course, we shall account it presumption for any to prescribe any time unto us for Parliaments, the calling, continuing, and dissolving of which is always in our own power, and shall be more inclinable to meet in Parliament again, when our people shall see more clearly into our interests and actions and when such as have bred this interruption shall have received their condign punishment."

This policy required other large measures. First, there must be peace with France and Spain. Without the support of Parliament Charles had not the strength to carry on foreign wars. It was not difficult to obtain peace. Indeed both the French and Spanish Governments showed their contempt of English exertions when they voluntarily returned the prisoners they had taken at La Rochelle and in the Netherlands. The second condition was the gaining of some at least of the Parliamentary leaders. Upon this there must have been a long discussion. In those days there were few men who did not seek the favour of the Crown. Some sought it by subservience, and others by opposition. Eliot was regarded as irreconcilable, but Sir Henry Savile, Thomas Digges, and Wentworth were deemed both possible and serviceable acquisitions. Digges had proved himself willing to endure prison for the Parliamentary case; he thawed somewhat readily in the royal sunshine. But Wentworth was the man of all others most worth winning. In the debates upon the Petition of Right he had taken a line marked by certain restraints. Behind the fierce invective of the Parliamentarian there had been noticed a certain willingness not to exclude the other side of the argument. His abilities were obviously of the first order, and so were his ambitions. His sombre force might mar or make the system the King now sought to establish.

To Wentworth therefore the King turned. Indeed, even before the death of Buckingham this champion of Parliament had made distinct overtures, all couched in dignified and reasonable guise. The securing of Wentworth had now become essential to the Personal Rule. Wentworth was more than willing. He knew he judged better than most other men; he was a born administrator; all he wanted was scope for his endeavours. In December 1628 he became Lord President of the Council of the North and a member of the Privy Council. From this moment he not only abandoned all the ideas of which he had been the ablest exponent, but all the friends who had fought at his side. He sailed on in power and favour while Eliot, his rival but for long his comrade, was condemned for contempt of the King's Government and languished to his death in the Tower. The very force of Wentworth's practical mind led him to a theme which was the exact contrary of all he had previously espoused. Elaborate explanations have been offered to mitigate the suddenness of this transformation. We are invited to regard him as the only man who could have achieved the reunion of Parliament and the monarchy. Allowance must be made for the different values assigned in those days to royal favour and public duty. As Ranke justly but severely observes: "The statesmen of England have always been distinguished from those of other countries by the combination of their activity in the Council and in the Cabinet with an activity in Parliament, without which they cannot win their way into the other sphere. . . . But there was as yet no clear consciousness of the rule, infinitely important for the moral and political development of remarkable men, that the activity of a Minister must be harmonious and consistent with his activity as a Member of Parliament. In the case of Wentworth especially it is clear that he opposed the Government of that day, by which he was kept down, only in order to make himself necessary to it. His natural inclination was, as he once avowed, to live not under the frown but under the smile of his sovereign. The words of opposition to the Government had hardly died away from his lips when, at the invitation of that Government, he joined it, although no change had been introduced into its policy." This was the reason why a hatred centred upon Wentworth different from that which even incompetence attracted to other Ministers. He was "the Satan of the Apostasy," "the lost Archangel," "the suborned traitor to the cause of Parliament." No administrative achievements, no address in business, no eloquence, no magnitude of personality, could atone to his former friends for his desertion. And they had eleven years to think about it all.

Savile and Digges had already accepted office; and a couple of eminent lawyers whose opinions had been adverse to the Crown were also persuaded to sing the opposite tune. Wentworth therefore was enlisted by the King. The lesser figures of the Parliamentary movement either suffered ill usage at the royal hands or, like Holles, Hazelrigg, and Pym, were allowed to brood and fume in obscurity.

But the third and least sentimental condition of the Personal Rule was dominant—money. How to get the money? First, an extreme frugality must be practised by the executive—no wars, no adventures of any kind, no disturbances; all State action reduced to a minimum; quietness by all means. These were the inevitable rules of King Charles's new system. Looking back, the modern eye may discern in this arbitrary régime some at least of those results at which Bright and Cobden aimed in the nineteenth century. The executive was at its weakest. All foreign enterprise was therefore barred. The Crown had to make shift with what it could scrape from old taxes. There even was in the Victorian day a casual saying, "An old tax is no tax." The wealth gained by national toil fructified in the pockets of the people. Peace reigned throughout the land. No large question could be stirred. The King, with his elegant, dignified Court, whose figures are portrayed by the pencil of Van Dyck, whose manners and whose morals were an example to all, reigned on the smallest scale. He was a despot, but an unarmed despot. No standing army enforced his decrees. There was more tolerance towards religious differences in the King's circle than anywhere else in the land. He sincerely believed, his judges vehemently asserted, and his people found it difficult to deny, that he was ruling according to many of the old customs of the realm. It is a travesty to represent this period of Personal Rule as a time of tyranny in any effective sense. In later years, under the yoke of Cromwell's Major-Generals, all England looked back to these placid thirties as an age of ease and tranquillity. But man has never sought tranquillity alone. His nature drives him forward to fortunes which, for better or for worse, are different from those which it is in his power to pause and enjoy.

The Prerogative of the Crown offered a wide and vaguely defined field within which taxes could be raised. The King, supported by his judges, strained all expedients to the limit. He not only persisted in levying tonnage and poundage, to which every one had become accustomed, but he raised or varied the rates upon certain articles. He empowered commissioners to confirm, at a price, defective titles to lands and to commute frauds in their sale. He profited greatly by exercising the Crown's rights of wardship over the estates of heirs who were minors. He mulcted all persons who had not obeyed the summons to receive knighthood at his coronation. Their attendance had long been regarded as a mere form; their absence now opened a source of revenue. He organised into a system the sporadic monopolies in which Queen Elizabeth and his father, to the resentment of Parliament, had indulged. Loopholes in the existing Act against monopolies enabled Charles to make new and more profitable grants, many of them to corporations, in which courtiers and landowners participated. This was in practice a system of indirect taxation farmed out through deeply interested taxgatherers. Large sums of money were paid for each concession, and a handsome due was yielded upon each year's trading. Those who benefited were all for the Personal Rule, while the many who did not swelled the opposition. The growth of London was widely viewed with apprehension. With its suburbs it numbered some two hundred thousand people. The plague lurked in their congested habitations, and public opinion had supported strict rules against new buildings. Nevertheless many had built houses and London and other cities grew. The King's commissioners now came along with the hard alternative, demolish or ransom. In some cases the poor, ill-housed society tore down the structures it had raised; in most they paid the fine.

Meanwhile Wentworth, now Lord-Lieutenant of Ireland, had, by a combination of tact and authority, reduced that kingdom to a greater submission to the British Crown than ever before or since. He assuaged internal feuds; he established order and prosperity; and with an undoubted measure of general acquiescence he produced an Irish army and a substantial Irish subvention for the upkeep of Charles's crown. His repute in history must rest upon his Irish administration. At the end of seven years he stood at the head of a country which he had disciplined and exploited, but which, without any apparent violent measures or bloodshed, lay docile in his hands.

By all these means under a modest frugal régime King Charles managed to do without a Parliament. Hungry forces still lay in shadow. All the ideas which they cherished and championed stirred in their minds, but they had no focus, no expression. The difficulties of travel, the dangers of gathering at any point, the pleasant, easy life of peaceful England, oppressed their movement. Many who would have been vehement if the chance had come their way were content to live their life from day to day. The land was good; springtime, summertime, autumn, had their joys; in the winter there was the Yule log and new amusements. Agriculture and fox hunting cast their compulsive or soothing balms upon restless spirits. Harvests were now abundant and the rise in prices had almost ceased. There was no longer a working-class problem. The Poor Law was administered with exceptional humanity. Ordinary gentlefolk might have no share in national government, but they were still lords on their own estates. In Quarter Sessions they ruled the shires, and as long as they kept clear of the law and paid their taxes with a grunt they were left in peace. It required an intense effort by the Parliamentary party to rouse in them under such conditions a national feeling and concern for the State. The malcontents looked about for points which would inflame the inert forces of the nation.

* * * * *

Presently Charles's lawyers and sleuth-hounds drew attention to an anomaly which had grown with the passage of years. According to the immemorial laws of England—perhaps of Alfred the Great—the whole land should pay for the upkeep of the Fleet. However, for a long time only the maritime counties had paid for the Navy. Yet was not this Navy the shield of all the peace and freedom which thrived in Britain? Why should not all pay where all benefited? There never was a juster demand made of its subjects by an island state than that all counties should share alike in the upkeep of the Fleet. Put properly to a loyal Parliament, it would have passed, with general consent, on its merits apart from ancient tradition. But the abuse of letting the inland counties go untaxed had grown into a custom not broken by Queen Elizabeth even in the days of the Armada. The project commended itself to the King. In August 1635 he levied "Ship Money" upon the whole country.

Forthwith a Buckinghamshire gentleman, a former Member of Parliament, solidly active against the Crown, stood forth among many others and refused to pay. His assessment was no more than twenty shillings; but upon the principle that even the best of taxes could be levied only with the consent of Parliament he faced the distraint and imprisonment which were the penalties of contumacy. John Hampden's refusal was selected by both sides as a test case. The Parliamentarians, who had no other means of expression, saw in it a trial upon which all eyes would be directed, and welcomed a martyr whose sacrifice would disturb the public tameness. They wished to hear the people groan at tyranny. The Crown, on the other hand, was encouraged by the logic of its argument. The case of Hampden therefore became famous at once and for ever. An obelisk at Princes Risborough records to this day his valiant assertion that the inland counties have no concern for the Royal Navy, except in so far as Parliament shall require them to pay. The Crown prevailed. The judges were justified in their decision. It does not even appear that the law was strained. But the grievance ran far and wide. Ninety per cent of ship money was eventually collected for the year 1637, but only 20 per cent for 1639. Everywhere persons of property looked up from their pleasant life and began to use again the language of the Petition of Right.

Yet this alone would not have sufficed to rouse the country. The Parliamentary party knew that upon the constitutional issue alone they could not succeed. They therefore continued to foster religious agitation as the surest means of waking England from its apathy. Here emerges the figure of the man who of all others was Charles's evil genius—William Laud, Archbishop of Canterbury. He was a convinced Anglican, wholehearted in his opposition both to Rome and to Geneva, and a leader in the movement away from Calvinism. But he had an itch for politics, had been a confidant of Buckingham, was indeed the reputed author of Buckingham's most successful speeches. He stepped with agility from an academic career at Oxford into national politics and the King's Council at a time when religious affairs were considered paramount. The Elizabethan settlement was dependent on the State. By itself the Church had not the strength to bear the strain. An informal compact therefore grew up between the secular and spiritual aspects of government, whereby the State sustained the Church in its property and the Church preached the duty of obedience and the Divine Right of Kings.

Laud by no means initiated this compact, but he set himself with untimely vigour to enforce it. Among his innovations was the railing off of the altar, and a new emphasis on ceremony and the dignity of the clergy. The gulf between clergy and congregation was widened and the rôle of authority visibly enhanced. Thus the King's religious ideas marched in step with his politics and resentments multiplied. Laud now found a new source of revenue for the Crown. Under the statutes of Elizabeth everyone was obliged to go to church; they might think as they liked, but they must conform in public worship. This practice had fallen into widespread disuse. Some did not trouble to go; to others it was abhorrent. Now all over England men and women found themselves haled before the justices for not attending church, and fined one shilling a time. Here indeed was something that ordinary men and women could understand. This was no question for lawyers and judges in the court of the Exchequer; it was something new and something teasing. The Puritans, already chafed, regarded it as persecution; they talked at large about the fires of Smithfield, to which this broad downward path must assuredly lead. The Parliamentary agitation which had been conducted during all these years with so much difficulty gained a widespread accession of strength at a time when the King's difficulties had already massed themselves into a stack.

The prosecutions before the Prerogative courts of Prynne and other Puritan writers, and the pillorying, branding, and cropping of ears which they suffered in punishment, were isolated blots upon a régime mild and good-natured compared with that of other countries in the recent past or the approaching future.[1] Indeed it is by no means certain that, left to herself, England would have broken into revolt. It was in Scotland, the home of the Stuarts and Charles's birthplace, that the torch was lighted which began the vast conflagration. Laud was dissatisfied with the spiritual conditions pre-

[1] Written in 1938.—W. S. C.

vailing in the Northern kingdom, and he moved the King to make some effort to improve them. The Scots must adopt the English Prayer Book, and enter broadly into communion with their English brethren.

Besides the desire for uniformity in religious ceremonies throughout the whole Island, King Charles had practical and secular aims. His father had re-established bishops in Scotland with the aim of disciplining the outspoken Presbyterian ministers. James had also adroitly backed the Scottish nobles in their resistance to the pretensions of the Kirk. Charles on his accession had alienated the nobles by an Act which sought to take away from them all the Church lands they had acquired since the Reformation. Furthermore, he was determined to reform the system of collecting tithes, which had largely fallen into their hands. The burden on the smaller landholders was to be reduced and the stipends of the clergy increased. Charles's plans for reinforcing episcopacy in Scotland thus drove the Scottish nobles into opposition. The bishops, for their part, as agents of the distant King, found themselves increasingly disliked by their own clergy as well as by the landowners. In order to strengthen the hands of the Scottish bishops a new exposition of Canon Law was framed emphasising the position of the Crown, and a new Prayer Book or Liturgy was drawn up in London to regulate the forms of public worship in Scotland. These books were promulgated in the year 1636. No one appears to have foreseen the consequences.

Charles and his advisers had no thought of challenging doctrine, still less of taking any step towards Popery. They desired to assert the Protestant High Church view. They defined with new stress the Royal Supremacy, and they prescribed, especially in the sacrament of the Lord's Supper, a somewhat more elaborate ritual. Thus in their course they

affronted at the same time the property interests of the powerful, the religious convictions of all classes, and the independent spirit of the Scottish nation. The resentment excited was
general, and was immediately turned into the channels of
most violent prejudice. The Scottish people believed, and
were told by their native leaders to believe, that they were
to be forced by the royal authority to take the first fatal steps
towards Roman Catholicism. Every tenet, every word, of the
new Prayer Book was scanned with profound suspicion.
Was not the King married to a Popish wife, who practised
idolatry in her private chapel? Were not Papists tolerated
throughout England in a manner increasingly dangerous to
the Protestant faith? Was there not a design to pave the way
to Rome?

When in July 1637 the dignitaries of Scottish Church and
State were gathered in St Giles's Church in Edinburgh for
the first solemn reading of the new Prayer Book it was evident that many ministers of religion and substantial laymen
from all over Scotland had come into the city. An outburst
of fury and insult overwhelmed the Dean when he sought
to read the new dispensation. A woman of the poorer classes
even threw her footstool at the wolf in sheep's clothing
now revealed in their midst. The ceremony became a riot.
A surge of passion swept the ancient capital before which
the episcopal and royal authorities trembled. Edinburgh had
defied the Crown, and no force was found to resist it. King
Charles was startled by the news. He tried to reassure his
Scottish subjects. He dwelt in forcible terms upon his hatred
of Popery, and professed himself willing to amend the new
Prayer Book. But this was vain: only the immediate with-
drawal of the offensive book could have availed. Instead a
long argument on minor points began, with repeated concessions on the part of the King and growing anger through-

out Scotland. Once again we see in a long period of wordy contention and legal interchanges the prelude to a violent convulsion. The Scots, shrewdly advised by their men of law, cast their resistance into the form of a Petition, a Grand Supplication, under the pressure of which the new Prayer Book was withdrawn. But too late. A tempest was blowing which bore men forward. Respect and loyalty were still professed to the King; the blast beat upon the bishops. At length the whole original policy of the King was withdrawn. It had served only to raise a counter-movement, which grew in intensity. All through the year 1637 King Charles was in appearance conceding and virtually apologising, though at the same time he was meditating the use of force. Meanwhile the Scottish nation was forming a union which challenged existing conditions both in Church and State.

At the beginning of 1638 the Petition was abandoned for the signing of a Covenant. There was little new in this Covenant. Much of it merely repeated the confession of faith agreed upon by all fifty years before under King James VI. At that time, amid the stress of the religious wars in Europe, there had been a desire to testify against the power and misdeeds of Rome. But the Covenant now became the solemn bond of a whole nation. All who signed pledged themselves to "adhere to and defend the aforesaid true religion, and forbear the practice of all novations in the matter of the worship of God till they be tried and allowed in free Assemblies and in Parliaments." Whatever was done against the weakest among them was to be the concern of all. On February 28, 1638, the Covenant was read in the Church of Blackfriars in Edinburgh. The Earl of Sutherland, the first to sign his name thereto, was followed by a long list of notables who felt themselves borne forward upon what is described as the "demoniacal frenzy" of the populace. The scroll was signed in the church by many who cut a vein for their ink, and copies were taken for signature to nearly every town and village. It embodied the unalterable resolve of a whole people to perish rather than submit to Popery. Nothing of this sort had ever been intended or dreamed of by the King; but this was the storm he had aroused.

He met it by a fresh semblance of concessions. The Marquis of Hamilton, an experienced Scottish statesman, who was to follow his King to the scaffold, was sent to the North as lay commissioner, with the supreme aim of making friends again. Hamilton fought for nothing more than some show of dignity to cover the temporary royal retreat. He was expostulating with a whirlwind. It was agreed that a General Assembly should be convoked. The Committee of the Covenanters, sitting in Edinburgh, set themselves to organise the elections as elections had never been managed before. The Assembly which met in St Mungo's Cathedral in Glasgow was found to be dominated by the religious convictions of the Northern kingdom, supported by a formidable lay element, who, surrounded by fervent adherents of all classes, sat armed with sword and dagger in the middle of the church.

*　　*　　*　　*　　*

Before Charles sent Hamilton to Scotland they had had a significant conversation. The King had said that if the reconciliation failed Hamilton should collect troops and put down rebellion. "But," said Hamilton, "what if there be not enough troops found in the country for this purpose?" "Then," answered Charles, "power shall come from England, and I will myself come in person with them, being resolved to hazard rather my life than to suffer the supreme authority to be contemned." This occasion now arose. The King was confronted with a hostile and organised Assembly, gathered to adjust religious differences, but now led by armed lay elders, whose aims were definitely political and whose demand was the actual and virtual abolition of the Episcopacy. He ordered the dissolution of the Assembly. That body declared itself resolved to continue in permanent session. They took this step with full knowledge of what it meant. The refusal of the General Assembly of Scotland in November 1638 to dissolve upon the demand of the King's commissioner has been compared to that of the French National Assembly in 1789, when for the first time the members resisted the royal will. The facts and circumstances no doubt were different; but both events led by unbroken chains of causation to the same end, namely, the solemn beheading of a king.

Hamilton, the baffled peacemaker, returned to Whitehall, full of self-reproach for the advice he had given to the King. He now declared himself in favour of drastic measures. The matter was long debated in the King's Council. On the one hand, it was asked, why draw the sword upon a whole people who still proclaimed their love and reverence for the Crown? And how levy war upon them without money or armed forces and without the support of a united England? Moreover, Charles's Ministers could not fail to see the deadly recoil of the Scottish revolt upon the English situation, so outwardly calm, so tense and brittle. If this succeeded where would it stop? The royal authority, supported by the courts of law, had reigned, not without challenge, but effectually, for more than ten years without a Parliament. Here in the North was open defiance. Laud in England and Wentworth in Ireland were in constant correspondence, and to stamp it out while time remained was the mood of both. That mood prevailed, and both King and Covenanters looked about for arms and means of war.

Force was now to be invoked. The King's Council turned its eyes to Wentworth's troops in Ireland, and even to Spain.

There was talk of hiring two thousand Spanish infantry to form the nucleus around which the well-affected in Scotland, of whom there were many, especially in the Eastern Highlands, might gather. But the Covenanters had far better resources overseas. The famous part played by the Scots brigades and by Scottish generals under Gustavus Adolphus in Germany had left Scotland with an incomparable military reserve. Alexander Leslie had risen in the Thirty Years War to the rank of Field-Marshal. He felt himself called upon to return and fight the same quarrel on his native soil. To him it was but a flanking operation in the vast conflict of the Protestants with the Catholic Church. The appeal of Scotland to her warriors abroad was not in vain. Back they flowed in thousands: trained officers and men, the hardened, experienced leaders of many harsh campaigns. They became instantly the core of a disciplined army, with an organised, competent staff and an outstanding, capable Commander-in-Chief. The nobles of Scotland bowed to Leslie's military reputation. They obeyed his orders. Their personal rivalries were allayed. In a few months, and long before any effective preparations could be made in the South, Scotland had the strongest armed force in the Island. It had military knowledge and good officers. It had more: it was inspired with earnest, slowly roused, and now fanatical religious passion. The preachers, sword at side, carbine in hand, aided the drill-sergeants with their exhortations. The soldiers stood ranked in humble supplication, chanting their psalms. Over all there was a rigorous restraint, not only in religious but political opinion. They still had reverence for the King. They would even on occasion cheer his name. But their banners displayed the motto "For Christ's Crown, and the Covenant." The lines of antagonism were drawn with cold, pedantic, inflexible resolve. In May 1639 this army, about twenty thousand strong, stood upon the

Scottish Border opposite the weaker, ill-disciplined, and uncertain forces which Charles and his advisers had gathered.

It was clear from the first that in the King's camp there was no united desire to make war upon the Scots; on the contrary, parleys were set on foot in a good spirit, and on June 18 the so-called "Pacification of Berwick" was agreed. The Scots promised to disband their army and restore the royal castles which they had seized. The King agreed to the summoning in the following August both of a General Assembly and of a Parliament; that these should henceforth be regularly summoned, and that one should have the decision of ecclesiastical and the other of temporal affairs. He declined to recognise the enactments of the Assembly at Glasgow, because they reflected upon his duty as a sovereign; but for the time being he accepted the abolition of the Episcopacy. So far had he travelled since the gay plan of a High Church Liturgy. Charles however thought of the Pacification as a device to gain time, and the Covenanters were soon convinced of this. The spirit of independence was now aroused throughout Scotland. Wrath was expressed at the restoration of the royal fortresses, and fears at the dispersal of the Scottish army. Hamilton, returning to Scotland, found himself in a world of rising antagonism. The Scottish Parliament, which met in Edinburgh at the end of August 1639, claimed forthwith that the King's Privy Council should be responsible to it, and that the King should follow its advice in appointing commanders of troops, and especially of fortresses. They repudiated the jurisdiction of the Treasury, particularly in the coinage, which was being debased; and they even required that honours and dignities should be bestowed in accordance with their wishes. When these intentions became apparent Hamilton could only at first temporise by adjournments, and finally by a prorogation until June 1640. Before the Assembly dispersed it left in full authority a powerful and representative committee, which was in fact the Government of Scotland.

In the complicated pattern of Western Europe the Scots were not only the ardent partisans of Protestantism, but the friends of France against the Austro-Spanish combination. They viewed the neutral and isolationist foreign policy of King Charles as unduly favouring the Catholic interest. They now sought to revive in an intimate form their traditional association with France. By the end of 1639 Charles saw himself confronted with an independent State and Government in the North, which, though it paid formal homage to him as King, was resolved to pursue its own policy both at home and abroad. It thus challenged not only the King's Prerogative, but the integrity of his dominions. He felt bound to fight. But how?

Hamilton, back from Scotland, posed the hard question, "If the Kingly way be taken, how money may be levied, and if that be feasible without a Parliament?" Wentworth was now summoned from Ireland to strengthen the Council. His repute at Court stood high. He had restored not only order but the appearance of loyalty throughout Ireland. Irish sympathies lay upon the Catholic side. Ruling as an enlightened despot, the Lord Deputy had raised and was paying and training an Irish army of eight thousand men. He believed himself capable of enforcing upon Scotland, and later upon England, the system of autocratic rule which had brought him success in the sister island. "Thorough" was his maxim; and we have no means of judging how far he would have pushed on in success. He now threw his weight in favor of war with Scotland. He hoped, once fighting started, to arouse the old antagonism of the English against the Scots. He dreamed of a new Flodden; and he was fully prepared to use his Irish army in Scotland whenever it might be necessary.

*   *   *   *   *

At this decisive moment England's monarchy might well have conformed to the absolutism which was becoming general throughout Europe. Events however took a different turn. The King was by no means resolved to depart from the ancient laws, as he understood them. He had a respect for tradition both in Church and State, of which Wentworth, the ruthless, capable adventurer, whose personal force grew with the crisis, was devoid. But Wentworth saw clearly enough that the royal revenues were not sufficient to support the cost of the campaign. He concluded therefore that Parliament must be summoned. In his over-confidence he thought that the Commons would prove manageable. He was wrong. But a momentous step was taken. After nearly eleven years of Personal Rule the King issued writs for a new Parliament, and elections were held throughout England. This opened the world-famous struggle of Parliament against the King. The Parliamentary forces, though without public expression, had been neither impotent nor idle. Under a mild despotism they had established a strong control of local government in many parts of the country. When suddenly elections were held they were immediately able to secure a Parliament which began where its predecessor had left off. More than this, they presented the issues of 1629 with the pent-up anger and embitterment of eleven years of gag and muzzle. Charles had now to come back cap in hand to those very forces which he had disdainfully dismissed. The membership had been changed by time and fortune. Only a quarter of the former Members reappeared. Eliot was dead in the Tower; Wentworth was now Earl of Strafford and the King's First Minister. But of the old lot one man stood forth, competent, instructed, and avenging. From the moment when the new, afterwards called the Short, Parliament met, Pym was the central figure. "He had observed the errors and mistakes in government," his contemporary Clarendon wrote of him, "and knew well how to make them appear greater than they were." In a long, majestic oration he restated the main case and the added griefs. Charles and his chief counsellors, Strafford and Laud, found no comfort from the new assembly. On the contrary, they were met by such a temper that by an act of extreme imprudence it was dissolved after a few days. Its calling had only served to excite and engage the whole of England in the controversy.

The expedient of calling Parliament had clearly failed and "Thorough" became for Strafford the order of the day. The Scottish army was on the Border, and only weak, ill-disciplined forces could be mustered against it. To place armed men in the field both money and a cause were needed. Neither could be found. Many of the great nobles gave or loaned money to the King for the defence of the realm. Catholic England, silent, banned, but still grateful, made its contribution, secretly given and received. But what did these poor sums avail for a war?

Strafford wished to bring over his Irish troops, but fear of the reactions which this step might provoke paralysed the Council. As Lord President of the North he harangued the nobility at York in rugged, violent terms. The reception was cool and disappointing. Presently the Scots crossed the Tweed in good order. The cavalry stood upstream to break the current while the foot waded across. They met with no opposition until they reached the Tyne. Then, as before the Pacification of Berwick, the two hosts faced one another. The Scottish leaders were encouraged in their invasion by the Parliamentary and Puritan movements throughout England, and in the centre of this combination stood Pym. For some days little happened, but one morning a Scottish horseman, watering his horse in the river, came too near the English outposts. Some one pulled a trigger; the shot went home; the imprudent rider was wounded; all the Scots cannon fired and all the English army fled. A contemporary wrote that "Never so many ran from so few with less ado." The English soldiers explained volubly that their flight was not due to fear of the Scots, but to their own discontents, mentioning especially that they had had no pay. This did not prevent the Scottish army arriving swiftly before the gates of Newcastle. Here the Scots generals declared that they stood for the liberties of England, and appealed for aid from all who agreed with the Parliamentary and Puritan cause. The magistrates however were only induced to open their gates on the blunt reminder that newcastle was in fact a conquered city. Meanwhile Strafford at York was frantically striving to form a front against the invasion, vainly hoping that the insult to English soil would produce the longed-for revival of the national spirit, trying without success to gain a majority upon the Council for the importation of Irish troops.

At this time many of the lords who were now meeting in London pressed on the King the proposal to summon a Magnum Concilium, which was an assembly of the Peers without the Commons. Centuries had passed since it had been convoked, but was not here a crisis which demanded it? Charles agreed, but this antique body could only recommend that Parliament should be called. The King could not defend the country himself. Only Parliament could save the land from what had now become an act of Scottish aggression. At this moment King Charles's moral position was at its worst. He had plumbed the depths of personal failure. His enemies, while compassing and finally achieving his destruction, now built and rebuilt for him a party and a cause for which any man could die.

The Revolt of Parliament

INEXORABLE forces compelled the King to do what he most feared. The invading Scottish army had possession of Durham and Northumberland. Their leaders were in close correspondence with the Parliamentary and Puritan party in England. They put forward not only demands which affected the Northern kingdom, but others which they knew would reverberate in the South. They were careful that the supply of sea-coal to London should not fail for a single day; but at the same time their marauding bands lay heavy on the occupied counties. The King could not prevail against them. Strafford believed that he could hold Yorkshire, but that was all. The Privy Council addressed itself to making a truce with the Scots, who demanded forty thousand pounds a month to maintain their army on English soil until their claims should be met. By haggling this was reduced to £850 a day. Thus the two armies, facing each other with sheathed swords, were each to be maintained during an indefinite period of negotiation at the cost of the Crown, which was penniless. The so-called "Bishops' War" was over; the real war had yet to begin.

There arose from all quarters a cry that Parliament should be summoned. At least half the lords had remained in London. A group of them, headed by the Earl of Bedford, who was in close touch with Pym, waited on the Privy Council and called for a Parliament. It was even implied that if the

King would not issue the writs himself a Parliament would be convened without him. The Queen and such counsellors as were with her wrote urgently to Charles that they saw no other course. The King had himself arrived at the same conclusion. In these days his outlook underwent a decided change. He recognised that his theory of monarchy must be modified. In summoning the new Parliament he accepted a different relationship between the people and the Crown.

The calling of Parliament relieved for a space the severe tension, and the choosing of Members employed the zeal of partisans. But it was only after long begging, supported by the very lords who were opposing the King, and on their personal security, that the City of London consented to advance £50,000, pending the meeting of Parliament, to keep the Scottish army in victorious possession of the North of England and the English army from dissolving in mutiny.

There is no surer way of rousing popular excitement than the holding of General Elections in quick succession. Passions ran high; beer flowed. Although there was nothing like the organisation of the Scottish elections in 1639, the leaders of the popular party hastened from county to county exhorting their adherents. The King too appealed, not without response, to the great lords who stood by him. In some places four or five rival candidates appeared; but the tide ran strong against the Court. "We elected," runs a pamphlet of 1643, "such as were not known to us by any virtue, but only by crossness to superiors." Three-fifths of the Members of the Short Parliament, 294 out of 493, were returned, and nearly all the newcomers were opponents of the Government. Of the men who had made a name in Opposition not one was rejected. The King could count on less than a third of the House.

Thus on November 3, 1640, was installed the second longest and most memorable Parliament that ever sat in England. It derived its force from a blending of political and religious ideas. It was upborne by the need of a growing society to base itself upon a wider foundation than Tudor paternal rule. It used for tactical purposes the military threat of the invaders from Scotland. Scottish commissioners and divines arrived in London. They were astonished at the warmth of their welcome, and were hailed as the deliverers of England. They found themselves outpaced in their hostility to the bishops by some of their English Parliamentary allies. The negotiations were protracted from week to week at an expense to the Crown which could only be defrayed by Parliament. Demands in both kingdoms for far-reaching changes in the civil and religious government which had lasted for centuries were pooled and set forth again with combined force. The accession of James I had involved the union of the Crowns of England and Scotland; but now in a manner very different from what James or his son had conceived there was a union of the dominant political parties in both countries, and they strove together for a common cause. Here then was an explosive charge, pent in a strong cannon and directed upon King Charles and those who were his trusted Ministers.

Of these the first and most obnoxious was Strafford. Pym and Hampden, the leading figures in the new House of Commons, were immediately in command of a large and indignant majority. The Crown now made no resistance to the principle that redress of grievances should precede supply; but the grievances of the Commons could be satisfied only by vengeance. Strafford possessed convincing proofs of the correspondence carried on by Pym and others with the invading Scots. This was plain treason if the King's writ ran. It was believed that Strafford meant to open this formidable case; but Pym struck first. All the rage of the Parliamentary party, all the rancour of old comradeship forsworn, all that self-preservation dictated, concentrated upon "the wicked Earl" a blast of fury such as was never recorded in England before or since. On the morning of November 11 the doors of St Stephen's Chapel were locked; the key placed upon the table; no strangers might enter, no Member might leave. Late in the afternoon Pym and Hampden, attended by three hundred Members, carried the articles of Strafford's impeachment up to the House of Lords. At the King's request Strafford had come to London. In the morning he had been greeted with respect by the peers. Hearing what was afoot, he returned to the Chamber. But now all was changed. He was received with a hollow murmur. Shouts were raised that he should withdraw while the issue was being debated. He was forced to do so. In less than an hour the powerful Minister saw himself transformed into an accused prisoner. He found himself to his own and the general surprise kneeling at the Bar to receive the directions of his peers. He was deprived of his sword and taken into custody by Black Rod. As he went through the crowd on his journey to Black Rod's house the hostility of the populace was terrible. Such a downfall recalls, in its swiftness at least, the fate of Sejanus, the hated Minister of Tiberius.

The proscription extended to all the Ministers, as they would now be called, of the King. Archbishop Laud, impeached in the Lords, silenced when he sought to reply, was removed by water to the Tower. Sir Francis Windebanke, the Secretary of State, and some others escaped to the Continent. Lord Keeper Sir John Finch, leaving the Woolsack, appeared before the House of Commons in his robes of office bearing the Great Seal of England in his embroidered bag, and defended himself in such moving words that all were hushed.

Nevertheless this produced no longer delay than was necessary for him to flee the country. All this was done by the fierce anger of the Commons, supported by the Londoners and by the distant military forces of Scotland, and accepted by the peers.

The main feature of the Puritan Revolution for our generation is its measured restraint. The issues were fought out with remorseless antagonism, not only in Parliament by men who glared upon one another and were prepared to send each other to the scaffold, but also in the streets of London, where rival mobs or bands came face to face or even mingled. Respect for law and for human life nevertheless prevailed. In this mortal struggle physical violence was long held in check, and even when it broke into civil war all those conventions were observed which protect even the sternest exercise of the human will from the animal barbarism of earlier and of later times.

*　　*　　*　　*　　*

The Commons were harassed by fears and rumours. They had been careful to pay the Scottish army for invading England; it was the English troops who had gone short. There were tales of mutinies and military plots. Pym, with cold-blooded skill, played upon these alarms, which indeed needed but a tremor of Parliamentary weakness to become real. The aggressive tendencies of the majority in the Commons shaped themselves into a demand for the abolition of Episcopacy. The Scots, now so influential in London and masters in the North, sought to establish the Presbyterian system of Church government. This was indeed turning the tables. A petition signed by fifteen thousand was presented to the House, and caught up by the majority, seeking to extirpate the Episcopate "root and branch." But now for the first time effective counter forces appeared. A second petition signed by seven hundred clergymen hostile to the principles of the King and the Archbishop proposed the restriction of the bishops' power to spiritual matters, and limited them at certain points in these. Here was a line of resistance upon which the other side could form. It was known that the King regarded the Episcopate, based upon the Apostolic Succession, as inseparable from the Christian faith. The English Episcopate went back to the days of St Augustine, and Henry VIII's break with Rome had made no difference to its continuity. The King held sincerely to his hereditary right of nominating bishops; his opponents saw in this a dangerous fount of power. Thus in the religious field the quarrel was between men who were all Christians and all Protestants, but who were divided upon the method of Church government. On this they were prepared to proceed to extremes against each other; but whereas in politics the opposition to Personal Rule was at this moment overwhelming, on the Church question the balance was far more even. Pym realised this and decided to delay a full debate. Both petitions were therefore sent to a committee.

Meanwhile the trial of Strafford had begun. Proceeding as they did upon admittedly rival interpretations of law and justice, the Commons at once found difficulty in establishing a case against the hated Minister. That he was the arch enemy of all that the majority championed, and indeed of the rights and liberties of the nation, was apparent. But to prove him guilty of the capital offence of treason was not possible. Within the large wooden structure erected in Westminster Hall the leaders of the nation, its magnates and politicians and divines, assembled. One third of the floor was thronged with the public. The King and Queen sat daily in their special box, hoping by their presence to restrain the prosecution. Strafford defended himself with magnificent ability. Each morning he knelt to the Lord Steward and bowed to the lords and to the assembly. Each day by logic and appeal he broke up the heads of accusation. He successfully derided the theory of "cumulative treason" to which the managers of the impeachment were soon reduced. How could a number of alleged misdemeanours be made to add up to treason? He drove home the massive doctrine of English liberty, "No law, no crime." What law had he broken? With every art of the orator, or, as his foes said, of the actor, he wrought not only upon the minds but upon the sentiments of the audience. The King worked night and day upon the peers. There was nothing he would not concede to save Strafford. He had assured him on his kingly word that he should not suffer in liberty or life. The sympathy not only of the galleries, crowded with the wives of all the leading men, but of the peers themselves, was gradually gained. On the thirteenth day the prisoner's hopes stood high.

Now Pym and his colleagues made a deadly stroke. Sir Henry Vane, Secretary of the Privy Council, had a son who was ardent for the popular cause. This son, by an act of bad faith which after many stormy years was to cost him his life, purloined a note which his father had preserved of the discussion in the King's Council on May 5, 1640. The cryptic sentiments ascribed to Strafford were: "Everything is to be done as power will admit, and that you are to do. They refused, you are acquitted towards God and man. You have an army in Ireland you may employ here to reduce this kingdom. Confident as anything under Heaven, Scotland shall not hold out five months."

The Commons declared that this convicted Strafford of advising the use of an Irish army to subdue England. The words in their context seem to mean that Scotland was intended, and Scotland at the time of their utterance was in rebellion against the King. Vane the elder, Secretary of the Council, in cross-examination could not, or would not, say whether the words "this kingdom" meant England or Scotland. The other members of the Council who were examined declared that they had no recollection of the words; that the debate regarded the means of reducing Scotland, not England; and that they had never heard the slightest hint of employing the Irish army anywhere but in Scotland. It must have been present in all minds that if an Irish army had been successfully used in Scotland it would assuredly have found other employment thereafter; but this was not the point in question. Strafford's answer covered all issues. "What will be the end," he said, "if words which are spoken in the King's Privy Council, half understood or misunderstood by its members, are to be turned into crime? No one will any longer have the courage to speak out his opinion plainly to the King." The lawyers also declared themselves on his side. There was no doubt that he had won his case.

The Commons, baffled, claimed to advance new evidence. Strafford demanded that if this were admitted he should have an equal right. The lords decided in his favour. And then suddenly there arose from the mass of Members gathered in the court loud cries of "Withdraw! Withdraw!" The Commons trooped back to St Stephen's Chapel and again locked their doors. Was this enemy of English rights to escape by legal processes? They knew he was their foe, and they meant to have his blood. They would dispense with a trial and have him declared guilty by Act of Parliament. Pym and Hampden did not themselves put forward the plan of a Bill of Attainder. They had it moved by one of their principal followers; but when it was launched they threw their weight behind it, and the weight of the angry, tumultuous City outside. The Lords affected to ignore what was known to be going forward in the Lower House, and listened with evident sympathy to Strafford's closing speech. He struck deep into their hearts. "My lords, it is my present misfortune, but forever yours . . . and except your lordships' wisdom provide for it, the shedding of my blood may make a way for the tracing of yours. You, your estates, your posterities, lie all at the stake if such learned gentlemen as these, whose lungs are well acquainted with such proceedings, shall be started out against you; if your friends, your counsel, were denied access to you; if your professed enemies admitted to witness against you; if every word, intention, circumstance of yours be alleged as treasonable, not because of a statute, but a consequence, a construction heaved up in a high rhetorical strain. I leave it to your lordships' consideration to foresee what may be the issue of so dangerous, so recent precedencies.

"These gentlemen tell me they speak in defence of the Commonweal against my arbitrary laws. Give me leave to say it, I speak in defence of the Commonweal against their arbitrary treason; for if this latitude be admitted, what prejudice shall follow to the King, to the country, if you and your posterity be disabled by the same from the greatest affairs of the kingdom. For my poor self, if it were not for your lordships' interest, and the interest of a saint in heaven [his first wife], who hath left me two pledges here on earth [at these words he was overcome with emotion], were it not for this, I should never take the pains to keep up this ruinous cottage of mine. . . . Nor could I leave it in a better time than this, when I hope the better part of the world think that, by this my misfortune, I had given testimony of my integrity to God, my King, and country."

But the Bill of Attainder passed the House of Commons on April 21 by 204 votes to 59. Among the minority was Lord Digby, who had come to Parliament as one of the leading opponents of the Crown. With all his gifts, which were exceptional, he pleaded against his own party. He gained nothing but the suspicion of being a renegade. A surge of panic and of wrath convulsed the assembly. When a board creaked overhead they thought of Gunpowder Plot. The names of the fifty-nine were spread abroad as traitors defending a traitor. The aspect of the multitude which daily beset the approaches to Parliament became more than ever threatening. The peers deemed to be favourable to Strafford were cowed by the frenzy they saw around them. When Oliver St John urged the case for the Attainder in a great conference between the Houses he used arguments not of law but of revolution. Parliament was not bound, like inferior tribunals, by existing laws, but was justified in making new ones to suit circumstances. Its only guide should be care for the public weal: it was the political body, embracing all, from the King to the beggar, and could deal with individuals for the good of the whole, could open a vein to let out the corrupted blood. It had been said that the law must precede the offence; that where no law was there could be no transgression. But that plea could not avail for the man who had desired to overthrow all laws. "It was never accounted either cruelty or foul play," said St John, "to knock foxes and wolves on the head because they be beasts of prey. The warrener sets traps for polecats and other vermin for the preserving of the warren."

When Strafford heard this harsh cry for vengeance he raised his hands above his head, as if to implore the mercy of Heaven, knowing that all was lost on earth. Only half the lords who had been present at the impeachment dared to vote upon the Bill of Attainder, and these in great preponderance sent Strafford to his doom. They had become convinced that if they let him go the King would use him to make war upon the Houses; and, as the Earl of Essex, the discontented son of Queen Elizabeth's favourite, brutally observed, "Stone-dead hath no fellow."

There were however other chances. The King tried to gain control of the Tower and of the prisoner. But the Governor, Sir William Balfour, closed his gates against the forces which sought to enter. He also spurned an immense bribe offered him by Strafford. The cry for "Justice!" rang through London streets. A mob of several thousand, many of them armed, appeared before the palace roaring for Strafford's head. In Parliament it was bruited that they would now impeach the Queen.

This was the agony of Charles's life, to which none of his other sufferings compared. The question was not now whether he could save Strafford, but whether the royal authority would perish with him. He appealed to the bishops, who, with two exceptions, advised him that he must separate his feelings as a man from those of a sovereign. But his real release came from Strafford himself. In a noble letter, written before the vote in the Lords, he had urged the King not to let any promise to him endanger the monarchy or the peace of the realm. At last Charles made the surrender which haunted him to the last moment of his life. He gave his assent to the Bill of Attainder. But conscience stirred in him still. Abandoning his kingly authority, on the next day he sent the young Prince of Wales to beg the House of Lords to reduce the sentence from death to perpetual imprisonment. Those peers who still attended refused, and even an appeal for a few days of grace in which the victim might settle his worldly affairs was denied.

An immense concourse of persons such as had never yet been seen in the Island crowded to the place of execution. Strafford died with fortitude and dignity. He was beyond doubt a man conscious of commanding gifts, impelled by high ambition and a desire to rule. He had sought power by the path of Parliament. He had found it in the favour of the Crown. He adopted a system which suited his interests, and it became interwoven with his strong character. The circumstances of his trial and of the Attainder threw odium upon his pursuers. They slaughtered a man they could not convict. But that man, if given his full career, would have closed perhaps for generations the windows of civic freedom upon the English people.

*   *   *   *   *

In the crash of the Strafford trial and execution the King let various matters slip. The Triennial Bill providing for the summoning of Parliament at least once in three years, if necessary in spite of the Crown, put a final end to the system of Personal Rule over which Charles had so far presided. The grant of tonnage and poundage for one year only was accompanied by a censure upon the exaction of Ship Money, and reparation to all who had suffered for their resistance to it. The King perforce subscribed to all this. But he must have been completely broken for the moment when he assented to a measure designed "to prevent inconvenience that may happen by the untimely prorogation or dissolving of this present Parliament" except by its own consent. He accepted this on the same day as the Bill of Strafford's Attainder. It was in fact a law making this Parliament, since called the Long Parliament, perpetual. Many other changes necessary to the times and remedial to the discontents were made. The judges, whose tenure had hitherto been dependent upon the pleasure of the Crown, now held office on good behaviour. The Court of Star Chamber, which, as we have seen, Henry VII had used to curb the baronage, but which had in the lapse of time become oppressive to the people, was abolished. So was the Court of High Commission, which had striven to impose religious uniformity. The jurisdiction of the Privy Council was strictly and narrowly defined. The principles of the Petition of Right about personal liberty, particularly freedom from arbitrary arrest, were now finally established. Charles endorsed these great decisions. He had realised that in his trusteeship of the rights of monarchy he had grasped too much. Henceforward he took his stand on broader ground. The whole Tudor system which the Stuarts had inherited was shaken from its base.

But everything was now fluid, and in that strong-willed, rugged, obstinate England men, without regard to their former actions, looked about them for sure foothold. From the day when Strafford's head fell beneath the axe there began a conservative reaction, partial but nationwide. Charles, who at the meeting of the Parliament had been almost alone with his cluster of hated Ministers, found himself increasingly sustained by strong and deep currents of public feeling. If he had only allowed these to have their flow he might have reached a very good establishment. The excesses and fanaticism of the Puritan party, their war upon the Church, their confederacy with the Scottish invaders, roused antagonisms of which the hitherto helpless Court was but a spectator, but from which the Crown might by patience and wisdom emerge, curtailed certainly but secure. Henceforward the quarrel was no longer between King and people, but between the two main themes and moods which have until the confusion of the modern age disputed for mastery in England. The twentieth century was to dawn before men and women became unable to recognise their political ancestors in this ancient conflict.

Charles now felt that his hope lay in a reconciliation with Scotland. The interplay of the Scots army in the North with the Puritan faction at Westminster was irresistible. He resolved to go to Scotland himself and open a Parliament in Edinburgh. Pym and his adherents could hardly object to this. Moderate opinion welcomed the plan. "If the King shall settle and establish a perfect quietness with the Scots," wrote his sagacious Secretary, Sir Edward Nicholas, "it will open a way for a happy and good conclusion of all differences here." To Scotland then the King proceeded. Far gone were the days of the new Liturgy and the dreams of uniformity in Church and State between the two kingdoms. Charles accepted everything he had most abhorred. He strove to win the hearts of the Covenanters. He listened devoutly to their sermons and sang the psalms in the manner of the Kirk. He assented to the establishment of total Presbyterianism in Scotland. But all was in vain. Charles was accused of complicity in an ill-starred attempt of Royalist partisans to kidnap the Scottish leader, the Marquess of Argyll. The Scots were confirmed in their obduracy, and the King returned to England crestfallen.

Upon this melancholy scene a hideous apparition now appeared. The execution of Strafford liberated all the elemental forces in Ireland which his system had so successfully held in restraint. The Irish Parliament in Dublin, formerly submissive, had hastened to voice their complaints against his rule. At the same time a Roman Catholic Celtic people regarded the English Protestantism with the utmost aversion. Strafford's disciplined Irish army was disbanded. Some efforts were made by Charles's Ministers to enlist the religious convictions of the Irish in the royal cause. But all this fused into inextricable ruin. The passions of the original inhabitants and of the hungry, downtrodden masses, bursting from all control, were directed upon the gentry, the landowners, and the Protestants, both within and without the Pale. A veritable Jacquerie, recalling the dark times in France, broke upon the land in the autumn of 1641. The propertied classes, their families and dependents, fled to the few garrisoned towns. "But," says Ranke, "no one can paint the rage and cruelty which was vented, far and wide over the land, upon the unarmed and defenceless. Many thousands perished, their corpses filled the land and served as food for the kites. . . . Religious abhorrence entered into a dreadful league with the fury of national hatred. The motives of the Sicilian Vespers and of the night of St Bartholomew were united."[1] Cruelties unspeakable were reported on all sides, and the Government, under the Lords Justices, struck back without mercy. A general slaughter of males and a policy of devastation were proclaimed throughout large parts of the countryside. As the tale of these atrocities crept home to England it gave a shock to men's minds which even amid their own preoccupations lasted long. It was deeply harmful to the King's interests. The Puritan party saw, or declared that they saw, in the Irish outrage the fate to which they would be consigned if the Popish tendencies of the bishops were armed with the sword of an absolute sovereign. They regarded the native Irish as wild beasts to be slain at sight, and the cruelties which they in their turn were to wreak in their hour of triumph took their impulse from this moment.

*　*　*　*　*

The mere fact of his absence from London, which had left the Parliamentary forces to their full play, had served the King's interests better than the closest attention to English affairs. During September and October conservative reaction had become a tide. Who could accuse the Court of army plots when the English and Irish armies had both been disbanded? Englishmen, irrespective of religious and constitutional convictions, were ill disposed to be taxed for the upkeep of invading Scottish troops. Presbyterianism made little

[1] Ranke, vol. ii, p. 287.

appeal to the bulk of the English people, who, so far as they were not satisfied with the Elizabethan Church tradition, sought spiritual comfort or excitement in the more vehement sects which had sprung up in the general turmoil of the Reformation, or in the Puritan body itself, such as Anabaptism and Brownism, both of which were as much opposed to Presbytery as to Bishops. The House of Commons at the end of 1641 had travelled far. Pym and his supporters were still dominant and more extreme. But there was an opposition equally resolute. The Lords were now at variance with the Commons, and a large majority, when they attended, sided with the King. From being the servants of the national cause, the Puritans had become an aggressive faction. But the argument, even in that persevering age, was becoming too long and harassing for mere words. Men felt their right hands itching to grasp the swords by which alone it seemed their case could be urged.

It was in this stormy weather that Pym and Hampden sought to rally their forces by bringing forward what was called the "Grand Remonstrance." This long document, on which committees had been at work for many months, was in fact a party manifesto. It was intended to advertise all that had so far been accomplished by Parliament in remedying old grievances, and to proclaim the future policy of the Parliamentary leaders. Pym's hope was to re-establish the unity of his diverse followers, and so the more extreme demands for religious reform were dropped. The power of Bishops was to be curtailed, but they were not to be abolished. Nevertheless the growing body of Conservatives, or "Episcopalian Party," as they were sometimes named, were affronted by the Remonstrance and determined to oppose it. They did not like the way that Pym was going. They wanted "to win the King by the sweeter way of concealing his errors than by publishing of them." Pym however was preparing to carry the struggle further; he would appeal to the people and win complete control for Parliament over the King's Ministers. Already, in a message about the Irish rebellion, he had demanded that the King should "employ such counsellors and Ministers as shall be approved by his Parliament." If this were not conceded he threatened that Parliament would take Irish affairs into its own hands. Here was a sweeping challenge to royal authority. But the King now had at his side very different counsellors from those of a year before. Many of his former opponents, chief among them Digby and his father, the Earl of Bristol, were hostile to Pym. Bishop Williams, foremost of Laud's critics, now stood against Laud's accusers. Falkland and Colepeper ranged themselves against the violence of the majority and were soon to take office in the King's Government. Edward Hyde, later famous as the historian Clarendon, opened the debate by insisting that the aim must now be peace: if the Remonstrance as a whole were carried, and especially if it were published, the disputes would be embittered and prolonged.

The debate was long and earnest, vehement with restrained passion. At last at midnight the Remonstrance, somewhat amended, was put to the vote. When Parliament had met a year earlier the King's party could not count on a third of its members. Now the Grand Remonstrance was carried only by eleven votes. A motion was put forward by the majority that it should be printed forthwith. On this the Commons rose to a clash of opposing wills. About one o'clock in the morning a lawyer of the Middle Temple, Mr Geoffrey Palmer, demanded that the clerk should record the names of all who protested. The procedure of protest by a minority was, and long continued to be, customary in the House of Lords, but the principle of the Commons was that the vote of the majority was the vote of the House. Palmer seemed to ask who was prepared to protest. A great crowd rose to their feet with the cry, "All! All!" Plumed hats were waved, men laid their hands upon their swords, some even drew them and rested their hands upon the pommels. "I thought," wrote a Member, Philip Warwick, of this moment in the crowded, dimly lighted room of the chapel, "we had all sat in the Valley of the Shadow of Death, that we, like Abner's and Joab's young men, had catched at each other's locks and sheathed our swords in each other's bowels." Only Hampden's suave, timely intervention prevented a bloody collision. But here the pathway of debate was broken, and war alone could promise further steppingstones.

A hitherto little-noticed Member for Cambridge, Oliver Cromwell, rather rough in his manners, but an offshoot of Thomas Cromwell's line, said to Falkland as they left the House, "If the Remonstrance had been rejected I would have sold all that I had next morning, and never have seen England any more; and I know there are many honest men of the same resolution." He, and Pym also, looked across the ocean to new lands where the cause for which they were prepared to die, or kill, could breathe, albeit in a wilderness. Their sentiments awoke echoes in America that were not to be stilled until more than a century later, and after much bloodshed.

* * * * *

The King, who, in spite of his failure in Scotland and the Irish catastrophe, had been conscious of ever-gathering support, was now drawn into various contradictory blunders. At one moment he sought to form a Ministry dependent upon the majority faction which ruled the House of Commons. A dozen of the Opposition lords were sworn members of the Privy Council. But when in a few weeks it was found that these noblemen began to speak of the King in terms of undue respect the London factions howled upon them as backsliders. Still seeking desperately for a foothold, Charles invited Pym himself to become Chancellor of the Exchequer. Such a plan had no contact with reality. Colepeper took the post instead, and Falkland became Secretary of State. Next, in violent revulsion, Charles resolved to prosecute five of his principal opponents in the Commons for high treason. Upon this wild course he was impelled by Queen Henrietta Maria. She taunted him with cowardice, and exhorted him, if he would ever see her again, to lay strong hands upon those who spent their nights and days seeking his overthrow and her life. He certainly convinced himself that Pym meant to impeach the Queen.

Thus goaded, Charles, accompanied by three or four hundred swordsmen—"Cavaliers" we may now call them—went down to the House of Commons. It was January 4, 1642. Never before had a king set foot in the Chamber. When his officers knocked at the door and it was known that he had come in person members of all parties looked upon each other in amazement. His followers beset the doors. All rose at his entry. The Speaker, William Lenthall, quitted his chair and knelt before him. The King, seating himself in the chair, after professing his goodwill to the House, demanded the surrender of the five indicted Members—Pym, Hampden, Holles, Hazelrigg, and Strode. But a treacherous message from a lady of the Queen's Bedchamber had given Pym a timely warning. The accused Members had already embarked at Westminster steps and were safe amid the train bands and magistrates of the City. Speaker Lenthall could give no information. "I have only eyes to see and ears to hear as the House may direct," he pleaded. The King, already conscious of his mistake, cast his eyes around the quivering assembly. "I see that the birds are flown," he said lamely, and after some civil reassurances he departed at the head of his disappointed, growling adherents. But as he left the Chamber a low, long murmur of "Privilege" pursued him. To this day the Members for the City take their places on the Treasury bench at the opening of a session, in perpetual acknowledgment of the services rendered by the City in protecting the five.

Upon this episode the wrath of London became uncontrollable. The infuriated mobs who thronged the streets and bellowed outside the palace caused Charles and his Court to escape from the capital to Hampton Court. He never saw London again except to suffer trial and death. Within a week of his intrusion into the House the five Members were escorted back to Parliament from the City. Their progress was triumphal. Over two thousand armed men accompanied them up the river, and on either bank large forces, each with eight pieces of cannon, marched abreast of the flotilla. Henceforth London was irretrievably lost to the King. By stages he withdrew to Newmarket, to Nottingham, and to York. Here he waited during the early months of 1642, while the tireless antagonisms which rent England slowly rebuilt him an authority and an armed force. There were now two centres of government. Pym, the Puritans, and what was left of the Parliament ruled with dictatorial power in London in the King's name. The King, round whom there gathered many of the finest elements in Old England, freed from the bullying of the London mob, became once again a prince with sovereign rights. About these two centres there slowly assembled the troops and resources for the waging of civil war.

The Great Rebellion

THE negotiations between King and Parliament which occupied the early months of 1642 served only to emphasise their differences while both were gathering their forces. "The question in dispute between the King's party and us," wrote a captain of the Roundheads, as the militant section of the Parliamentary party was now called, "was whether the King should govern as a god by his will, and the nation be governed by force like beasts; or whether the people should be governed by laws made by themselves and live under a Government derived from their own consent." To balance more evenly he might have added "or said to be derived from their own consent." On June 1, 1642, Parliament presented nineteen Propositions to the King. This ultimatum demanded that the Council, the King's Great Officers of State, and his children's tutor should be appointed by Parliament; that Parliament should be given complete control over the militia, and over the army required for the reconquest of Ireland—that is to say, "the power of the sword"; and that a Church Settlement should be determined by the wishes of Parliament. In brief, the King was invited to surrender his whole effective sovereignty over Church and State. But underlying the apparently clear-cut constitutional issue was a religious and class conflict. The Puritans were predominant in Parliament, High Churchmen at Court. The "new classes" of merchants and manufacturers and the substantial tenant-farmers in some counties were claiming a share of political power, which had hitherto been almost monopolised by the aristocracy and the hereditary landlords.

Yet when the alignment of the parties on the outbreak of the Civil War is surveyed no simple divisions are to be found. Brother fought against brother, father against son. The Royalists' appeal was negative, but none the less potent. Against loyalty to Parliament they invoked loyalty to the Crown; against Puritan ardour Anglican unity. They preferred the ancient light of divinely blessed authority to the distant glimmer of democracy. "God saith, 'Touch not Mine anointed,' " wrote a Cavalier knight as he reluctantly girded on his sword for the battle. On both sides men went into the fight doubtfully, but guided by their belief in high-souled ideals. On both sides were others—dissolute courtiers, ambitious politicians spoiling for a fight, out-of-work mercenaries, ready to profit from the national dissensions; but, broadly, the contest now became a tragic conflict of loyalties and ideals.

The arrogant tone and ever-growing demands of the Parliamentary party shaped the lines of the struggle and recruited the forces of the King. The greater part of the nobility gradually rallied to the Royalist cause; the tradesmen and merchants generally inclined to the Parliament; but a substantial section of the aristocracy were behind Pym, and many boroughs were devotedly Royalist. The gentry and yeomen in the counties were deeply divided. Those nearer London generally inclined to Parliament, while the North and West remained largely Royalist. Both sides fought in the name of the King, and both upheld the Parliamentary institution. The Roundheads always spoke of "King and Parliament." The orders given to their first Commander-in-Chief, the Earl of Essex, directed him to "rescue" the King and princes, if necessary by force, from the evil counsellors into whose power they had fallen. Charles vowed himself to live as a

ENGLAND
DURING THE
CIVIL WAR

COUNTRY HELD BY THE
ROYALISTS AT THE END OF 1643

× BATTLES

SCOTLAND

Dunbar
Edinburgh
Berwick

Newcastle

Scarborough

Bridlington

Marston
Moor York
Preston Hull
Adwalton Moor Selby
Lathom House Winceby
Winnington Newark
Bridge
Nottingham
Shrewsbury
Naseby Newmarket
Edge
Worcester Hill Northampton
Gloucester Cropredy Bridge
Oxford
Chalgrove Field LONDON
Brentford
Bristol Newbury Turnham Green
Lansdown Roundway Down

Carisbrooke
Castle
Lostwithiel
Plymouth

constitutional monarch and to respect the laws of the realm. The issue was never Autocracy against Republicanism, but, in Ranke's compact phrase, "One party desired Parliament not without the King, and the other the King not without Parliament." Behind all class and political issues the religious quarrel was the driving power. In Cromwell's words, "Religion was not the thing at first contested for, but God brought it to that issue at last; and gave it unto us by way of redundancy; and at last it proved that which was most dear to us."

For more than seventy years absolute peace had reigned in England. Except for a few officers who had seen service on the Continent, no one knew anything about military matters. At first the Cavaliers, trained in fencing, inured to the chase, with their gamekeepers and dependents, had a military advantage over the Roundheads. From York the King looked to Hull, where the weapons of his disbanded army against the Scots had been stored. The Prince of Wales and the Duke of York, who were but boys aged twelve and nine, paid a visit to Hull and were courteously received, but when the King himself sought entry the Governor, Sir John Hotham, closed the gates and manned the ramparts against him. As he had only a few thousand local levies or train bands the King had to accept the rebuff. It was more, it was a heavy blow. Arms were vital. At Nottingham, where town and county alike had proclaimed devotion, Charles set up his standard on August 22 and called his loyal subjects to his aid. This was the ancient signal for feudal duty, and its message awoke ancestral memories throughout the land. The genius of De Quincey has lighted the tragedy of those "who met in peace, and sat at the same tables, and were allied by marriage or by blood; and yet, after a certain day in August 1642, never smiled upon each other again, nor met but in the field of battle; and at Marston Moor, at Newbury, or at Naseby, cut asunder all ties of love by the cruel sabre, and washed away in blood the memory of ancient friendship."

* * * * *

At Nottingham the King had only eight hundred horse and three hundred foot, and at first it seemed doubtful whether any royal army could be raised. But the violence of Parliament served him well. By the end of September he had with him two thousand horse and six thousand foot. A few weeks later their numbers were more than doubled, and other forces were raised for him all over the country. The Queen, who had found refuge in Holland, sent arms and trained officers, procured by the sale of the Crown jewels. But the Navy, which Charles had quarrelled with his subjects to sustain, adhered to Parliament and the blockade was hard to run. The great nobles supplied the King with money. The Marquis of Newcastle is said to have spent nearly a million pounds upon the Royalist cause, and the Marquis of Worcester seven or eight hundred thousand. The University of Oxford melted their plate, and this example was followed in many a hall and manor. When Cambridge University was found in the same mood Cromwell intervened with armed force. Meanwhile the Roundheads, sustained by ample funds from the wealth and regular taxation of London, levied and trained an army of twenty-five thousand men under Essex. As on the Royalist side, most of the regiments were raised personally by prominent people. But whereas the King could give only a commission to raise a regiment or a troop Parliament could provide the equipment as well. The quality of the Parliamentary forces was inferior, but they made up in zeal what they lacked in discipline and military skill. The London militia, drilled by German instructors, were already to be respected.

The King, skilfully avoiding Essex's army, now moved west

to join his Welsh reinforcements, and then struck south for the Thames valley and London. There was a panic in the capital when this became evident. An address was hastily dispatched to the King, proposing that he should return to his Parliament, and at the same time Essex was enjoined to overtake him. Charles did not dare to be caught between the troops in London and those who followed hard upon him. At Edgehill, in Warwickshire, on October 23 the royal army turned on its pursuers and attacked them before their rearguard, which was approaching the village of Kineton, had come in. The battle was marked by abundant ignorance and zeal on both sides. Prince Rupert of the Rhine, the King's nephew, who, with his younger brother, Prince Maurice, both fresh from the European wars, had hastened to his side and taken command of the cavalry, charged and overthrew all the Parliamentary horse on their left wing. Carried away by his own ardour or the indiscipline of his troopers, he pursued the Roundheads into Kineton village, where he plundered the baggage train. Meanwhile the King and the royal infantry, unsupported by any cavalry of his own, had to withstand the assault of the Parliamentary foot and several strong bodies of horse. After confused and bloody fighting even Charles's own guards were broken. His cannon were captured. The royal standard was for a time taken, and its bearer, Sir Edmund Verney, was cut down. But the approach of the Parliamentary rearguard under Hampden drove Rupert and his cavalry from the baggage train. They returned to the battlefield in time to avert defeat. Both sides retired to their morning positions and gazed at each other in doubt and confusion. At least five thousand Englishmen lay upon the field; twelve hundred were buried by the vicar of Kineton.

Edgehill, which might so easily have ended the war in the King's favour, was judged a drawn battle. Essex rightly resumed his march to cover London, which was in fact however a retreat. The King occupied Banbury, and in triumph entered Oxford, which now became his headquarters and remained so to the very end.

It has often been asked whether Charles could have reached London before Essex, and what would have happened when he got there. Prince Rupert urged this course on the morrow of Edgehill. It seems probable that the royal army would have been involved in heavy fighting with the Londoners, while Essex, still himself superior in numbers, came steadily in upon them. But now the advance was made from Oxford and the King contented himself with disarming and dispersing the local forces that stood in the way. At the same time the Parliamentary envoys were presenting a new address to the King, and negotiations were in progress without any formal truce. While Essex's leading regiments were rapidly approaching the capital, and were already in touch with its defenders, Rupert attacked them, reinforced by some of Essex's troops at Brentford, on the Thames, and routed and pursued them with great severity. Each side accused the other of treachery. Parliament declared that their innocent men had been fallen upon and treated with German cruelty while parleys were proceeding. The Royalists pointed to the military fact that Essex was hourly effecting his junction with the London forces. Neither side had ground for complaint. Charles was unjustly reproached with perfidy. This ignores the conditions of war and movement of troops towards key points.

A few days later, at Turnham Green, a few miles west of London, the King found himself confronted with the combined forces of Essex's field army and the London garrison. He was outnumbered by more than two to one. After a cannonade he withdrew towards Oxford, being, as some held, lucky in getting clear. From this we may judge better the heavy argument against a dash on London after Edgehill. Everything might have gone with a run; on the other hand, he might have been entangled, caught, and destroyed amid superior forces. Thus closed the fighting of the year 1642.

* * * * *

Throughout angry England, divided in every shire, in every town, in every village, and often in the very bosom of families, all eyes had been fixed upon the clash and manœuvre of the two main armies. The hopes of both sides were that these would give a decision, and thereafter peace. When it was seen that nothing of the kind would happen, and that a long, balanced struggle lay ahead, all suspended antagonisms started into action. Fighting and pillage spread throughout the country. The constitutional issue, the religious quarrel, and countless local feuds were combined in a new surge of party hatred. The lines of strife correspond geographically in a broad degree to those upon which the Conservative and Liberal Parties voted and vociferated in the nineteenth century. The cleavages of the great Civil War dominated English life for two centuries, and many strange examples of their persistency survive under universal suffrage in English constituencies to-day.

From the beginning of 1643 the war became general. Classes and interests as well as parties and creeds did their best against one another. The ports and towns, the manufacturing centres, mostly adhered to the Parliament; what might be called Old England rallied to Charles. In the two great areas of the North and the West the King's cause prospered. In the North Queen Henrietta Maria arrived from Holland. Braving the blockade, she brought a considerable shipload of cannon and munitions to Bridlington, on the Yorkshire coast. The Parliamentary warships were hard upon her wake.

Coming as close inshore as the ebb tide would permit, they fired their guns upon the house where she was sleeping. Her men assured the Queen that her ship and its priceless cargo would be defended, and in barefoot haste she sheltered from the whistling shot in the village. This personal cannonade upon the Queen, by the Parliamentary admiral Batten, was deemed unwarrantable and indecent in an age where sex, rank, and chivalry still counted. In our own time we have seen an Empress slaughtered in a cellar without any marked reaction upon the collective mind of civilisation.

Henrietta Maria entered York amid intense rejoicing. Enormous crowds of loyal people cheered the imposing train of cannon which followed behind her. Some had thought that she, a woman, would urge the King to peace. On the contrary, she brought with her a spirit of war as tameless and indomitable as Margaret of Anjou.

At first the decisive action was not in the North. Parliament was already in some doubts about the capacity of Essex as a general. The peace party favoured him, but the fancy of those who wanted all-out war was for Sir William Waller, now sent to command the Parliamentary army in the West. The Cornishmen however showed a lively devotion to the royal cause and uncommon nimbleness and courage in fighting. Here also the most sagacious and skilful of the Royalist generals, Sir Ralph Hopton, commanded. Three fierce battles on a small scale were fought by Hopton and Waller. A warm personal friendship subsisted between them, but, as Waller wrote to his opponent, "each had to bear his part in a matter of honour and fidelity." At Lansdowne, outside Bath, Hopton's Cornishmen stormed Waller's position. The feature of Waller's army was the London cavalry. These were so completely encased in armour that they looked like "moving fortresses," and were called by both sides "the Lobsters." The

Lobsters were charged uphill by the Royalists, who wrought great havoc among them. Waller was defeated, but Hopton's losses were so severe that he took refuge in Devizes. Hopton himself was wounded by the explosion of almost the only powder wagon in his army. His horsemen, under Prince Maurice, ran away. But the Prince, returning by a rapid march with fresh cavalry from Oxford, found Waller drawn up to receive him on Roundway Down. The Royalists attacked and drove the Lobsters headlong down the steep slopes, while Hopton moved out from the town and completed the victory with his infantry.

Fired with these successes, Rupert, with the Oxford army joined to Hopton's forces, summoned, assaulted, and procured the surrender of the city of Bristol. This was the second city in the kingdom, and on the whole its inhabitants were Royalists. They had undermined the resistance of the Parliamentary garrison; they looked upon Rupert as a deliverer. The warships in the port declared for the King, and hope dawned of a royal squadron which could command the Bristol Channel. King Charles was master in the West.

His cause had also prevailed in Yorkshire. Here Lord Fairfax and his son, Sir Thomas, led the Parliamentary forces. These were mainly drawn from Leeds, Halifax, and Bradford, "three very populous and rich towns," which, according to Clarendon, writing a few years after the event, "depending wholly upon clothiers, naturally maligned the gentry." The Fairfaxes besieged York; but the Marquis of Newcastle, a man of no military aptitude, rich, corpulent, proud, but entirely devoted, led his territorial retainers, the valiant "whitecoats," to its relief, and later in the summer overwhelmed the Fairfaxes at Adwalton Moor. Upon the Parliamentary side there now appeared numbers of peasants armed with scythes or bludgeons—"the Clubmen," as they were called. These shared in the slaughter to the full. The defeat left Parliament with Hull as their only stronghold in the North. The Governor of Scarborough, Hugh Cholmley, a distinguished Member of Parliament, had already deserted the Roundheads, carrying over his forces and bringing about the surrender of the town. Now in Hull Governor Hotham, hitherto so steadfast for the Roundheads, was converted to the royal side in part by the persuasions of one of his captives, Lord Digby, and also, no doubt, by the King's successes. Eighteen months before, when Hull and its munitions might have been decisive, he could have delivered all with ease. But now he had built up a spirit of resistance among the townsfolk, who did not change with him. He and his son were arrested and carried by sea to London. Meanwhile in the Midlands also the Royalists made head. The Hastings family had the upper hand in Leicestershire and the Cavendishes in Lincolnshire, though Charles Cavendish himself was defeated and slain in a sharp fight near Gainsborough by Colonel Cromwell, who for the first time brought into the field the mounted troops of the Eastern Counties Association, which he had organised and trained. But they could not stop the Royalists from capturing Lincoln. On neither side did cavalry ever succeed in holding the towns.

*　　*　　*　　*　　*

Charles possessed a certain strategic comprehension. He had not that intense clarity of view and promptitude to act which are the qualities of great commanders, but his military outlook took all things in, and he was brave in action. From the beginning of 1643 his design was for a general advance on London. Hopton from the West, Newcastle from the North, himself from Oxford, would converge on the capital and break the prime centre of rebellion. Till midsummer the results of the fighting seemed to favour this decisive plan; but the King had neither the resources nor the authority for so large a combination. The heavy fighting in the West had cost him his best adherents. Hopton's little army marched steadily east through Hampshire and Sussex, and was checked, while the Western Royalists, who ought to have reinforced it, were content to sit down before Plymouth, whose Parliamentary garrison had been raiding far and wide. Indeed, the loyalty to Parliament of a single town in a generally Royalist region made it hard for the King to draw off local troops for a national campaign. Newcastle could not be dissuaded from a land attack upon Hull, where the strong tides prevented the building of a boom to cut the port from the sea. Without his Northern forces nothing could be expected from the evenly matched conflict in the Midlands. The Queen and other vehement counsellors urged a singlehanded advance on London. On the other hand, Gloucester was the sole stronghold remaining to the Parliament between Bristol and York. Its fall would open the Severn to the Royalist flotillas and supply barges, as well as uniting Oxford and the West to Royalist Wales. Thus the King, in the zenith of his military fortune, resolved to besiege Gloucester. He was probably right. England was an obstinate country, and people fought out their part locally, undeterred by bad news from elsewhere, and were not at all likely to be swept by sensational revulsions. Moreover, the Governor, Massey, was believed, on the strength of serious promises, to be ready to change sides. Accordingly on August 5 the city was invested.

Meanwhile in London Pym, the master of the Parliament, the heart and soul of the Roundhead war, was in grievous straits. So far all had gone ill and every hope had been broken. As head of the Government he was obliged to raise money for an increasingly unpopular war by methods as little conformable to the principles he championed as those which

Charles had used against the Scots in 1640. Forced loans and direct taxation of almost everyone were among his devices. Strong currents of Royalism now flowed in the capital. These joined themselves to the peace movement. The Common Council of the City was unyielding; but Royalist opinion was too strong to be silenced. At one time seventy merchants were in prison for refusing to pay taxes which they judged illegal. On another occasion hundreds of women crowded to Westminster to present a petition for peace. When the troopers rode in among them the frantic women tried to drag them from their saddles. "Let us throw the dog Pym into the Thames," they cried. But the soldiers drew their swords and slashed the women with extreme brutality, chasing them round Palace Yard, so that many were injured before they could escape. The House of Lords, consisting now of fewer than twenty sitting peers, carried a precise and solemn resolution for peace negotiations. Even the Commons, by a narrow majority in a thin House, agreed to the Lords' propositions. Pym's life was ebbing to its close. He had cancer. His greatest colleague, Hampden, had died of wounds early in the year after a clash with Rupert's cavalry at Chalgrove Field. The ruin of his cause and the approach of death in an array of disaster seemed to be the only reward of Pym's struggles. Undaunted, he bore up against all; and the last impulse of his life may well have turned the scale. All the Puritan forces in London were roused to repudiate peace. The preachers exhorted their congregations, and warlike crowds beset Westminster. The House of Commons rescinded their conciliatory resolution, and now the relief of Gloucester was the cry.

The Earl of Essex had fallen into just disrepute as a general, and was suspected of political lukewarmness. Although ever faithful to the cause he had espoused, he sought a peaceful settlement. His project was fantastic in form but serious in purpose. He proposed that the King should withdraw from his army and stand aside, an august neutral, and that Cavaliers and Roundheads, horse, foot, and artillery, should meet in equal numbers at an appointed place and fight till God gave His decision, which should be accepted by all. This was a peace proposal in martial guise. Now however he was ordered and conjured to relieve Gloucester. He accepted the duty, perhaps hoping this would give him strength to stop England tearing herself to pieces. The London militia, or train bands, in a surge of resolve clamoured to march. There were enthusiastic scenes in the streets when they departed through cheering crowds. The dominant elements in the capital once again appeared in undisputed sway.

At Gloucester Governor Massey had failed the King. The violent Puritanism within his walls left him no choice of treacheries. When Charles summoned the city two surly fellows were sent out to say that "they could only obey His Majesty's commands when sent to them through both Houses of Parliament." They had scarcely withdrawn from the royal presence when they stuck the orange cockades of Essex's army in their caps. This was thought most ill-behaved. But the orange cockades were soon to be seen to some effect. The King's resources, indeed the art of war in England at this time, afforded no satisfactory method of making a siege. Compared with the gigantic systematised operations of later times the sieges of the English Civil War were feeble and primitive. A few batteries of cannon, with scanty powder and ball, tried to make a hole in the wall in which both sides could fight with sword and musket until food ran short or the inhabitants in fear of sack forced a capitulation. The King had made no progress against Gloucester when, in the early days of September, Essex and the London army drew near in superior numbers. There was no choice but to raise the siege and retire upon Oxford.

*　　*　　*　　*　　*

Essex entered Gloucester in triumph, but found himself immediately short of supplies and food, with a formidable enemy between him and home. Both armies headed for London, and on September 20 they clashed at Newbury, in Berkshire. There was a long and bitter conflict. Once again Rupert's cavalry beat their opponents; but they could make no impression on the London pikemen and musketeers. A third of the troops were casualties, and on the Royalist side many nobles fell. Among them Lord Falkland found in death the release he had for some time sought from a world and a quarrel which he could no longer endure. The battle was undecided when darkness fell. Essex had no choice but to renew it at dawn; but the King withdrew, stricken by the loss of so many personal friends, and short of powder, and the London road lay open to the Roundheads.

*　　*　　*　　*　　*

The King's large plan for 1643 had failed. Nevertheless the campaign had been very favourable to him. He had gained control of a great part of England. His troops were still, on the whole, better fighting-men than the Roundheads. Much ground lost at the beginning of the war had been recovered. A drift of desertion to the royal camp had begun. All could see how even were the forces which rent the kingdom. On both sides men's thoughts turned to peace. Not so the thoughts of Pym; he looked to the Scots; by substantial money payments he induced a Scots army of not less than eleven thousand men to intervene. He led Parliament on September 25 into signing a Solemn League and Covenant among themselves and with the Scots to wage war with untiring zeal. It was a military alliance expressed in terms of a

· 245 ·

religious manifesto. Then on December 8 Pym died, un-cheered by success, but unwearied by misfortune. He had neglected his private affairs in the public cause, and his estate would have been bankrupt had not Parliament, as some ex-pression of their grief and gratitude, paid his debts. He re-mains the most famous of the old Parliamentarians, and the man who more than any other saved England from absolute monarchy and set her upon the path she has since pursued.

Ranke pays a high tribute to Pym. "He possessed," he says, "talents created for times of revolution, capable at once of shaking and destroying existing institutions and of estab-lishing new ones, as resolute in passing great measures as in devising small means: audacious in his projects, but practical in executing them, at once active and unyielding, bold and prudent, systematic and pliant, full of thought for his friends, devoid of all consideration for those against whose rights he was battling. In Pym there is something both of Siyès and of Mirabeau: he is one of the greatest revolutionary leaders known to history. Characters like his stand midway between the present, which they shatter for ever, and the future, which however generally develops itself on principles different from those which they have laid down." [1]

*   *   *   *   *

There was a lull during the winter. Charles was encour-aged by the death of the great French Minister, Richelieu, which restored power to his Queen's brother, Louis XIII, and by the friendly aid of the King of Denmark. In Ireland the Earl of Ormonde, Lord-Lieutenant, had made a truce with the Catholics, who, in spite of all atrocities committed and suffered, still accepted the monarchy. The Royalist camp even considered bringing Irish Papists into England, and rumours of this did harm to the King's cause. But the "Cessation" in Ireland, as it was called, enabled Irish Protestant regiments

[1] *History of England*, vol. ii, p. 394.

and other royal troops to be brought to England, where they played a recognisable part.

Charles had never dissolved the Parliament which was warring against him, because in so doing he would have invalidated his assent not only to the Act which he had unwisely accepted in 1641, making it virtually perpetual, but many other laws which counted with his own supporters. Declaring therefore that the Parliament at Westminster was no longer a free Parliament, he summoned all who had been expelled or who had fled from it to a Counter-Assembly. The response was remarkable. Eighty-three peers and a hundred and seventy-five Members met in Oxford on January 22, 1644.

But these advantages were overwhelmed by the arrival in England of a Scottish army of eighteen thousand foot and three thousand horse, who crossed the Tweed in January. For this succour the London Parliament paid £31,000 a month and the cost of equipment. But the Scots, though in a sense hired, had other objects besides money. They now aspired to outroot the Episcopacy and impose by armed force the Presbyterian system of Church government upon England. This was indeed a change from the days, scarcely six years gone by, when Charles and Laud were pressing the English Liturgy upon them. Now no longer were the Scots defending their own religious liberties; they sought to compel the far larger and stronger English nation to conform to their ideas. Glittering prospects were opened to Scottish ambition. They had the best of both worlds; they were invited to invade a wealthy country at its own expense in the cause of Almighty God and their own particular style of public worship. Punctual cash payments and assured salvation awaited them across the Border. For the honour of Scotland it must be said that the Edinburgh Assembly, which lent itself to such a policy, contained a strong minority. It was effectively suppressed.

Marston Moor and Naseby

THE King at the beginning of 1644 had the larger part of the country behind him and a considerable Parliament of his own which met in Oxford. Military victory in England seemed within his grasp. The Scots reversed the balance. As their army advanced southwards they dominated the Royalist counties in the North; they stormed the city of Newcastle, and sent the bill to Westminster. Their ascendancy became decisive. Their Commissioners arrived in London with three principal aims: first, the imposition of Presbyterianism upon all England; secondly, a share in the government of England by means of the Committee of Both Kingdoms, set up in pursuance of the Solemn League and Covenant, not only for the conduct of the war but for general policy; thirdly, the maintenance of the monarchy. They paid elaborate lip-service to the majesty and sanctity of the Crown, and opposed Republican tendencies because they liked to see a Scottish line on the English throne. All this was good for them.

Grim as were the straits to which the cause of the dead Pym and Hampden was now reduced, these transactions did not pass without protest. The Parliamentary taxpayers resented the expense of the Scottish army. The House of Lords, or what was left of it at Westminster, resisted the plan for the Committee of Both Kingdoms as subverting their constitutional rights. They were answered that the war must be fought in common by the two united nations. But the most serious difference was on religion. It was now that Oliver Cromwell came into prominence. The Member for Cambridge was deemed the best officer on the Parliamentary side, though he had not yet held a supreme command. At the head of the troops of the Eastern Counties Association, he had triumphed at Gainsborough in a dark hour. His regiment had a discipline and quality surpassing, as it seemed, any other formation on either side. He could not be ignored. He could not be suppressed. The rise of Cromwell to the first rank of power during 1644 sprang both from his triumphs on the battlefield and his resistance to the Presbyterians and the Scots at Westminster. Except for Papists and Episcopalians, he declared for liberty of conscience. All the obscurer Protestant sects saw in him their champion.

When the joint Westminster Assembly of English and Scottish divines fervently and passionately debated the awful issues of Church government among Christian men there was a formidable division between the Presbyterians and the Congregationalists or Independents. The Congregationalists were but a seventh of the Assembly, but their zeal and valour made them powerful in the Army. They rejected all forms of ordination by the laying on of hands. These, they declared with some logic, savoured of Episcopacy. The Reformation could only be fulfilled by going back to the original institution of independent Churches. They were less strict than the Presbyterians, or the older Puritans, about correctness of demeanour, but every member must be in a state of grace, of which the congregation must be judge. They had their ministers, but they refused to give them any portion of the spiritual authority claimed by Anglican priest or Presbyterian minister. These congregations were a breeding ground of extreme views in politics. Presbyterian discipline was as ab-

horrent to them as Episcopacy. The Scottish Commissioners
and divines were shocked by such doctrines of spiritual anarchy, but neither they nor their English colleagues could afford to quarrel with Cromwell and his Independents while
the Royalists were unsubdued. They thought it better for their
Army to penetrate deeply into England and become involved
in the war before dealing with these "dissenting brethren" as
they deserved. Thus not for the first or last time theology
waited upon arms; and in the long run it was the alliance of
the Anglican and Presbyterian against their common enemy
the Independent that restored both the monarchy and the
Established Church.

In the North the Marquis of Newcastle had now to con-
tend with the Scottish army on one side and the two Fairfaxes on the other. He made the military movements usual
under such conditions. In the spring he marched north against
the Scots and left Lord Bellasis to ward off the Roundheads.
Bellasis was overwhelmed at Selby on April 11 by the Fairfaxes. Newcastle's rear was thereby exposed, and he could do
no more than maintain himself in York, where he was presently vigorously besieged. The loss of York would ruin the
King's cause in the North. Charles therefore sent Prince Rupert with a strong cavalry force, which gathered strength as
it marched, to relieve the city and sustain the harassed and
faithful Marquis. Rupert fought his way into Lancashire,
striking heavy blows on all sides. Lathom House, defended
by the Countess of Derby, was freed and the besiegers destroyed. Stockport was plundered; Bolton stormed. On
June 1 Lord Goring with five thousand horse joined the
Prince. Together they took Liverpool.

The King now wrote Rupert a letter which contained the
following passage: "If York be lost I shall esteem my crown
little less, unless supported by your sudden march to me, and

a miraculous conquest in the South, before the effects of the Northern power can be found here. . . . Wherefore I command and conjure you, by the duty and affection which I know you bear me, that, all new enterprises laid aside, you immediately march according to your first intention, with all your force, to the relief of York; but if that be lost . . . that you immediately march with your whole strength directly to Worcester to assist me and my army, without which, or your having relieved York by beating the Scots, all the successes you can afterwards have most infallibly will be useless to me." [1]

Rupert needed no spur, and took these involved sentences as an order to fight an immediate battle on the first chance. "Before God," said Colepeper to Charles when he heard that the letter had been sent, "you are undone, because upon this peremptory order he will fight whatever comes on't." So it fell out.

Rupert saved York at its last gasp: the mine was sprung; the walls were already breached. The Scots and Roundheads withdrew together westwards, covering Leeds and joining the forces from East Anglia under Lord Manchester and Cromwell. The three Puritan armies were thus combined, and numbered twenty thousand foot and seven thousand horse. Their outposts lay upon a ridge at Marston Moor. Rupert met the Marquis of Newcastle, and their united forces reached eleven thousand foot and seven thousand horse. The Marquis was against fighting. He regarded the Northern theatre as relieved for the time being. He expected reinforcements from Durham. He was vexed that Rupert should have command over him. He would have been content to see the Prince march back southwards to join the King, but Rupert said he "had a letter from the King with a positive and absolute command

[1] Gardiner, *History of the Great Civil War* (1901), vol. i, p. 371.

to fight the enemy." "Happen what will," said the Marquis to his friends, "I will not shun to fight, for I have no other ambition than to live and die a loyal subject of his Majesty." Accordingly the Royalist army followed the enemy to Marston Moor, and on July 2 found themselves near their encampments. Opinion, though divided, has on the whole condemned Rupert's resolve to fight, but his tactics were still more questionable. Though he kept his infantry in the centre of the line, he split into squadrons his hitherto invincible cavalry, and had not therefore that mass in his own command wherewith he had so often gained and squandered victory. He inquired anxiously of a prisoner, "Is Cromwell there?"

The whole day passed in alternating rain and sunshine, with both armies in close contact. Rupert imagined that it rested with him to begin the battle on the morrow, but at six o'clock in the evening he was himself attacked by the whole force of the Roundheads, who outnumbered his infantry by nearly two to one. A heavy column of steel-clad cavalry was seen approaching at a fast trot. It was Cromwell and his Ironsides. The royal army, who, though drawn up, were preparing to eat their evening meal, had neither the advantage of a defensive position nor the impulsion of attack. None the less they made a glorious fight. Goring's cavalry of the left wing beat the Roundhead right, and, falling upon the Scots in the centre, threw them into disorder and retreat. The veteran Alexander Leslie, now Lord Leven, quitted the field, declaring all was lost, and was arrested by a constable ten miles away. But Cromwell, with the help of the remaining Scots under David Leslie, restored the day. Now for the first time the heroic, dreaded Cavaliers met their match, and their master. "We drove the entire cavalry of the Prince off the field," wrote Cromwell. "God made them as stubble to our swords.

Then we took their regiments of foot with our cavalry, and overthrew all that we encountered."

Marston Moor was the largest and also the bloodiest battle of the war. Little quarter was given and there were four thousand slain. Newcastle's "white-coats" fought to the death, and fell where they stood. They had boasted they would dye these white coats with the blood of the foe. They were indeed reddened, but with their own blood. Night alone ended the pursuit. A disaster of the first magnitude had smitten the King's cause. His Northern army was shattered and the whole of the North was lost. The prestige of Rupert's cavalry was broken. The Marquis, brokenhearted, fled into exile. Rupert, whom nothing could appal, gathered up the remnants of his army and led them safely south to Shrewsbury.

*   *   *   *   *

The success of the King's campaign in the South veiled, at least for a time, the disaster at Marston Moor. Charles revealed unexpected qualities as a general. He had begun to like the life of a camp, with its stir and movement of war. Sabran, the French Ambassador, who had a long audience with him on horseback, praised him highly. "He is full of judgment and sagacity, never lets himself be led to any precipitate action through his dangerous position, orders everything himself, both great and small, never signs anything that he has not read, and on horseback or on foot is ever at the head of his troops." By May Charles could only gather ten thousand men to meet the two armies of Essex and Waller, who each had as many. He hoped that the ill feeling between the Roundhead generals would give him a chance to strike at them separately. But instead they moved in concert upon Oxford. The city was ill supplied for a siege, and could certainly not maintain the Royalist field army as well as its garrison. It was expected, not only by the Parliament, but in his own circles, that the King would be caught in Oxford and compelled to surrender. However, after providing for the defence of the city, Charles, with great skill, eluded both of the converging armies and reached Worcester.

The two Roundhead generals were then forced to divide their forces, as he had foreseen. Waller manœuvred against the King, who gradually moved northwards, while Essex broke into the Royalist West. Then, turning east, the King inflicted a severe check on Waller at Cropredy Bridge, in Oxfordshire, on June 6, capturing all his artillery. He was undaunted by Marston Moor. Outmarching and outwitting Waller, he suddenly during August began to march westward, with the intention of taking Essex in the rear. Essex had made some progress, and had relieved both Lyme and Plymouth from siege; but he found himself obstinately opposed in districts where the whole countryside was hostile to the Roundheads. Now the King himself came suddenly upon him. Essex was outnumbered, his supplies were cut off, and after rejecting a proposal for surrender he rode off himself with his officers to Plymouth, ordered his cavalry to cut their way out of the trap, and left the rest of his army to its fate. All the infantry and artillery, to the number of eight thousand men, surrendered at Lostwithiel, in Cornwall, on September 2.

Winter approached, but the war did not slacken. The Cavaliers, undiscouraged by their dwindling territory, and the superior numbers and resources of the Roundheads, defended themselves in every county where they had a stronghold. The main forces of the Parliament were now thrown against the King. Manchester and Waller were reinforced by Cromwell. The Royalist position, centred in Oxford, comprised a system of fortified towns which covered Wales and the West of England. Among these the King manœuvred. Once again on October 27 the armies met at Newbury, and once again there was a drawn battle, followed by a Royalist retirement. It was late in November before active warfare paused. Charles re-entered Oxford in triumph. The campaign had been his finest military achievement. In the teeth of adversity he had maintained himself with little money or supplies against odds of two or three to one. Moreover, on the side of the Parliament there lay always the hard weight of a greatly superior artillery.

*   *   *   *   *

Cromwell rode in from the Army to his duties as a Member of Parliament. His differences with the Scots and his opposition to Presbyterian uniformity were already swaying Roundhead politics. He now made a vehement and organised attack on the conduct of the war, and its mismanagement by lukewarm generals of noble rank, namely Essex and Manchester. Essex was discredited enough after Lostwithiel, but Cromwell also charged Manchester with losing the second Battle of Newbury by sloth and want of zeal. He himself was avid for the power and command which he was sure he could wield; but he proceeded astutely. While he urged the complete reconstitution of the Parliamentary Army upon a New Model similar to his own in the Eastern Counties, his friends in the House of Commons proposed a so-called "Self-denying Ordinance," which would exclude members of either House from military employment. The handful of lords who still remained at Westminster realised well enough that this was an attack on their prominence in the conduct of the war, if not on their social order. But there were such compelling military reasons in favour of the measure that neither they nor the Scots, who already dreaded Cromwell, could prevent its being carried. Essex and Manchester, who had fought the King from the beginning of the quarrel, who had raised regiments and served the Parliamentary cause in all fidelity, were discarded. They pass altogether from the story.

During the winter months the Army was reconstituted in accordance with Cromwell's ideas. The old personally raised regiments of the Parliamentary nobles were broken up and their officers and men incorporated in entirely new formations. These, the New Model, comprised eleven regiments of horse, each six hundred strong, twelve regiments of foot, twelve hundred strong, and a thousand dragoons, in all twenty-two thousand men. Compulsion was freely used to fill the ranks. In one district of Sussex the three conscriptions of April, July, and September 1645 yielded a total of 149 men. A hundred and thirty-four guards were needed to escort them to the colours.

At the King's headquarters it was thought that these measures would demoralise the Parliamentary troops; and no doubt at first this was so. But the Roundhead faction now had a symmetrical military organisation led by men who had risen in the field and had no other standing but their military record and religious zeal. Sir Thomas Fairfax was appointed Commander-in-Chief. Cromwell, as Member for Cambridge, was at first debarred from serving. However, it soon appeared that his Self-denying Ordinance applied only to his rivals. The urgency of the new campaign and military discontents which he alone could quell forced even the reluctant Lords to make an exception in his favour. In June 1645 he was appointed General of the Horse, and was thus the only man who combined high military command with an outstanding Parliamentary position. From this moment he became the dominant figure in both spheres.

Amid these stresses Archbishop Laud, who languished ailing in the Tower, was brought to the scaffold. Roundheads, Scots, and Puritans alike could all combine upon this act of hatred. The House of Commons upon a division rejected his appeal to be decapitated rather than hanged, drawn, and quartered. Overnight however this barbarous decision was mitigated, and after he had uttered an unyielding discourse the old man's head was chopped off in a dignified manner.

The desire of all Englishmen for an end to the unnatural strife forced itself upon the most inflamed partisans. "Clubmen" reappeared. Large numbers of farmers and their labourers, together with townsfolk, assembled in many parts of the country with such weapons as they could find, protesting against the exactions and pillage of the contending forces. They now showed themselves rather more favourable to the King than to the Parliament. Largely to please the Scots, a parley for a peace settlement was set on foot at Uxbridge, near London, and on this many hopes were reposed, though not by the die-hards in Parliament. For twenty days the village and its inns were divided between the delegates of the two sides. They met and argued with grave ceremony. But neither King Charles nor the Roundhead executive had the slightest intention of giving way upon the two main points— Episcopacy and the control of the armed forces. In the fourth year of the war these still presented themselves as issues upon which no compromise was possible. Uxbridge only proved the ferocious constancy of both parties in their struggle for supreme power.

The antagonism of the Scots towards Cromwell and the pressure to enforce by law Presbyterian conformity against independent sectarianism were now at their height. Echoes of Marston Moor mingled with doctrinal differences. The Independents made strong play with the episodes of the battle. Leven and a part of the Scottish army had run away, while Cromwell and his Ironsides had remained to conquer. The Scots retorted by accusing Cromwell of personal cowardice in action; but this theme did not carry conviction. Their unwarrantable and intolerant interference in English life, though well paid, had drawn upon them a formidable animosity, and their main object of enforcing Presbyterianism was now frustrated by forces hitherto unimagined but wielding a sharp and heavy sword.

At the same time the Marquis of Montrose sprang upon the scene. He had been a Covenanter, but having quarrelled with Argyll went over to the King. Now he made himself known to history as a noble character and brilliant general. He pledged his faith to Charles, and distracted all Scotland by a series of victories gained against much larger forces, although sometimes his men had only stones to throw before falling on with the claymore. Dundee, Aberdeen, Glasgow, Perth, and Edinburgh were at one time or another in his power. He wrote to Charles assuring him that he would bring all Scotland to his rescue if he could hold out. But a decisive battle impended in the South.

On June 14, 1645, the last trial of strength was made. Charles, having taken Leicester, which was sacked, met Fairfax and Cromwell in the fine hunting country about Naseby. The Cavaliers had so often saved themselves by the offensive spirit, which Rupert embodied to the eclipse of other military qualities, that they did not hesitate to attack uphill the Roundhead army of twice their numbers. The action followed what had almost become the usual course. Rupert shattered the Parliamentary left, and though, as at Edgehill, his troopers were attracted by the Parliamentary baggage column, he returned to strike heavily at the central Roundhead infantry. But Cromwell on the other flank drove all before him, and also took control of the Roundhead reserves. The royal foot, beset on all sides by overwhelming numbers, fought with devotion. The King wished himself to charge to their rescue with the last reserve which stood about his person. He actually gave the order; but prudent hands were laid upon his bridle by some of his staff, and the royal reserves wheeled to the right and retreated above a mile. Here they were joined by Rupert, who had seen nothing but success, the Royalist cavalry quitting the field intact. The foot were killed or captured. Quarter was given, and the butchery was less than at Marston Moor. A hundred Irish women who were found in the Royalist camp were put to the sword by the Ironsides on grounds of moral principle as well as of national prejudice. Naseby was the expiring effort of the Cavaliers in the open field. There still remained many sieges, with reliefs and manœuvrings, but the final military decision of the Civil War had been given.

Cromwell later recorded his impressions in repellent sentences: "I can say this of Naseby, that when I saw the enemy draw up and march in gallant order towards us, and we *a company of poor, ignorant men*"—thus he described veterans for the most part, the best-equipped, best-disciplined, and most highly paid troops yet seen in England, and twice as numerous as their opponents—"to seek how to order our battle, the General having commanded me to order all the horse, I could not, riding alone about my business, but smile out to God in praises in assurance of victory, because God would, by things that are not, bring to naught things that are. Of which I had great assurance—and God did it."

The Axe Falls

BY the spring of 1646 all armed resistance to the Parliamentary Army was beaten down. Sir Jacob Astley, caught and defeated with the last troops of the King at Stow-on-the-Wold, said to his captors, "Well, boys, you have done your work, and may go home and play—unless you fall out with one another."

The Puritans had triumphed. In the main the middle class, being more solid for Parliament, and beaten the aristocracy and gentry, who were divided. The new money-power of the City had beaten the old loyalties. The townsfolk had mastered the countryside. What would some day be the "Chapel" had beaten the Church. There were many contrary examples, but upon the whole this was how it lay. The Constitution however was still unsettled. All that Charles had stood for in the days of his Personal Rule was swept away; but much wider issues, for which the nation and the times were unripe and unready, had been opened. All these focused in the office and the person of the King. Charles was now ready to yield upon the control of the armed forces, but for the sake of the Episcopal establishment of the Church of England he was prepared to continue the struggle singlehanded. Montrose had been defeated in the autumn of 1645 at Philiphaugh, near the Border, by detachments from the regular Scottish army in England. Yet it was to the Scots Government that Charles eventually turned. He saw the deep division which was now open between Scotland and the Ironsides. He had no physical resources, but he hoped that his Sovereign Majesty, though stripped of power, might yet raise, from what seemed a most adverse quarter, a new resource for his unquenchable purpose. He also had expectations of aid from France, where Queen Henrietta Maria had taken refuge. In the event all her efforts on his behalf came to nothing, and she never saw her husband again.

After some agonising months, in which Rupert too easily surrendered Bristol, and one Royalist fortress after another was reduced, the King thought to come to London alone and argue what had been lost in war with his subjects. There was a great desire for this in many quarters. He apparently had no fear for the security of his person. The Common Council in the City and a potent element in Parliament and in the Roundhead army favoured the plan; but in the end he resolved to place himself in the hands of the Scots. A French agent obtained from them a verbal promise that the King should be secure in his person and in his honour, and that he should not be pressed to do anything contrary to his conscience. On this he resorted to the headquarters of the Scottish army, which, with the Roundheads, was besieging Newark. Newark fell, and the Scots immediately turned northwards.

The King had persuaded himself he was a guest; but he soon found he was a prisoner. When on the march he asked a Scottish officer to tell him how he stood, General David Leslie peremptorily forbade the conversation to continue. Although treated with ceremony, he was closely guarded, deprived of all intercourse with his personal followers, and his windows were watched lest an uncensored letter should be thrown into the street. Kept at Newcastle in these hard circumstances, he entered upon nearly a year's tenacious bargainings on the national issues at stake. He wrangled with the Scots, who strove to force him to accept the Covenant and impose Presbyterianism upon England. At the same time he argued the constitutional issues which the English Parliament presented to him. Parliament's plan was to keep Charles captive till they had built him a constitutional and religious cage, and meanwhile to use his name and sign manual for all that they wished to do in their party interest. He was to subscribe to the Covenant; the bishops were to be abolished. The Fleet and militia were for twenty years to be in the hands of Parliament. An immense catalogue of pains and penalties, described as "branches" and "qualifications," flung all his faithful friends and supporters into a kind of Attainder as wholesale as that which had smitten the house of Lancaster after Towton. As a modern writer of remarkable insight has it, "Charles had only to abandon his crown, his Church, and his friends, and he might, for what it was worth, be King of England still. . . . King of England—a prisoner in a foreign camp, forbidden to have his own chaplains, reduced to reading the Prayer Book alone in his bedroom, so becoming that dangerously attractive figure, the Injured Man." [1]

The King naturally hoped to profit by the differences between Parliament and the Army and between the English and Scottish Governments. He delayed so long that the Governments came to terms without him. In February 1647 the Scots, having been paid an instalment of half the sum due to them for their services in England, handed over Charles under guarantee for his safety to Parliamentary Commissioners and returned to their own country. This transaction, though highly practical, wore and still wears a sorry look. The jingle

> Traitor Scot
> Sold his King for a groat

[1] G. M. Young, *Charles I and Cromwell.*

was on many lips. The confusion and distresses of the year 1646, with its interminable constitutional and religious discussion and the paralysis of national life, created fierce and general discontent, and from every quarter eyes were turned in new loyalties towards the King.

When the Scots had taken their payment Charles was led with the greatest deference southward to Holmby House in Northamptonshire by his new owners. His popularity became at once manifest. From Newcastle southwards the journey was a progress of cheering crowds and clashing bells. To greet the King, to be freed from the cruel wars, to have the Old England back again, no doubt with some important changes, was the national wish. Completely broken in the field, as previously in the Parliamentary struggle, Charles was still incomparably the most important figure in England. Every one was for the King, provided he would do what they wished. Stripped of all material weapons, he was more than ever conscious of the power of the institution which he embodied. But a third and new partner had appeared upon the English scene. The Ironside Army, twenty-two thousand strong, was not yet the master, but was no longer the servant, of those who had created it. At its head stood its renowned and trusted generals: Thomas Fairfax, Commander-in-Chief; Oliver Cromwell, its sun of glory; Henry Ireton, its brain and in a large degree its conscience. Beneath them, upon the grim parades, stirred political and religious controversies sufficient in themselves for civil and social wars far more embittered than that which had been finished.

Parliament had been refreshed by the election of new Members to fill the Royalist vacancies. It contained a strong Independent group which supported the Army. But the majority still represented the Presbyterian interest and strove for a strictly limited monarchy. The Army in no way shared the religious views of its Presbyterian employers. Their fiercest fighters, their most compulsive preachers, their most passionate sectaries, were almost as much opposed to a Presbyterian Establishment as to the Episcopacy. They differed from the Scots as much as from Archbishop Laud. Freedom of religious conviction was wrought in them by the variety and vigour of their sects. They were ready indeed to dragoon others; but who should dragoon them?

Now that the war was won most Members of Parliament and their leaders had no more need of the Army. It must be reduced to modest proportions. The civil power must reign. The expenses must be curtailed. A large number of regiments should be employed in Ireland to avenge the Irish massacres of 1641. Suitable garrisons must be maintained in England. As for the rest, let them go to their homes with the thanks of the House of Commons to cheer them in their later life. But here a matter very awkward on such occasions obtruded itself. The pay of the Army was in arrears. In March 1647 the foot were owed for eighteen weeks and the horse for forty-three. At Westminster in this once great Parliament it was felt that a six-weeks' payment should efface the debt. The soldiers did not look upon all this in the same way. Differing in many great things from one another, they were united upon the question of pay. They were resolved not to go to Ireland or be disbanded to their homes until it was settled—and other matters as well in which they took an interest. A serious dispute between Parliament and the Army thus began, both sides flushed with the sense of having a victory in their hands for which they deserved a reward.

In the first phase of the dispute Parliament assumed it had the power to give orders. Cromwell, as Member for Cambridge, assured them in the name of Almighty God that the

Army would disband when ordered. But he must have used a different language in the other quarter, because when the Army received the Parliamentary decisions they responded by a respectful petition from the officers. In this document, drawn up probably by Ireton, they asked for themselves and their men arrears of pay, indemnity for acts done in the war, guarantees against future conscription, and a pension for disabled men, widows, and children. "Whereas," they said, "the necessity of war has put us upon many actions, which the law would not warrant (nor have we acted in time of settled peace); we humbly desire that before our disbanding a full and sufficient provision may be made by ordinance of Parliament (to which the royal assent may be desired) for our indemnity and security in all such services." Even after Marston Moor and Naseby the victorious Ironsides did not feel sure that anything counted without the royal authority. They sought a guarantee which would be national and permanent, and for all the tight-knit majority organisation at Westminster this guarantee the kingly office alone could supply. Here is the salient fact which distinguishes the English Revolution from all others: that those who wielded irresistible physical force were throughout convinced that it could give them no security. Nothing is more characteristic of the English people than their instinctive reverence even in rebellion for law and tradition. Deep in the nature of the men who had broken the King's power was the conviction that law in his name was the sole foundation on which they could build.

The Parliamentary leaders received the officers' petition with displeasure. They seemed to imagine themselves in full control. Eventually they ordered each regiment to proceed to a different station in order that they might be separately disbanded or sent to Ireland. The reply of the Army was to concentrate at Newmarket. There they made a Solemn Engagement not to disband until their desires were met. As the balance between authority and physical force seemed fairly even both sides sought allies. The Presbyterians in Parliament looked to the Scots and the Army leaders looked to the King. The generals—Cromwell, Ireton, and Fairfax, Commander-in-Chief, to put them in their order of power—saw themselves about to be reduced to something lower than the venomous faction-politicians, who thought the victory was their own property and that all they had to do was to enjoy and distribute its spoils in a narrowly selected circle. Up to this point the Army, generals, officers, and men, were at one.

Cromwell and Ireton felt that if they could get hold of the King physically, and before Parliament did so, it would be much. If they could gain him morally it would be all. Ireton was already secretly in touch with the King. Now in early June, on his and Cromwell's orders Cornet Joyce, with near four hundred Ironside troopers, rode to Holmby House, where the King, surrounded by his household and attended by the Parliamentary Commissioners, was agreeably residing. The colonel of the Parliamentary guard fled. Charles, convinced of his personal inviolability, passed the night in calm serenity. Civilities were interchanged between the officers of his household and the troops.

In the morning Cornet Joyce intimated with due respect that he had come to remove the King. Charles made no protest. He walked out on to the terrace and eyed the solid buff and steel array with an almost proprietary air. "I have promised," said Joyce to his troopers, "three things in your name. You will do no harm to His Majesty's person; you will force him to nothing against his conscience; you will allow his servants to accompany him. Do you all promise?" "All," was the cry. "And now, Mr Joyce," said the King, "tell me, where is

your commission? Have you anything in writing from Sir
Thomas Fairfax?" Cornet Joyce was embarrassed. He looked
this way and that, but finally he said, pointing to the regiment, "Here!" "Indeed," said the King, with the compulsive
smile and confidence of sovereignty and Divine Right. "It is
one I can read without spelling: as handsome and proper a
company of gentlemen as I have seen this many a day. . . .
Where next, Mr Joyce?"

The Cornet and those who had sent him thought only of
studying the King's wishes so long as they had him in their
power. Oxford —but the King thought it unhealthy. Cambridge—this was more agreeable. The King found Newmarket attractive. The Army at any rate lay there. Off they all
rode together, a jingling and not unhappy company, feeling
they had English history in their hands. For three days the
King lay at Childerley, near Newmarket. Cambridge University flocked out with loyal addresses, which had been lacking
in the Civil War. Soon arrived Cromwell, Ireton, and Fairfax.
The royal captive was removed to Hatfield, thence to Hampton Court, where the officers of the household were astonished to see the King walking up and down the garden for
hours conversing and laughing with the rebel generals, all apparently in the highest good humour. Eventually the following royal message was framed: "His Majesty conceives the
Propositions of Parliament as being destructive to the main
principal interests of the Army, and of all those whose affections concur with them; and His Majesty, having seen the
Proposals of the Army . . . believes his two Houses will
think with him that they much more conduce to the satisfaction of all interests and may be a fitter foundation for a lasting peace than the Propositions now tendered by Parliament.
He therefore propounds (as the best way in his judgment in

order to peace) that his two Houses would instantly take into consideration those Proposals." [1]

Behind all this was a great political and personal deal. No one has probed its precise details. There was a religious compromise which the nation could have stomached. There was a Constitution where power was balanced between Parliament and Crown. There was substantial indemnity and reward for the Army when disbanded. There is the outline of a Cromwell, Earl and Knight of the Garter, quelling, as Viceroy, the Irish disorders, renewing in a different form the "Thorough" administration for which Strafford had lost his life. As Lord Keeper, Ireton, the most constructive political mind of the hour, might have shaped the Island Constitution and outrun the toilsome marches of the generations. At this moment there was at finger tips a settlement in the power of the English people and near to their hearts' desire. But of course it was too good to be true. Not so easily can mankind escape from the rigours of its pilgrimage. Charles was never wholly sincere in his dealings with the Army leaders; he still pinned his hopes on help from the Scots. Parliament for their part rejected the military and royal proposals. They stood by faction and the party policy, and they too hoped that the Scots might be brought to put down the warriors who had saved them in their need. Here were checks. But another came from the Army itself.

Hitherto the generals had held the officers, and the officers had held the men; but all was boiling with force and thought, surging upwards upon religious passion. The soldiers were deep in the Old Testament. Ehud and Eglon, Saul and Samuel, Ahab and Jehu, were in their minds. They particularly admired the conduct of Samuel when before the Lord he hewed to pieces Agag, delicately though he walked. The gen-

[1]Young, p. 67.

erals wished to make a good arrangement for the country, for the King, and for themselves. The rank and file had deeper-cutting convictions. The only chance for the arrangement between Charles and Cromwell was that it should be carried swiftly into effect. Instead there was delay. The main preoccupation of the generals was to hold their men. But the old harangues did not seem effective in a military assembly which already looked upon the King as "the Man of Blood," and were astonished that their honoured leaders should defile themselves by having truck with him. The mood of the soldiers became increasingly morose; and the generals saw themselves in danger of losing control over them.

The Presbyterian party in the House of Commons now realised they could not quell the Army. But the City of London, its apprentices and its mob, as yet unconvinced, held them to their duty. They were forced by riot and violence to rescind the conciliatory resolutions which, much against their will, they had offered to the Army. In fear of the London mob, the Speaker and fifty or sixty Members resorted to Army headquarters at Hounslow, claiming the protection of Cromwell. This was granted. The Army marched on London, occupied Westminster, entered the City, and everything except their problems fell prostrate before them.

*   *   *   *   *

At Putney in the autumn of 1647 the Army held keen debate. The generals, and especially Ireton, sought to canalise their turbulence. A military Parliament or Army debating society was formed. The regiments had elected their delegates. These were called by them the "agents," or "agitators." Ireton had drawn up the military constitution. He was prepared to go to all lengths short of disturbing the social order or the rights of property. At Putney they wrestled with one another and with their ideas long and earnestly for weeks. They set a secretary to record their proceedings; his records eventually found their way to an Oxford college, and the nineteenth century was presented with a window on the vivid scene. All sorts of new figures sprang up: Sexby, Rainborow, Wildman, Goffe the preaching colonel. These spoke with fervour and power, and every time they hit the bull's-eye. Cromwell listened to sentences like these: "The poorest he that is in England hath a life to live as the greatest he," and "A man is not bound to a system of government which he hath not had any hand in setting over him." It was a brew of hot Gospel and cold steel.

The doctrine of natural right to political equality shocked Ireton as much as it would have shocked Burke or Fox. He sought rigidly the middle course between a Parliament which could not be dissolved and the rank and file of an Army which would not be disbanded. His precise arguments commanded Cromwell's intellectual assent, but not his political judgment. They fell flat with the soldiers' "agents." When General Ireton dwelt upon the principle that only those should vote who had what is now called "a stake in the country" his audience became thoughtful. When he pointed out that a claim for political equality based on the law of God or the law of Nature would affect the rights of property, when he said, "By the same right of Nature he hath an equal right in any goods he sees," the soldiers did not recoil in horror from this conclusion. Their ideas were soon abreast of those of the Chartists in the nineteenth century—manhood suffrage at twenty-one, equal electoral districts, biennial Parliaments, and much more in prospect.

Cromwell heard all this and brooded over it. His outlook was Elizabethan. He thought such claims would lead to anarchy. When orators raised the cheers of the assembly for the day when King, lords, and property would all be cast down together his thoughts wandered back to his landed estate. Clearly this was dangerous nonsense. Ireton's would-be calming arguments only opened up new vistas of subversion. Apart from all this political talk, Cromwell had to think of discipline. He still held power. He used it without delay. He carried a resolution that the representative officers and agitators should be sent back to their regiments. He replaced the General Council of the Army by a General Council of his officers. The political conceptions of the Putney Ironsides were only to be realised in our own day.

Late in this autumn of 1647 Cromwell and Ireton came to the conclusion that even with the pay and indemnity settled they could not unite King and Army. They could not carry the troops. Religious notions which Pym and Hampden would have detested, a Republicanism which the Long Parliament had persistently eschewed, and behind these questions of property manhood suffrage, and, in terms then unknown, Socialism and Communism, all seethed in the conclaves and conventicles of the soldiers. It remained only to find occasion to break the dangerous, glittering contacts which had been made. There was no difficulty. Royalist England, beaten in arms, mulcted in estate, still lived and breathed, watching for its chance. Parliament continued to formulate its solidly based political aims. The Scots, imbued with religious fervour and personal cupidity, hung on the Border. Charles, who was aware of all these movements, began to look elsewhere. Under these stresses the combination between the defeated King and the victorious generals finally splintered. It was easy for an Ironside colonel, by the directions of his chiefs, to hint to Charles that his life was in danger, that meetings were held openly at which his assassination in the public interest was debated by ruthless men. At the same time no restriction was placed upon his movements.

In November the King, convinced that he would be murdered by the soldiery, whom their officers could no longer restrain, rode off in the night, and by easy stages made his way to Carisbrooke Castle, in the Isle of Wight. Here, where a donkey treads an endless water wheel, he dwelt for almost a year, defenceless, sacrosanct, a spiritual King, a coveted tool, an intriguing parcel, an ultimate sacrifice. There still resided in him a principle which must be either exploited or destroyed; but in England he no longer had the power to make a bargain. There remained the Scots. With them he signed a secret Engagement by which Royalism and Presbyterianism were to be allied. From this conjunction there shortly sprang the Second Civil War.

How near to the verge both Cromwell and Charles had pushed their effort to agree was meanwhile to be shown. The Army was about to revolt. A plot was made to arrest or murder the generals. Colonels talked of impeaching Cromwell. He was "going the same way as Hotham." On December 15 the generals faced their men. Some of the regiments submitted at once; but those of Robert Lilburne and Thomas Harrison were mutinous. The historian Gardiner has described the scene: "They appeared on the field with copies of the *Agreement of the People* stuck in their hats, with the addition of the motto 'England's Freedom! Soldiers' Rights!' Harrison's regiment was soon brought to submission by a few words of reproof from Fairfax, but Lilburne's was not in so compliant a mood. Cromwell, seeing that persuasion alone would not avail him here, rode along the ranks, sharply ordering the men to tear the papers from their hats, and on finding no signs of obedience dashed among the mutineers with his sword drawn. There was something in his stern-set face and resolute action which compelled obedience. The instincts of military discipline revived, and the soldiers, a moment before so defiant, tore the papers from their hats and craved for mercy. The ringleaders were arrested, and three of them condemned to death by an improvised court-martial. The three were, however, allowed to throw dice for their lives, and the loser, whose name was Arnold, was shot in the presence of his comrades. Thus at the cost of a single life discipline was restored, without which the Army would have dissolved into chaos." [1]

* * * * *

The Second Civil War was very different in cause and conditions from the first. The parts played by almost all the principals were altered, or even reversed. The King and his Prerogative were now seen, not as obstacles to Parliamentary right, but as the repository of ordinary English freedom. A large proportion of the Members of the Long Parliament, and almost all the House of Lords, if they had been allowed to meet, would have expressed this view. The Scots, formerly so exacting against the King, were now convinced that their peril lay in the opposite quarter. Wales was solid in its Royalism. London, formerly the main prop of Pym and Hampden, was now deeply inclined to a restoration of the royal authority. The apprentices, who had hounded Charles out of the capital, still rioted in their exuberance; but now they insulted the soldiery and cried "Long live the King!" Half the Navy, hitherto a deadly weapon against Charles, mutinied in his favour. Most of the ships involved sailed off to Holland and entreated the Prince of Wales to become their admiral. All the Royalist forces, smarting, bleeding in pocket and in person, outraged in sentiment and social interest, were eager to draw the sword. The mass of the people still remained comparatively inert. There was not at this moment the universal passion which produced the Restoration of 1660; but

[1] *History of the Great Civil War* (1901), vol. iv, p. 23.

all the leading forces in English society were moving together, and even in the mass the feeling prevailed that the King and Parliament had been swept aside by a new tyranny, which would bring bad times to the toilers. Prisoner at Carisbrooke, Charles was now more truly King than he had ever been in the palmiest days of the Personal Rule.

The story of the Second Civil War is short and simple. King, Lords and Commons, landlords and merchants, the City and the countryside, bishops and presbyters, the Scottish army, the Welsh people, and the English Fleet, all now turned against the New Model Army. The Army beat the lot. And at their head was Cromwell. Their plight at first might well have seemed desperate; but this very fact wiped out all divisions among them. Fairfax, Cromwell, Ireton, were now once again united to their fierce warriors. The Army marched and fought. They marched to Wales; they marched to Scotland, and none could withstand them. A mere detachment sufficed to quell a general rising in Cornwall and the West. They broke the Royalist forces at Colchester; and here a new rigour became apparent. The Royalist commanders, Lucas and Lisle, contrary to all previous conventions, were by Fairfax's order shot outside the walls after the surrender. Cromwell, having subdued the Welsh rising, moved swiftly to the North, picked up his forces, and fell on the Scottish army as it was marching through Lancashire. Although David Leslie led it this was not the old Army of Scotland. The trained Scottish forces, under Lord Leven, stood aside. The invaders were cut off, caught, and destroyed at Preston. The Fleet, which had been so potent a few years back against a struggling King, could do little against this all-mastering, furious Army which stalked the land in rags, almost barefoot, but with bright armour, sharp swords, and sublime conviction of its wrongheaded mission.

By the end of 1648 all was over. Cromwell was Dictator. The Royalists were crushed; Parliament was a tool; the Constitution was a figment; the Scots were rebuffed, the Welsh back in their mountains; the Fleet was reorganised, London overawed. King Charles, at Carisbrooke Castle, where the donkey treads the water wheel, was left to pay the bill. It was mortal.

* * * * *

We must not be led by Victorian writers into regarding this triumph of the Ironsides and of Cromwell as a kind of victory for democracy and the Parliamentary system over Divine Right and Old World dreams. It was the triumph of some twenty thousand resolute, ruthless, disciplined, military fanatics over all that England has ever willed or ever wished. Long years and unceasing irritations were required to reverse it. Thus the struggle, in which we have in these days so much sympathy and part, begun to bring about a constitutional and limited monarchy, had led only to the autocracy of the sword. The harsh, terrific, lightning-charged being, whose erratic, opportunist, self-centred course is laid bare upon the annals, was now master, and the next twelve years are the record of his well-meant, puzzled plungings and surgings.

Plainly the fruit of the victory that could most easily be gathered was the head of the King. True, he had never moved from Carisbrooke, but was he not the mainspring of the whole of this vast movement of England against the Army, its rule, and even its pay? Was he not the pivot upon which all public opinion turned? Did he not embody all those courses which the Ironsides either hated or could not unravel? Was he not a trophy gained by march and battle? At a moment of great hesitancy in matters of government, when everything was fluid and uncertain, here was a supreme act which all could understand and upon which the Army could unite. The execution of Charles Stuart, "the Man of Blood," could alone satisfy the soldiers and enable their leaders to hold their obedience.

One stormy evening, with the rain beating down, in the Isle of Wight, it was noticed that many boat-loads of Ironside soldiery were being rowed across the Solent and landed at Newport and Cowes. The King's household made inquiries and kept vigilant watch. His trusty friends urged flight, which was not, it seemed, as yet impossible. Charles, who was deep in new and hopeful negotiations with Parliament, had enough confidence in the strength of his position to reject the opportunity. It was his last. A few days later he was brought to the mainland and confined in Hurst Castle. Here the new severities of the Second Civil War marked the rules to which he was subjected. Hitherto his personal dignity and comfort had always been consulted. Now, with scarcely a personal attendant, he found himself shut in the candleless gloom of a small tower prison. There was still a further interlude of negotiations; they were nothing but parleyings with a doomed man. And in this darkness the King rose to his greatest height. His troublous, ill-starred reign had shown him in many wrong attitudes; but at the end he was to be granted by Fate the truly magnificent and indisputable rôle of the champion of English—nay, British, for all the Island was involved—rights and liberty. After some delay he was during the Christmas season brought towards London. At first he feared that Colonel Harrison, the officer who fetched him, would be his assassin; but nothing of the kind was intended. The Army meant to have his blood in the manner which would most effectively vindicate their power and their faith. Cromwell, who had nothing else to give his burning legions, could at least present them with an awful and all-dominating scene of expiation. To Colonel Harrison, one evening, on the journey to the capital, Charles put a blunt question, "Are you come to murder me?" "It is not true, sir," said the Colonel. "The law is equally bound to great and small." Charles slept in peace. He was reassured against murder; by law he was inviolable.

It must have been a vivid contrast with the privations of Hurst Castle when the King rested for nearly a week at Windsor. Here all again was respect and ceremony. A nucleus of the staff and household were in attendance. The King dined every night in ancient state, served on the knee. The Parliamentary officers joined him at table, saluted, and quitted him with the deepest bows. A strange interlude! But now forward to London; much is afoot there. "Will Your Majesty graciously be pleased to set forth?"

London lay locked under the guard and countersign of the Army. Some Parliamentary time-server had stood by Colonel Pride, when the Members sought to take their seats in the House of Commons, and had ticked off all those not likely to obey the Army's will. Forty-five Members who tried to enter were arrested, and out of a total of over five hundred three hundred did not take their seats again. This was "Pride's Purge." The great trial of "the Man of Blood" was to be presented to the nation and to the world. English law and precedent were scoured from the most remote times, but no sanction or even cover for such a proceeding could be found. The slaying of princes had many examples. Edward II at Berkeley Castle, Richard II at Pontefract, had met terrible fates; but these were deeds wrapped in secrecy, disavowed by authority, covered at the time by mystery or the plea of natural causes. Here the victorious Army meant to teach the English people that henceforward they must obey; and Cromwell, who eighteen months before might have been King Charles's Viceroy of Ireland, now saw in his slaughter his only chance of supremacy and survival. In vain did Fairfax point out that the stroke which killed the captive King would make his son in Holland the free possessor of all his rights. No English jurist could be found to frame the indictment or invent the tribunal. A Dutch lawyer, Isaac Dorislaus, who had long lived in England, was able to deck what was to be done in the trappings of antiquity. The language of the order convening the court had no contact with English history; it looks back to the classical age, when the ruin of tyrants was decreed by the Senate or the Prætorian Guard. An ordinance passed by the docile remnant of the Commons created a court of a hundred and thirty-five Commissioners, of whom barely sixty would serve, to try the King. The carpenters fitted Westminster Hall for its most memorable scene. This was not only the killing of a king, but the killing of a king who at that time represented the will and the traditions of almost the whole British nation.

*　*　*　*　*

The more detail in which the famous trial has been described the greater is the sense of drama. The King, basing himself upon the law and Constitution he had strained and exploited in his years of prosperity, confronted his enemies with an unbreakable defence. He eyed his judges, as Morley says, "with unaffected scorn." He refused to acknowledge the tribunal. To him it was a monstrous illegality. John Bradshaw, the president of the court, could make no logical dint upon this. Cromwell and the Army could however cut off the King's head, and this at all costs they meant to do. The overwhelming sympathy of the great concourse gathered in Westminster Hall was with the King. When, on the afternoon of the final sitting, after being refused leave to speak, he was conducted from the Hall it was amid a low, intense murmur of "God save the King." But the soldiers, primed by their corporals, and themselves in high resolve, shouted, "Justice! Justice! Execution! Execution!"

Personal dignity and convenience were consulted to the last. Every facility was accorded the King to settle his temporal affairs and to receive the consolations of religion. This was not a butchery, but a ceremony, a sacrifice, or, if we may borrow from the Spanish Inquisition, "an act of faith." On the morning of January 30, 1649, Charles was conducted from St James's, whither he had been removed from his comfortable lodgings by the river, to Whitehall. Snow fell, and he had put on his warm underclothes. He walked briskly amid the Ironside guard, saying, "Step out now," across the half mile which led him to the Banqueting House. There no attempt was made to interfere with his wishes so far as they did not conflict with what had been resolved. But most of those who had signed the death warrant were aghast at the deed of which they were to bear the weight, and the ultimate vengeance. Cromwell had found great difficulty in holding together enough of his signatories. Fairfax, no mean person, still Commander-in-Chief, was outraged. He had to be mastered. Ireton and Harrison remained in the building with the doomed King. Cromwell was there, and wherever else was necessary.

At one o'clock in the afternoon Charles was informed that his hour had come. He walked through a window of the Banqueting House on to the scaffold. Masses of soldiers, many ranks deep, held an immense multitude afar. The King looked with a disdainful smile upon the cords and pulleys which had been prepared to fasten him down, upon the fantastic assumption that he would carry his repudiation of the tribunal which had condemned him even to physical lengths. He was allowed to speak as he chose. His voice could not reach beyond the troops; he therefore spoke to those who gathered on the scaffold. He said that "he died a good Christian, he had forgiven all the world, yea, chiefly those who had caused his death (naming none). He wished their repentance and that they might take the right way to the peace of the kingdom, which was not by way of conquest. He did not believe the happiness of people lay in sharing government, subject and sovereign being clean different. And if he would have given way to an arbitrary Government and to have all laws changed according to the sword he need not have suffered, and so he said he was a martyr to the people."

He resigned himself to death, and assisted the executioner in arranging his hair under a small white satin cap. He laid himself upon the block, and upon his own signal his head was struck off at a single stroke. His severed head was shown to the people, and someone cried, "This is the head of a traitor!"

An incalculable multitude had streamed to the spot, swayed by intense though inarticulate emotions. When they saw the severed head "there was such a groan by the thousands then present," wrote a contemporary diarist, "as I never heard before and desire I may never hear again."

A strange destiny had engulfed this King of England. None had resisted with more untimely stubbornness the movement of his age. He had been in his heyday the convinced opponent of all we now call our Parliamentary liberties. Yet as misfortunes crowded upon him he increasingly became the physical embodiment of the liberties and traditions of England. His mistakes and wrong deeds had arisen not so much from personal cravings for arbitrary power as from the conception of kingship to which he was born and which had long been the settled custom of the land. In the end he stood against an army which had destroyed all Parliamentary government, and was about to plunge England into a tyranny at once more irresistible and more petty than any seen before or since. He did not flinch in any respect from the causes in which he believed. Although, no doubt, in bargainings and manœuvres with his enemies he had practised deceit and ill faith, these arose from the malignancy and ever-shifting character of the quarrel, and were amply matched upon the other side. But he never departed from his central theme either in religion or State. He adhered unswervingly to the Prayer Book of the Reformed Church and to the Episcopacy, with which he conceived Christianity was interwoven. By his constancy, which underlay all the shifts and turns of tumultuous and swiftly changing years, he preserved the causes by which his life was guided. He was not a martyr in the sense of one who dies for a spiritual ideal. His own kingly interests were mingled at every stage with the larger issues. Some have sought to represent him as the champion of the small or humble man against the rising money-power. This is fanciful. He cannot be claimed as the defender of English liberties, nor wholly of the English Church, but none the less he died for them, and by his death preserved them not only to his son and heir, but to our own day.

BOOK SIX

THE RESTORATION

The English Republic

THE English Republic had come into existence even before the execution of the King. On January 4, 1649, the handful of Members of the House of Commons who served the purposes of Cromwell and the Army resolved that "the people are, under God, the original of all just power . . . that the Commons of England in Parliament assembled, being chosen by and representing the people, have the supreme power in this nation." On the 9th it was voted that the name of a single person should no longer be mentioned in legal transactions under the Great Seal. A new seal was presented, bearing on one side a map of England and Ireland and on the other a picture of the House of Commons, with the inscription "In the first year of freedom, by God's blessing restored." A statue of Charles I was thrown down, and on the pedestal were inscribed the words "Exit the tyrant, the last of the Kings." On February 5 it was declared that the House of Lords "is useless and dangerous and ought to be abolished." Thereafter it ceased to meet. Vengeance was wrought upon a number of peers taken prisoner in the Second Civil War, and Lords Hamilton and Holland, statesmen of high intellectual qualities and long record, were beheaded.

The country was now to be governed by a Council of State chosen annually by Parliament. Its forty-one members included peers, judges, and Members of Parliament, among them most of the principal regicides. It was found to be fearless, diligent, and incorrupt. The judiciary hung for a time in the balance. Six of the twelve judges refused to continue, but the rest, their oath of allegiance being formally abrogated, agreed to serve the Commonwealth. The highly conservative elements at the head of the Army held firmly to the maintenance of the Common Law and the unbroken administration of justice in all non-political issues. The accession of the lawyers to the new régime was deemed essential for the defence of privilege and property against the assaults of the Levellers, agitators, and extremists. This had now become the crucial issue. Fierce and furious as was the effort of the Levellers, there was no hesitation among the men in power to put them down. Even Ireton was excluded from the new Council of State, with which all power rested. Cromwell and his colleagues were familiar with the extremists' demands. They had originally been put forward by five cavalry regiments who had signed the "Agreement of the People," promoted by John Lilburne at the time of the abortive negotiations between Cromwell and the King in 1647.

It was essential to divide and disperse the Army, and Cromwell was willing to lead the larger part of it to a war of retribution in the name of the Lord Jehovah against the idolatrous and bloodstained Papists of Ireland. It was thought that an interprise of this character would enlist the fanaticism of the rank and file. Lots were drawn which regiments should go to Ireland, and were drawn again and again until only the regiments in which the Levellers were strongest were cast. A pamphlet on *England's New Chains* spread through the Army. Mutinies broke out. Many hundreds of veteran soldiers appeared in bands in support of "the sovereignty of the people," manhood suffrage, and annual Parliaments. This mood was not confined to the soldiers. Behind these broad principles the idea of equal rights in property as well as in citizenship was boldly announced by a group led by Gerard Winstanley, which came to be known as "the Diggers."

Numbers of persons appeared upon the common lands in Surrey and prepared to cultivate them on a communal basis. These "Diggers" did not molest the enclosed lands, leaving them to be settled by whoever had the power to take them; but they claimed that the whole earth was a "common treasury" and that the common land should be for all. They argued further that the beheaded King traced his right to William the Conqueror, with whom a crowd of nobles and adventurers had come into England, robbing by force the mass of the people of their ancient rights in Saxon days. Historically the claim was overlaid by six centuries of custom and was itself highly disputable; but this was what they said. The rulers of the Commonwealth regarded all this as dangerous and subversive nonsense.

No one was more shocked than Cromwell. He cared almost as much for private property as for religious liberty. "A nobleman, a gentleman, a yeoman," he said, "that is a good interest of the land and a great one." The Council of State chased the would-be cultivators off the common land, and hunted the mutinous officers and soldiers to death without mercy. Cromwell again quelled a mutiny in person, and by his orders Trooper William Thompson, a follower of Lilburne, was shot in an Oxfordshire churchyard. His opinions and his constancy have led some to crown him as "the first martyr of democracy." Cromwell also discharged from the Army, without their arrears of pay, all men who would not volunteer for the Irish war. Nominated by the Council as Commander, he invested his mission not only with a martial but with a priestly aspect. He joined the Puritan divines in preaching a holy war upon the Irish, and made a religious progress to Charing Cross in a coach drawn by six Flemish horses. All this was done as part of a profound calculated policy in the face of military and social dangers which, if not

strangled, would have opened a new ferocious and measureless social war in England.

*   *   *   *   *

Cromwell's campaign of 1649 in Ireland was equally cold-
blooded, and equally imbued with those Old Testament sentiments which dominated the minds of the Puritans. The spirit
and peril of the Irish race might have prompted them to
unite upon Catholic toleration and monarchy, and on this
they could have made a firm alliance with the Protestant
Royalists, who, under the Marquess of Ormonde, had an organised army of twelve thousand men. But the arrival of the
Papal Nuncio Rinuccini had aggravated the many forces of
incoherence and strife. Ormonde's army was grievously
weakened before Cromwell landed. He had already in 1647
ceded Dublin a Parliamentary general; but he had later
occupied the towns of Drogheda and Wexford and was resolved to defend them. Upon these Cromwell marched with
his ten thousand veteran troops. Ormonde would have done
better to keep the open field with his regulars and allow
the severities of the Puritan invaders to rally the Irish nation behind him. Instead he hoped that Cromwell would
break his teeth upon a long siege of Drogheda, in which he
placed a garrison of three thousand men, comprising the
flower of the Irish Royalists and English volunteers. Cromwell saw that the destruction of these men would not only
ruin Ormonde's military power, but spread a helpful terror
throughout the island. He therefore resolved upon a deed of
"frightfulness" deeply embarrassing to his nineteenth-century
admirers and apologists.

Having unsuccessfully summoned the garrison to surrender, he breached the ramparts with his cannon, and at the
third assault, which he led himself, stormed the town. There
followed a massacre so all-effacing as to startle even the opin-

ion of those fierce times. All were put to the sword. None escaped; every priest and friar was butchered. The corpses were carefully ransacked for valuables. The Governor, Sir Arthur Ashton, had an artificial leg, which the Ironsides believed to be made of gold; however it was only in his belt that they found his private fortune. The ferreting out and slaughter of those in hiding lasted till the third day.

There is no dispute about the facts, for Oliver told his own tale in his letter to John Bradshaw, President of the Council of State. "It hath pleased God to bless our endeavours at Tredah [for thus he spelt Drogheda]. After battery, we stormed it. The Enemy were about 3000 strong in the Town. They made a stout resistance; and near 1000 of our men being entered, the Enemy forced them out again. But God giving a new courage to our men, they attempted again, and entered: beating the Enemy from their defences. . . . Being thus entered, we refused them quarter: having, the day before, summoned the Town. I believe we put to the sword the whole number of the defendants. I do not think Thirty of the whole number escaped with their lives. Those that did, are in safe custody for the Barbados. . . . This hath been a marvellous great mercy. The Enemy, being not willing to put an issue upon a field-battle, had put into this Garrison almost all their prime soldiers . . . under the command of their best officers. . . . I do not believe, neither do I hear, that any officer escaped with his life, save only one. . . . The Enemy upon this were filled with much terror. And truly I believe this bitterness will save much effusion of blood, through the goodness of God. . . .

"I wish that all honest hearts may give the glory of this to God alone, to whom indeed the praise of this mercy belongs."

In another letter to Speaker Lenthall he gave further details. "Divers of the Enemy retreated into the Mill-Mount: a place very strong and of difficult access. . . . The Governor, Sir Arthur Ashton, and divers considerable Officers being there, our men getting up to them, were ordered by me to put them all to the sword. And indeed, being in the heat of action, I forbade them to spare any that were in arms in the Town: and, I think, that night they put to the sword about 2000 men;—divers of the officers and soldiers being fled over the Bridge into the other part of the Town, where about 100 of them possessed St Peter's Church-steeple. . . . These being summoned to yield to mercy, refused. Whereupon I ordered the steeple of St Peter's Church to be fired, when one of them was heard to say in the midst of the flames, 'God damn me, God confound me; I burn, I burn.' " "I am persuaded," Cromwell added, "that this is a righteous judgment of God upon these barbarous wretches, who have imbrued their hands in so much innocent blood." [1] A similar atrocity was perpetrated a few weeks later at the storm of Wexford.

In the safe and comfortable days of Queen Victoria, when Liberals and Conservatives, Gladstone and Disraeli, contended about the past, and when Irish Nationalists and Radical Nonconformists championed their old causes, a school grew up to gape in awe and some in furtive admiration at these savage crimes. Men thought such scenes were gone for ever, and that while moving into a broad age of peace, money-making, and debatings they could afford to pay their tributes to the rugged warriors who had laid the foundations of a liberal society. The twentieth century has sharply recalled its intellectuals from such vain indulgences. We have seen the technique of "frightfulness" applied in our own time with Cromwellian brutality and upon a far larger scale. We

[1] Thomas Carlyle, *Oliver Cromwell's Letters and Speeches,* 1846, vol. ii, pp. 59–62.

know too much of despots and their moods and power to practise the philosophic detachment of our grandfathers. It is necessary to recur to the simpler principle that the wholesale slaughter of unarmed or disarmed men marks with a mordant and eternal brand the memory of conquerors, however they may have prospered.

In Oliver's smoky soul there were evident misgivings. He writes of the "remorse and regret" which are inseparable from such crimes. While brazening them out, he offers diverse excuses, eagerly lapped up by Carlyle. By a terrifying example he believed that he had saved far greater bloodshed. But this did not prove true. The war continued in squalid, murderous fashion for two years after he had left Ireland. In his hatred of Popery, which he regarded as a worldwide conspiracy of evil, he sought to identify the Royalist garrison of Drogheda with the Roman Catholic Irish peasantry who had massacred the Protestant landlords in 1641. He ought to have known that not one of them had the slightest connection with that eight-year-old horror. He shielded himself behind "the heat of action" when his troops had not suffered a hundred casualties, and when, in Ranke's impartial judgment, "there throughout mingled a cold-blooded calculation and a violence which is deliberate." Above all, the conscience of man must recoil from the monster of a faction-god projected from the mind of an ambitious, interested politician on whose lips the words "righteousness" and "mercy" were mockery. Not even the hard pleas of necessity or the safety of the State can be invoked. Cromwell in Ireland, disposing of overwhelming strength and using it with merciless wickedness, debased the standards of human conduct and sensibly darkened the journey of mankind. Cromwell's Irish massacres find numberless compeers in the history of all countries during and since the Stone Age. It is therefore only necessary to strip men capable of such deeds of all title to honour, whether it be the light which plays around a great captain of war or the long repute which covers the severities of a successful prince or statesman.[2]

We have seen the many ties which at one time or another have joined the inhabitants of the Western islands, and even in Ireland itself offered a tolerable way of life to Protestants and Catholics alike. Upon all these Cromwell's record was a lasting bane. By an uncompleted process of terror, by an iniquitous land settlement, by the virtual proscription of the Catholic religion, by the bloody deeds already described, he cut new gulfs between the nations and the creeds. "Hell or Connaught" were the terms he thrust upon the native inhabitants, and they for their part, across three hundred years, have used as their keenest expression of hatred, "the curse of Cromwell on you." The consequences of Cromwell's rule in Ireland have distressed and at times distracted English politics down even to the present day. To heal them baffled the skill and loyalties of successive generations. They became for a time a potent obstacle to the harmony of the English-speaking peoples throughout the world. Upon all of us there still lies "the curse of Cromwell."

*   *   *   *   *

At the moment when the axe severed the head of Charles the First from his body his eldest son became, in the opinion of most of his subjects and of Europe, King Charles the Second. Within six days, as soon as horsemen could bear the tidings northward, the Scottish Estates proclaimed him King of Great Britain, France, and Ireland. Their representatives in London demanded his recognition. The oligarchs who called themselves "Parliament" thereupon expelled the envoys, declaring that they had "laid the grounds of a new and

[2] Written 1938–39.—W. S. C.

bloody war." Charles II sheltered at The Hague. The predominant sentiment in Holland was friendly to him, and shocked by his father's execution. Dorislaus, the Dutch lawyer who had been so helpful in drawing up the regicide tribunal, was murdered by Scottish Royalists as he sat at dinner; and although the law was set in motion against the assassins their crime was widely applauded.

Montrose, when his army fell to pieces, had on the advice of the late King quitted Scotland, believing at first that the Whitehall execution robbed his life of all purpose. His spirit was revived by a priest who preached to him a duty of revenge. With a handful of followers he landed in Caithness, was defeated by the Government forces and betrayed for a paltry bribe into their power. He was dragged through many Scottish towns, and hanged at Edinburgh on a specially high gallows amid an immense agitated concourse. Uplifted by his commanding spirit above physical misfortune, he regarded his sufferings as glorious martyrdom, abashed his fiercest foes by his noble gaze, and has left a name long cherished in Scottish ballad and romance. His body, cut into an unusual number of pieces, was distributed for an example through the scenes of his triumphs. Yet at the same time that Argyll and the Covenanters inflicted this savage punishment upon an unorthodox Royalist they themselves prepared for war with England in the cause of monarchy and entered into urgent treaty with the young King.

Hard courses were laid before Charles II. If, said the Scottish Government, you will embrace the Covenant and become the champion of the Presbyterian cause not only will we bring all Scotland under your sovereignty, but we will march with you into England, where Presbyterians and Royalists alike will join to reestablish the sacred majesty of the Crown against Republicans and regicides. Here at the darkest moment was the proclamation of the continuance of the monarchy. But the price was extortionate and deadly. Charles II must bind himself to destroy the Episcopacy and enforce upon England a religious system odious to all who had fought for his father. He had been carefully and strictly brought up, and was versed in the religious and political controversies of the times. He hesitated long before taking the grim decision of selling his soul to the Devil, as he conceived it, for the interest of the Crown and betraying the cause to save its life. The exacting Scottish Commissioners who waited upon him day by day in Holland understood all that was involved in the bargain. "We made him," said one of them, "sign and swear a Covenant which we knew from clear and demonstrable reasons that he hated in his heart. . . . He sinfully complied with what we most sinfully pressed upon him." Even Queen Henrietta Maria, with the blood of her beloved husband to avenge, and to whom one Protestant heresy was no worse or better than another, was doubtful whether her son should subscribe.

The fulfilment of the contract was as harsh as the signing. On the ship before the King landed in Scotland the most precise guarantees were extracted. When the King looked out from the windows of the house in which he was lodged at Aberdeen a grisly object met his view. It was the shrivelled hand of Montrose, his devoted servant and friend, nailed to the wall. He found himself virtually a prisoner in the hands of those who had besought him to be their sovereign. He listened to endless sermons, admonitions, and objurgations. He bowed the knee in what was to him the temple of Baal. We may admire as polished flint the convictions and purposes of the Scots Government and its divines, but one must be thankful never to have been brought into contact with any of them.

It was the essence of Scottish policy to separate their new war with England from the invasion which had so lamentably failed at Preston two years before. All those who had taken part in that ill-starred attempt—"the Engagers," as they were called, after the name of the agreement with Charles I— were barred from the new venture. A purge of the Army stripped it of three or four thousand of its most experienced officers and men; their places were filled with "ministers' sons, clerks, and such other sanctified creatures, who hardly ever saw or heard of any sword but that of the spirit." Still there was again an army to fight for the Crown, and both Cardinal Mazarin in France and Prince William of Orange in Holland lent their aid to Scotland. The unhappy young King was forced, by the need to fight and the desire to win, to issue a declaration in which he desired to be "deeply humbled before God because of his father's opposition to the Solemn League and Covenant; and because his mother had been guilty of idolatry, the toleration of which in the King's house could not but be a high provocation to a jealous God visiting the sins of the fathers upon the children." Charles wondered whether he would dare to look his mother in the face again, and in fact she told him she would never again be his political adviser. On this strange foundation a large Scottish army gathered on the Border.

The menace in the North brought Cromwell back from Ireland. Fairfax, thoroughly estranged from his former colleagues, refused to invade Scotland, and the Council of State at last appointed Cromwell Commander-in-Chief in form as he had long been in fact. In his Ironside troops, fresh from their Irish slaughters, he grasped a heavy, sharp, and reeking sword. He did not shrink from argument before strife. He wrestled in soulful stress with men who believed that many of the tenets he knew and measured as political counters were matters of salvation or damnation. "I beseech you," he exclaimed, in tremendous challenge, "in the bowels of Christ Jesus, think it possible you may be mistaken." It was in vain. But for the expense and danger of keeping armies in the field, they would have wrangled heartily till Doomsday. Meanwhile however the English troops had invaded the Lowlands, hugging the coast, where they could be victualled from the sea by their Fleet. The armies manœuvred against each other. David Leslie was no mean opponent, and his army far more numerous. Cromwell was forced back upon Dunbar, dependent on wind and weather for his daily bread. He might still escape south by sea, picking up supplies at the East Coast ports. But this was no culmination to a career of unbroken success.

In the Scottish camp there were two opinions. The first, held by Leslie, was for letting Cromwell go. The second was urged by the six leading ministers of religion; now was the time to wreak the Lord's vengeance upon those guilty ones who would bring spiritual anarchy into the Reformed Church. Bigotry prevailed over strategy. The pious Scottish army descended from their blockading heights and closed down upon Cromwell and his saints to prevent their embarkation. Both sides confidently appealed to Jehovah; and the Most High, finding so little to choose between them in faith and zeal, must have allowed purely military factors to prevail. It was again September 3. A year had passed since the massacre at Drogheda. Further manifestations of the divine favour might well be expected. "We have much hope in the Lord, of whose mercy we have had large experience," remarked Oliver cheerfully. A Yorkshire officer, John Lambert, of whom more was to be heard, convinced him of the weakness of the southern Scottish flank, which he overlapped. At the first grey light Cromwell, feinting with his right wing, attacked heavily on the left. "Now," he ex-claimed, as the sun rose over the sea behind him, "let God arise and let his enemies be scattered." Once the battle was joined among these politico-religious warriors the end was speedy. The Scots, finding their right turned, fled, leaving three thousand dead on the field. Nine thousand were prisoners in Oliver's hungry camp, and the Army of the Presbyters was broken.

*   *   *   *   *

The disaster carried Scots policy out of the trammels of dogma. National safety became the cry. All haste was made to conciliate the Engagers and reinforce the depleted ranks with the officers and men so improvidently cashiered. The services of English Royalists were gratefully accepted. The King was crowned at Scone. Political ideas supervened upon the religious war. The plan of marching south, leaving Cromwell behind in Edinburgh, which he had occupied, and rousing the Royalist forces in England, captivated the majority of the Scots Council. But the religious, and what would later be called Radical, influences still retained enough strength to spoil this. The six Presbyterian ministers who professed to know what would be pleasing to the Almighty spread about the belief that the defeat at Dunbar was due to the estrangement of the Lord Jehovah from an army which espoused the cause of the son of an Uncovenanted King. Upon this reason or pretext many quitted the ranks.

A Scottish army now invaded England in 1651 upon a Royalist rather than a Presbyterian enterprise. It is proof of Cromwell's political and military sagacity that he allowed them to pass. He could by timely marches have overtaken them almost at the Border, but his intention was to cut them off from their supplies. The event justified his calculation. The English Royalists, bled white, mulcted, cowed, were found incapable of any fresh response; most of their active leaders had already been executed. Charles II trod his native soil as King. He marched in a chilling silence at the head of his troops. But Cromwell could now follow easily upon his track, and his concentration of all the forces of the Commonwealth against the Northern invaders was masterly. On his day of fate, September 3, sixteen thousand Scots were brought to battle at Worcester, not only by the twenty thousand veterans of the New Model, but by the English militia, who rallied in large numbers against this fresh inroad of the hated and interfering Scots. Leslie, who commanded, lingered in the city with the Scottish cavalry till the day was lost. Charles acquitted himself with distinction. He rode along the regiments in the thick of the fighting, encouraging them in their duty. The struggle was one of the stiffest contests of the civil wars, but it was forlorn, and the Scots and their Royalist comrades were destroyed as a military force. Few returned to Scotland. To Cromwell this was "the crowning mercy." To Charles II it afforded the most romantic adventure of his life. He escaped with difficulty from the stricken field; a thousand pounds was set upon his head. The land was scoured for him. He hid for a whole day in the famous oak tree at Boscobel, while his pursuers passed by. On every side were men who would have rejoiced to win the price of catching him. But also on every side were friends, if they could be found, secret, silent, unflinching. Nearly fifty persons recognised him, and thus became privy to his escape and liable to grave penalties. The magic of the words "the King, our master," cast its spell upon all classes. "The King of England, my master, your master, and the master of all good Englishmen, is near you and in great distress: can you help us to a boat?" "Is he well? Is he safe?" "Yes." "God be blessed." This was the temper of all who were trusted with or discovered the secret.

Thus after six weeks of desperate peril did the King find himself again in exile. His most faithful surviving supporter, Lord Derby, paid the last forfeit of loyalty on the scaffold, Lady Derby, who had gallantly defended her home at Lathom House, still hoped to keep the royal standard flying in the Isle of Man, the independence of which the Derbys had proclaimed; but Parliamentary ideas and later Parliamentary troops reduced this last asylum of Royalism. The valiant chieftainess was long imprisoned, and afterwards dwelt in penury. This was the end of the Civil War or Great Rebellion. England was mastered; Ireland was terrorised; Scotland was conquered. The three kingdoms were united under a Government in London which wielded autocratic power. The most memorable chapter in English history was closed by irresistible forces, which ruled absolutely for a while, but settled nothing. In harsh or melancholy epochs free men may always take comfort from the grand lesson of history, that tyrannies cannot last except among servile races. The years which seem endless to those who endure them are but a flick of mischance in the journey. New and natural hopes leap from the human heart as every spring revives the cultivated soil and rewards the faithful, patient husbandmen.

The Lord Protector

THE monarchy had gone; the Lords had gone; the Church of England was prostrate; of the Commons there remained nothing but the few survivors contemptuously named the Rump. The Rump sat high in its own estimation. It was the surviving embodiment of the Parliamentary cause. Its members felt that the country would need their guidance for many a long year. While Cromwell was fighting in Ireland and Scotland these Puritan grandees through their chosen Council of State ruled with efficiency. Though they expatiated with fervour upon religion they shaped a practical policy which, if it incurred odium, did not lack strength. They were an oligarchy born of war, and still warring. The money must be found. It came mainly from an excise and property tax which have not been displaced from the British financial system by the wisdom of later times. The defeated Royalists and proscribed Roman Catholics were obvious sources of revenue. Heavy fines were imposed upon them. They could only preserve a portion of their estates by paying the rest in ransom. There were large sales of land; and since only land directly confiscated was released when Charles II regained his throne there came about a lasting redistribution of landed property, which, though carried out within the same class, provided a core of self-interest among the new proprietors round which in after years the Whigs and their doctrines gradually gathered. The dualism of English life after the Restoration found its secular counterpart in two kinds of gentry, divided in interest, traditions, and ideas, but each based upon landed property. Here was one of the enduring foundations of the long-lived party systems.

It was a nationalistic Rump, at once protectionist and bellicose. Their Navigation Act forbade all imports not carried either in English ships or in those of the country of origin. Their rivalry with the Dutch, who controlled the Baltic trade and the spice trade with the Indies, and dominated the herring fisheries, provoked against a sister Protestant republic the first war in English history which was fought for primarily economic reasons. Robert Blake, a Somerset merchant, distinguished in the Civil War, but with no seafaring experience, was appointed admiral. He was the first and most famous of the "generals at sea," who, like Prince Rupert, proved that naval war is only the same tune played on different instruments. The English Navy more than held its own against the Dutch and the numerous Royalist privateers. Blake soon learned how to give the sea captains orders, taught the Fleet discipline and unity, and in his final campaign against the Mediterranean pirates proved that land batteries, then deemed unassailable, could be silenced by broadsides from ships afloat.

The Rump prospered only so long as their Lord General was at the wars. When he returned victorious he was struck by their unpopularity. He was also shocked at their unrepresentative character. Above all, he observed that the Army, hitherto occupied about God's business in other directions, looked sourly on their civilian masters and paymasters. He laboured to mediate between the shrunken Parliament and its gigantic sword, but even he could not withhold his criticism. He loathed the war against the Protestant Dutch. He deprecated Licensing Acts and Treason Acts, which overrode customary liberties. Finally he convinced himself of the "pride, ambition, and self-seeking" of the remaining Mem-

bers of Parliament. He foresaw sad dangers should they succeed in what he now feared was their design of perpetuating
their rule. He looked upon them with the same disparaging
glance as Napoleon, returned from Egypt, cast upon the Directory. The oligarchs, dwelling under the impression that
Parliamentary supremacy had been for ever established by
the execution of the King, and heedless of their tottering
foundations, remained obdurate. The Lord General's outlook
was clear and his language plain. "These men," Oliver said,
"will never leave till the Army pull them down by the ears."

He accordingly went to the House on April 20, 1653, accompanied by thirty musketeers. He took his seat and for a
time listened to the debate. Then, rising in his place, he made
a speech which grew in anger as it proceeded. "Come, come,"
he concluded, "I will put an end to your prating. You are no
Parliament." He called in his musketeers to clear the House
and lock the doors. While the indignant politicians, most of
whom were men of force and fire, were being hustled into
the street the General's eye fell on the Mace, symbol of the
Speaker's authority. "What shall we do with this bauble?" he
asked. "Take it away!" That night a Cockney wit scribbled
on the door of St Stephen's, "This House to let—unfur-
nished." To this halt then had come that famous effort in
which Selden and Coke had pleaded, and Pym and Hampden had consumed their lives. Here sank for the moment all
the constitutional safeguards and processes built and treas-
ured across the centuries, from Simon de Montfort to the
Petition of Right. One man's will now ruled. One puzzled,
self-questioning, but explosive spirit became for a spell the
guardian of the slowly gathered work of ages, and of the
continuity of the English message.

When the Abbé Siyès returned to Paris after Napoleon's
expulsion of the Republican legislature upon the 18th Bru-

maire, to which he was a party, he remarked to his colleagues in the Directory, "Gentlemen! We have a master." England —nay, England, Scotland, and Ireland—had a master now; and that was all they had. But how different was this master from the glittering adventurer of the eighteenth century! Napoleon was sure of himself. He had no scruples. He knew what he wanted to do. He intended to have supreme power in his hands, and to use that power without limit till he and his family controlled the world. He cared nothing for the past; he knew he had no means of governing the distant future; but the present was his prize and his spoil.

Cromwell, although crafty and ruthless as occasion claimed, was at all times a reluctant and apologetic dictator. He recognised and deplored the arbitrary character of his own rule, but he had no difficulty in persuading himself that his authority sprang both from Above and below. Was he not the new Moses, the chosen Protector of the people of God, commanded to lead them into the Promised Land, if that could indeed be found? Was he not also the only available constable to safeguard "the several forms of godliness in this nation," and especially in the civil sphere the property of God's servants who had been on the right side, against Royalist conspirators or crazy, ravening Levellers? Was he not the Lord General set up by Parliament, now defunct, captain of all the armed forces, the surviving holder of the whole authority of the State, and, as he said, "a person having power over the three nations without bound or limit set"?

Cromwell only desired personal power in order to have things settled in accord with his vision, not of himself or his fame but of the England of his youthful dreams. He was a giant laggard from the Elizabethan age, a "rustic Tudor gentleman, born out of due time," who wished to see Scotland and Ireland brought to their due allegiance, and England "the awe of the Western world, adorned and defended with stout yeomen, honourable magistrates, learned ministers, flourishing universities, invincible fleets." [1] In foreign policy he was still fighting the Spanish Armada, ever ardent to lead his Ironside redcoats against the stakes and faggots of some Grand Inquisitor, or the idolatrous superstitions of an Italian Pope. Were these not now ripe for the sickle; aye, for the same sickle which had shorn down the malignant Cavaliers at Marston Moor and Naseby and had exterminated the Papists of Wexford and Drogheda? In vain did John Thurloe, the able and devoted Secretary to the Council of State, point out, what was already so plain, that Spain was in decay, and that in the ever-growing power of the united France which Richelieu and Mazarin had welded lay the menace of the future. None of this was apparent to the Master. He sharpened his heavy sword for Don Quixote and the successors of Torquemada.

*   *   *   *   *

Cromwell's successes and failures in foreign policy bore consequences throughout the reign of Charles II. He sought to advance the world-interests of Protestantism and the particular needs of British commerce and shipping. In 1654 he ended the sea war against the Dutch which had begun two years earlier. He made ardent proposals for an alliance between the republics of England and Holland, which should form the basis of a Protestant League, capable not only of self-defence but of attacking the Catholic Powers. The Dutch leaders were content to wind up with the least cost to their trading prospects a war in which they knew they were beaten.

Conflict between France and Spain was meanwhile proceeding. Cromwell could choose his side. In spite of grave

[1] G. M. Young, *Charles I and Cromwell*.

arguments to the contrary urged by the Council, he sent a naval expedition to the West Indies in September 1654, and Jamaica was occupied. This act of aggression led slowly but inevitably to war between England and Spain, and a consequent alliance between England and France. In June 1658 six thousand veteran English soldiers in Flanders under Marshal Turenne defeated the Spaniards at the Battle of the Dunes and helped to capture the port of Dunkirk. The blockade of the Spanish coasts disclosed the strength of Britain's sea-power, and one of Blake's captains destroyed a Treasure Fleet off Teneriffe. Cromwell's imperial eye rested long upon Gibraltar. He examined schemes for capturing the marvellous rock. This was reserved for the days of Marlborough, but England retained Dunkirk and Jamaica as a result of Cromwell's war with Spain.

Cromwell found no difficulty in reconciling the predatory aims of the Spanish war with his exertions for a European Protestant League. He was ever ready to strike against the religious persecution of Protestants abroad. When in 1655 he heard that a Protestant sect in the valleys north of Piedmont called the Vaudois were being oppressed and massacred by order of the Duke of Savoy he suspended his negotiations with France and threatened to send the Fleet against the Savoyard port of Nice. When he learnt that war had begun between such good Protestant neighbours as the Swedes and the Danes he tried to persuade the Dutch to take part in joint mediation, and for a time arranged a truce. In the main however Cromwell's foreign policy was more successful in helping British trade and shipping than in checking or reversing the Counter-Reformation. The Mediterranean and Channel were cleared of pirates, foreign trade expanded, and the whole world learnt to respect British sea-power. The poet Waller could write:

The sea's our own; and now all nations greet
With bending sails, each vessel of our fleet;
Your power extends as far as winds can blow
Or swelling sails upon the globe may go.

And Dryden:

He made us freemen of the Continent
    Whom nature did like captives treat before;
To nobler preys the English lion sent
    And taught him first in Belgian walks to roar.

*   *   *   *   *

But how to find a worthy, docile Parliament, with the fear
of God and the root of the matter in their hearts, to aid and
comfort the Lord Protector in his task? He sought a Parliament whose authority would relieve him from the reproach
of a despotism similar to that which he had punished in "the
Man of Blood," which would sustain, and within respectful
limits correct, his initiative, without of course diverging from
his ideals or hampering his sword or signet. But such Parliaments do not exist. Parliaments are awkward things. They
have a knack of developing collective opinions of their own,
which they derive from those who elect them. Cromwell
sought the right kind of Parliament to limit his own dictatorship without crossing his will, and he boxed the compass in
his search. He tried in succession a Puritan oligarchy, an upper middle-class Assembly sprinkled with men who had risen
through military service, then in despair a naked military dictatorship, and finally a return to constitutional monarchy in
all but name. He had expelled the Rump in the cause of an
overdue popular election. He replaced it not by an elected
but by a handpicked body of Puritan notables, who became
known to history as "Barebone's Parliament," after one of

their members, Praise-God Barebone. This was to be a Parliament of Saints, with trustworthy political records. The independent or congregational Churches drew up a panel, from which the Council of Officers chose a hundred and twenty-nine English representatives and—thus revealing their sense of proportion—five Scottish and six Irish nominees. They were, said Cromwell in his address to the Assembly in July 1653, "a people chosen by God to do His Work and to show forth His Praise." But a pregnant unfinished sentence from his speech showed his pricks of conscience about nomination instead of election: "If it were a time to compare your standing with those that have been called by the suffrages of the people, who can tell how soon God may fit the people for such a thing, and none can desire it more than I."

The political behaviour of the Saints was a sad disappointment to their convoker. With breath-taking speed they proceeded to sweep the board clear of encumbrances in order to create a new Heaven and earth. They sought to disestablish the Church and abolish tithes without providing any livelihood for the clergy. In a single day's debate they abolished the Court of Chancery. They threatened rights of property and proclaimed Levelling ideas. With a temerity justified only by spiritual promptings, they reformed taxation in a manner which seemed to weaken the security for the soldiers' pay. This was decisive. The Army bristled. Cromwell, to whose advice the Saints no longer hearkened, saw them as a set of dangerous fools. He afterwards referred to his action in convening them as "a story of my own weakness and folly." The Army leaders, wishing to avoid the scandal of another forcible ejection, persuaded or compelled the more moderate Saints to get up very early one morning before the others were awake and pass a resolution yielding back their power to the Lord General from whom it had come. Cromwell did not waste his strength in wrestling against their wish. He declared that his own power had again "become as boundless and unlimited as before," and cast about for other means of cloaking it as decently as possible.

His high place, for all its apparent strength, depended on the precarious balance of Parliament and Army. He could always use the Army against Parliament; but without a Parliament he felt himself very much alone with the Army. The Army leaders were also conscious of the gulf of military rank and social class which separated them from their formidable rank and file. They too held their position by being the champions of the interests and the doctrines of the soldiery. They must find something to fight against or they would be needed no longer. Thus the whole cluster of these serious, practical, and hitherto triumphant revolutionaries needed to set up a Parliament, if only to have something to pull down. Ireton had died in Ireland, but Lambert and other Army leaders of various ranks drew up an "Instrument of Government," which was in fact the first and last written English Constitution. The executive office of Lord Protector conferred upon Cromwell was checked and balanced by a Council of State, nominated for life, consisting of seven Army leaders and eight civilians. A single Chamber was also set up, elected upon a new property qualification in the country. The old one had been the possession of a forty-shilling-a-year freehold; the new one was the ownership of personal estate with a capital value of two hundred pounds. It was probably not a narrower franchise, but all those who had fought against Parliament were disqualified from voting. Cromwell gratefully accepted the Instrument and assumed the title of Lord Protector.

But once again all went wrong with the Parliament. It no sooner met in September 1654 than it was seen to contain a fierce and lively Republican group, which, without the slightest gratitude to the Army leaders or to the Protector for their apparent deference to Republican ideas, set themselves to tear the new Constitution to pieces. Cromwell at once excluded the Republicans from the House. But even then the remaining Parliamentary majority sought to limit the degree of religious toleration guaranteed by the Instrument, to restrict the Lord Protector's control of the Army, and to reduce both its size and pay. This was carrying the farce too far. At the earliest moment allowed by the Instrument Cromwell dissolved the Commons. His farewell speech was a catalogue of reproaches; they had, he said, neglected their opportunities, and by attacking the Army had undermined national security and polluted the political atmosphere. "It looks," he added severely, "as if a laying of grounds for a quarrel had been designed, rather than to give the people a settlement." So here he was back at the old and ever-recurring problem. "I am as much for government by consent as any man," he told a critical Republican. "But"—pertinent inquiry—"where shall we find consent?"

Military dictatorship supervened, naked if not wholly unashamed. A Royalist colonel named Penruddock managed to capture Salisbury in March 1655. The rising was easily suppressed. But the outbreak, combined with the discovery by Thurloe, who directed the highly efficient secret service, of a number of abortive plots, convinced the Protector of great danger. "The people," Cromwell had told Parliament, "will prefer their safety to their passions and their real security to forms." He now proceeded to divide England and Wales into eleven districts, over each of which a Major-General was placed, with the command of a troop of horse and a reorganised militia. The Major-Generals were given three functions—police and public order, the collection of special taxes upon acknowledged Royalists, and the strict enforcement of Puritan morality. For some months they addressed themselves with zeal to their task.

None dared withstand the Major-Generals; but the war with Spain was costly and the taxes insufficient. Like Charles I, Cromwell was driven again to summon a Parliament. The Major-Generals assured him of their ability to pack a compliant House. But Levellers, Republicans, and Royalists were able to exploit the discontent against the military dictatorship, and a large number of Members who were known enemies of the Protector were returned. By a strained use of a clause in the Instrument of Government Cromwell managed to exclude a hundred of his opponents from the House, while another fifty or sixty voluntarily withdrew in protest. Even after this purge his attempt to obtain a confirmation of the local rule of the Major-Generals met with such vehement opposition that he was compelled to do without it. Indeed, many of the remaining Members "were so highly incensed against the arbitrary acting of the Major-Generals" that they "searched greedily for any powers that will be ruled and limited by law."

It was at this stage that a group of lawyers and gentry decided to offer Cromwell the crown. "The title of Protector," said one of them, "is not limited by any rule or law; the title of King is." Thus the "Humble Petition and Advice" in 1657 which embodied the proposed Constitution provided not only for the restoration of kingship, but also for the firm re-establishment of Parliament, including a nominated Upper House and a substantial reduction in the powers of the Council of State. Though he called it but "a feather in his cap," Cromwell was not unattracted by the idea of becoming King, and announced that he was "hugely taken with the word settlement." But the Army leaders and still more the soldiers showed at once their inveterate hostility to the trappings of monarchy, and Cromwell had to content himself with the right to nominate his successor to the Protectoral throne. In May 1657 he accepted the main provisions of the new Constitution without the title of King.

The Republicans rightly foresaw that this virtual revival of the monarchy opened the way for a Stuart restoration. Under the terms of the "Humble Petition" Cromwell had agreed to allow the Members whom he had excluded to return to Westminster, while his ablest supporters were taken away to fill the new Upper House. The Republicans could therefore act both inside and outside Parliament against the new régime. Cromwell, in the exaggerated belief that a hostile design was on foot against him, suddenly, in January 1658, dissolved the most friendly Parliament which he had ever had. He ended his speech of dissolution with the words, "Let God judge between you and me." "Amen," answered the unrepentant Republicans.

* * * * *

The maintenance of all privilege and authority in their own hands at home and a policy of aggression and conquest abroad absorbed the main energies of Cromwell and his Council. They were singularly barren in social legislation. Their treatment of the Poor Law has been called "harshness coupled with failure." Much better conditions and more improvements were established under the personal rule of Charles I between 1629 and 1640 than under those who claimed to rule in the name of God and the sovereignty of the Saints. They considered that poverty should be punished rather than relieved.

The English Puritans, like their brethren in Massachusetts, concerned themselves actively with the repression of vice. All betting and gambling were forbidden. In 1650 a law was

passed making adultery punishable by death, a ferocity mitigated by the fact that nothing would convince the juries of
the guilt of the accused. Drunkenness was attacked vigorously
and great numbers of alehouses were closed. Swearing was
an offence punishable by a graduated scale of fines: a duke
paid 30s. for his first offence, a baron 20s., and a squire 10s.
Common people could relieve their feelings at 3s. 4d. Not
much was allowed for their money; one man was fined for
saying "God is my witness," and another for saying "Upon
my life." These were hard times. The feast days of the
Church, regarded as superstitious indulgences, were replaced
by a monthly fast day. Christmas excited the most fervent
hostility of these fanatics. Parliament was deeply concerned
at the liberty which it gave to carnal and sensual delights.
Soldiers were sent round London on Christmas Day before
dinnertime to enter private houses without warrants and seize
meat cooking in all kitchens and ovens. Everywhere was pry-
ing and spying.

All over the country the Maypoles were hewn down, lest
old village dances around them should lead to immorality or
at least to levity. Walking abroad on the Sabbath, except to
go to church, was punished, and a man was fined for going
to a neighbouring parish to hear a sermon. It was even proposed to forbid people sitting at their doors or leaning against
them on the Sabbath. Bearbaiting and cockfighting were effectually ended by shooting the bears and wringing the necks
of the cocks. All forms of athletic sports, horse racing, and
wrestling were banned, and sumptuary laws sought to remove
all ornaments from male and female attire.

One may easily see how desire for office or promotion led
to hypocrisy. If sour looks, upturned eyes, nasal twang,
speech garnished with Old Testament texts, were means to
favour, there were others who could assume them besides

those naturally afflicted by such habits. But behind all this apparatus of cant and malignity stood an army of disciplined sectaries, who constantly extorted increases both of their numbers and their pay, and against whom none could make head. Their generals and colonels soon engrossed to themselves rich landed estates carved out of the Crown lands: Fleetwood became the owner of Woodstock Manor, Lambert of Wimbledon, Okey of Ampthill, and Pride of Nonesuch. Hazelrigg and Birch secured large holdings from the bishoprics of Durham and Hereford. To the mass of the nation however the rule of Cromwell manifested itself in the form of numberless and miserable petty tyrannies, and thus became hated as no Government has ever been hated in England before or since. For the first time the English people felt themselves governed from a centre in the control of which they had no say. Anger and hatred welled the stronger because their expression was difficult. The old kings might have harried the nobles and taxed the rich; but here were personages who had climbed up by lawless, bloody violations, and presumed to order the life and habits of every village and to shift custom from the channels which it had cut in the flow of centuries. What wonder that under the oak leaves, broad and far throughout the countryside, men dreamed fondly of what they called the good old times and yearned for the day when "the King shall enjoy his own again"?

The repulsive features fade from the picture and are replaced by colour and even charm as the summit of power is reached. We see the Lord Protector in his glory, the champion of Protestantism, the arbiter of Europe, the patron of learning and the arts. We feel the dignity of his bearing to all men, and his tenderness toward young people. We feel his passion for England, as fervent as Chatham's, and in some ways more intimate and emotional. No one can remain unconscious of his desire to find a moral basis for his power, or of his sense of a responsibility to his country and his God ranging far beyond the horizon of his life. Although Cromwell easily convinced himself that he had been chosen the Supreme Ruler of the State, he was ever ready to share his power with others, provided of course that they agreed with him. He was willing, indeed anxious, to govern through a Parliament, if that Parliament would carry the laws and taxes he required. But neither his fondlings nor his purgings induced his Parliaments to do his will. Again and again he was forced to use or threaten the power of the sword, and the rule which he sought to make a constitutional alternative to absolutism or anarchy became in practice a military autocracy.

*   *   *   *   *

Nevertheless the dictatorship of Cromwell differed in many ways from modern patterns. Although the Press was gagged and the Royalists ill used, although judges were intimidated and local privileges curtailed, there was always an effective vocal opposition, led by convinced Republicans. There was no attempt to make a party around the personality of the Dictator, still less to make a party state. Respect was shown for private property, and the process of fining the Cavaliers and allowing them to compound by surrendering part of their estates was conducted with technical formality. Few people were put to death for political crimes, and no one was cast into indefinite bondage without trial. "What we gain in a free way," Cromwell had told the Army in 1647, "is better than twice as much in a forced, and will be more truly ours and our posterities'. . . . That which you have by force I look upon as nothing."

Liberty of conscience as conceived by Cromwell did not extend to the public profession of Roman Catholicism,

Prelacy, or Quakerism. He banned open celebration of the Mass and threw hundreds of Quakers into prison. But such limitations to freedom of worship were caused less by religious prejudice than by fear of civil disturbance. Religious toleration challenged all the beliefs of Cromwell's day and found its best friend in the Lord Protector himself. Believing the Jews to be a useful element in the civil community, he opened again to them the gates of England, which Edward I had closed nearly four hundred years before. There was in practice comparatively little persecution on purely religious grounds, and even Roman Catholics were not seriously molested. Cromwell's dramatic intervention on behalf of a blaspheming Quaker and Unitarian whom Parliament would have put to death as well as tortured proves that he was himself the source of many mitigations. A man who in that bitter age could write, "We look for no compulsion but that of light and reason," and who could dream of a union and a right understanding embracing Jews and Gentiles, cannot be wholly barred from his place in the forward march of liberal ideas.

Although a very passionate man when fully roused, he was frequently harassed by inner doubts and conflicts. His strict Puritan upbringing and the soul-stressing of his youth had left him, even though convinced that he belonged to the Chosen People of God, without any certainty as to his own righteousness. Though he attributed his political and military victories to the special interventions of Providence, he could write to a friend that he feared he was liable to "make too much" of "outward dispensations." This uncertainty about himself excused opportunism, and reflected itself in his famous utterance, "No man goes so high as he who knows not where he is going." His doubts about political objectives became increasingly marked in his last years, and he grew more and more dependent on the advice and opinions of others. And thus there was ever a conflict in the man between his conviction of his divine right to rule for the good of the people and a genuine Christian humility at his own unworthiness. "Is it possible to fall from grace?" he inquired of his chaplain on his deathbed. On being reassured, he said, "Then I am saved, for I know that once I was in grace."

On September 3, 1658, the anniversary of the Battles of Dunbar and Worcester and of the massacre of Drogheda, in the crash and howling of a mighty storm, death came to the Lord Protector. He had always been a good and faithful family man, and his heart had been broken by the death of his favourite and least Puritan daughter. He nominated his eldest son, Richard, a harmless country gentleman, as his successor, and for the moment none disputed his will. If in a tremendous crisis Cromwell's sword had saved the cause of Parliament, he must stand before history as a representative of dictatorship and military rule who, with all his qualities as a soldier and a statesman, is in lasting discord with the genius of the English race.

Yet if we look beneath the surface to the rock he is revealed as its defence not only against the ambitions of generals, but from the wild and unimaginable forms of oppression in which the Ironside veterans might have used their power. With all his faults and failures he was indeed the Lord Protector of the enduring rights of the Old England he loved against the terrible weapon which he and Parliament had forged to assert them. Without Cromwell there might have been no advance, without him no collapse, without him no recovery. Amid the ruins of every institution, social and political, which had hitherto guided the Island life he towered up, gigantic, glowing, indispensable, the sole agency by which time could be gained for healing and regrowth.

The Restoration

I T proved impossible to fill the void which the death of the Lord Protector had created. In his last hours Cromwell had in terms "very dark and imperfect" nominated his eldest son, Richard, to succeed him. "Tumbledown Dick," as his enemies nicknamed him, was a respectable person with good intentions, but without the force and capacity required by the severity of the times. He was at first accepted by the Army and duly installed in his father's seat; but when he attempted to exercise authority he found he had but the form. The first appointment Richard Cromwell sought to make in the Army, of which his own brother-in-law, Charles Fleetwood, was Commander-in-Chief, was objected to by the Council of Officers. Richard was made aware alike that the command of the Army was not hereditary, and also that it could not remain unfilled. His brother, Henry, who was both able and energetic, strove like Richard to strengthen the civil power even at the expense of the monarchical attributes of the Protector's office. Upon Henry Cromwell's advice Parliament was summoned.

It was of course a Parliament from which all Royalists were formally excluded, and one which the ever-active Thurloe made a supreme effort to pack with Protectorate supporters. Nevertheless it immediately raised the large issues of government. After Richard had opened it in due state and delivered his "speech from the throne" the Commons set themselves without delay to restore the principles of the Commonwealth and to control the Army. They questioned the validity of all Acts since the purge of 1657 had robbed Parliament of its representative integrity. They sought to transfer the allegiance of the Army from the Protector to themselves. The Army leaders were however determined to preserve their independent power. They complained of the conduct of the Commons and that the "good old cause" was endangered. "For this cause," they said, "we have covered ourselves with blood; we shudder when we think of the account which we must one day give if we suffer the blood-bought liberties of the people to be again destroyed." The Commons thought it unbearable that the Army should establish itself as a separate Estate of the Realm. They called upon the assembled officers to return to their military duties. "It would fare ill with Parliament," they declared, "if they could no longer order them to return to their posts." They resolved that every officer should pledge himself in writing not to interrupt the sittings and debates of Parliament.

In their conflict with the Army they became willing to entrust the chief command to the Protector. This brought the dispute to a head. Both sides marshalled their forces; but although at first it seemed that both the Protectorate and Parliament had a proportion of the officers and a number of the regiments at their disposal, the will of the inferior officers and the rank and file prevailed over all. Within four months of succeeding to his august office Richard Cromwell found himself deserted even by his personal guard. The immediate dissolution of Parliament was demanded, and a Committee of Officers waited all night for compliance. In the morning they were obeyed. The Commons Members who sought to assemble were once again turned back by the troops. The Army was master, with Fleetwood and Lambert rivals at its head. These generals would have been content to leave Richard a limited dignity, but the spirit of the troops had become hostile to the Protectorate. They were resolved upon a pure republic, in which their military interest and sectarian and Anabaptist doctrines should hold the chief place.

Even in this hour of bloodless and absolute triumph the soldiery felt the need of some civil sanction for their acts. But where could they find it? At length an expedient was suggested to them. They declared that they recollected that the members of the Parliamentary assembly which sat in April 1653 had been "champions of the good old cause and had been throughout favoured with God's assistance." They went to the house of the former Speaker, Lenthall, and invited him and his surviving colleagues of 1653 to renew the exercise of their powers, and in due course, to the number of forty-two, these astonished Puritan grandees resumed the seats from which they had been expelled six years earlier. Thus was the Rump of the Long Parliament exhumed and exhibited to a bewildered land.

A Council of State was formed in which the three principal Republican leaders, Vane, Hazelrigg, and Scott, sat with eight generals and eighteen other Members of Parliament. Provision was made for Oliver Cromwell's sons, whose acquiescence in the abolition of the Protectorate was desired. Their debts were paid; they were provided with residences and incomes. Richard accepted these proposals at once, and Henry after some hesitation. Both lived unharmed to the end of their days. The Great Seal of the Protectorate was broken in two. The Army declared that they recognised Fleetwood as their Commander-in-Chief, but they agreed that the commissions of high officers should be signed by the Speaker in the name of the Commonwealth. A Republican Constitution based on the representative principle was set up, and all the authorities in the land submitted themselves to it. But the inherent conflict between the Army and Parliament continued. "I know not why," observed General Lambert, "they should not be at our mercy as well as we at theirs."

While these stresses racked the Republican administration in London a widespread Royalist movement broke out in the country. The recent changes at the centre of government had brought to power inveterate opponents of the Stuart house. There seemed good reason for an appeal to force. In the summer of 1659 Cavaliers, strangely consorting with Presbyterian allies, appeared in arms in several counties. They were at their strongest in Lancashire and Cheshire, where the Derby influence was lively. Sir George Booth was soon at the head of a large force. Against him Lambert marched with five thousand men. At Winnington Bridge, on August 19, the Royalists were chased from the field, although, as Lambert said in his dispatch, "the horse on both sides fought like Englishmen." Elsewhere the Cavalier gatherings were dispersed by the local militia. The revolt was so swiftly crushed that Charles II, fortunately for himself, had no chance of putting himself at its head. The Army had with equal ease overthrown the adherents of the Protectorate and of the monarchy. The clatter of arms reminded the generals of their power, and they were soon again in sharp dispute with the truncated Parliament they had resuscitated.

At this moment Lambert became the most prominent figure. He had returned to London from the victory at Winnington Bridge with most of his troops. In October, when Parliament, offended at his arrogance, sought to dismiss him and his colleagues from their commands he took the lead in bringing his regiments to Westminster and barred all the entrances to St Stephen's Chapel. Even Speaker Lenthall, who had signed the generals' commissions, was prevented from entering. When he asked indignantly "did they not know him" the soldiers replied that they had not noticed him at Winnington Bridge. No blood was shed, but the chief power passed for the moment into Lambert's hands.

Lambert was a man of high ability, with a military record second only to Oliver Cromwell's and a wide knowledge of politics. He did not attempt to make himself Lord Protector. Far different were the ideas that stirred him. His wife, a woman of culture and good family, cherished Royalist sympathies and family ambitions. A plan was proposed, to which she and the General lent themselves, for the marriage of their daughter to Charles II's brother, the Duke of York, as part of a process by which Lambert, if he became chief magistrate of the Republic, would restore the King to the throne. This project was seriously entertained on both sides; and the extreme lenience shown to all the Royalists taken prisoner in the recent rising was a part of it. Lambert seems to have believed that he could satisfy the Army, both in politics and religion, better under a restored monarchy than under either the Rump or a Protectorate. His course was secret, tortuous, and full of danger. Already Fleetwood's suspicions were aroused, and a deep antagonism grew between these two military chiefs. At the same time the Army, sensing its own disunity, began to have misgivings about its violent actions against Parliament.

Sternest and most unbending of the Republican Members was Hazelrigg, whose pale face, thin lips, and piercing eyes imparted to all the impression of Brutus-like constancy. Hazelrigg, barred from the Commons, hastened to Portsmouth, and convinced the garrison that the troops in London had done wrong to great principles. When Fleetwood and Lambert, themselves divided, sent a force to invest Portsmouth Hazelrigg converted the besiegers to his views. This portion of the Ironside Army presently set out for London in order to take a hand in the settlement of affairs. The schism in the rank and file was beginning to destroy the self-confidence of the troops and put an end to the rule of the sword in England. At Christmas the Army resolved to be reconciled with Parliament. "Let us live and die with Parliament," they shouted. They marched to Chancery Lane and drew up before the house of Speaker Lenthall. Instead of the disrespect with which they had so recently treated him, the soldiers now expressed their penitence for having suspended the sittings of the House. They submitted themselves to the authority of Parliament and hailed the Speaker as their general and the father of their country. But obviously this could not last. Someone must set in train the movement which would produce in England a Government which stood for something old or new. It was from another quarter that deliverance was to come.

*　*　*　*　*

The Cromwellian commander in Scotland, though very different in temperament from Lambert, was also a man of mark. Once again England was to be saved by a man who was not in a hurry. George Monk, a Devonshire gentleman, who had in his youth received a thorough military training in the Dutch wars, had come back to England at the beginning of the Great Rebellion equipped with rare professional knowledge. He was a soldier of fortune, caring more for plying his trade than for the causes at stake. He had fought for Charles I in all three kingdoms. After being captured and imprisoned by the Roundheads he went over to their side, and soon gained an important command. He fought in Ireland, and at sea against the Dutch. He had steered his way through all the hazardous channels and storms, supporting in turn and at the right moment Parliament, the Commonwealth, and the Protectorate. He brought Scotland, in Oliver Cromwell's day, into complete subjection, but without incurring any lasting animosity. He ranged himself from the first against the violence of the Army in London. Moving with the sentiments of the Scottish people, he gained from a Convention supplies to maintain his army without causing offence. He purged his command of all officers whom he could not trust. Lambert, still pursuing his ill-assorted designs, now found himself confronted by Monk. Monk used the watchwords of Parliament and Law; he commanded the sympathy of the English Republicans and the complete confidence of the Scots, whose interests he promised to safeguard. Lambert, who had marched North from London in November 1659 with a powerful army, was devoid of any acknowledgeable cause, seemed to stand for nothing but military violence, and had to maintain his troops by forced contributions from the countryside, to its extreme disgust and scandal.

Monk was one of those Englishmen who understand to perfection the use of time and circumstances. It is a type which has thriven in our Island. The English are apt to admire men who do not attempt to dominate events or turn the drift of fate; who wait about doing their duty on a short view from day to day until there is no doubt whether the tide is on the ebb or the flow; and who then, with the appearance of great propriety and complete self-abnegation, with steady, sterling qualities of conduct if not of heart, move slowly, cautiously, forward towards the obvious purpose of the nation. During the autumn of 1659 General Monk in his headquarters on the Tweed with his well-ordered army of about seven thousand men was the object of passionate solicitations from every quarter. They told him he had the future of England in his hands, and all appealed for his goodwill. The General received the emissaries of every interest and party in his camp. He listened patiently, as every great Englishman should, to all they had to urge, and with that simple honesty of character on which we flatter ourselves as a race he kept them all guessing for a long time what he would do.

At length when all patience was exhausted Monk acted. Informed of events in London, he crossed the Tweed from Coldstream on the cold, clear New Year's Day of 1660. In spite of all his precautions his anxieties about his troops were well founded. In the general uncertainty he held them only from day to day. The Roundhead veteran Thomas Fairfax now appeared in York, and rallied a large following for a Free Parliament. Monk had promised to be with him or perish within ten days. He kept his word. At York he received what he had long hoped for, the invitation of the House of Commons, the desperate Rump, to come to London. He marched south through towns and counties in which there was but one cry—"A free Parliament!" When Monk and his troops reached London he was soon angered by the peremptory orders given him by the Rump, including one to pull down the City gates in order to overawe the capital. For the City was now turning Royalist and collecting funds for Charles II. Unlike Cromwell and Lambert, Monk decided to tame the Rump by diluting, not by dissolving it. In February he recalled the Members who had been excluded by Pride's Purge. These were mainly Presbyterians, most of whom had become at heart Royalists. The restoration of the monarchy came into sight. On the night of the return of the excluded Members Samuel Pepys saw the City of London "from one end to another with a glory about it, so high was the light of the bonfires and so thick round it, . . . and the bells rang everywhere." The restored Parliament as their first act declared invalid all Acts and transactions since Pride's Purge in 1648. They had been ejected by one general. They were restored by another. The interval of twelve years had been filled by events without name or sanction. They declared Monk Commander-in-Chief of all the forces. The Rump of the Long Parliament was dissolved by its own consent. Monk was satisfied that a free Parliament should be summoned, and that such a Parliament would certainly recall Charles II. He was genuinely convinced after his march from Scotland that the mass of the English people were tired of constitutional experiments and longed for the return of the monarchy.

It was most plainly the wish of the people that the King should "enjoy his own again." This simple phrase, sprung from the heart of the common folk, also made its dominating appeal to rank and fortune. It was carried, in spite of Major-Generals and their myrmidons, on the wings of a joyous melody from village to village and manor to manor.

> Till then upon Ararat's hill,
> My hope shall cast her anchor still,
> Until I see some peaceful dove
> Bring home the Branch she dearly love:
> Then will I wait, till the waters abate,
> Which now disturb my troubled brain:
> Else never rejoice till I hear the voice
> That the King enjoys his own again.

But there was a vast pother of matters which must be settled. This was no time for vengeance. If the Parliamentary Army was to bring back the King it must not be by any stultification of their vigorous exertions against his father. But here the latent wisdom of the Island played its part. In the hour of victory there had been excesses, and the principles of the Great Rebellion had been unduly extended. It was necessary to recur to the original position in theory, but not in practice. Monk sent word to Charles II advising him to offer a free and general pardon, subject only to certain exceptions to be fixed by Parliament; to promise full payment of the soldiers' arrears, and to confirm the land sales. Here was an England where a substantial part of the land, the main source of wealth and distinction, had passed into other hands. These changes had been made good in the field. They could not be entirely undone. The King might enjoy his own again, but not all the Cavaliers. There must be a full recognition that men should keep what they had got or still had left. There must be no reprisals. Everyone must start fair on the new basis.

But sacred blood had flowed. Those living who had shed it were few and identifiable. If everyone else who had profited by the Parliamentary victory could be sure they would not be affected or penalised there would not be much objection on their part to punishing the regicides. The deed of 1649 was contrary to law, against the presumptive will of Parliament, and abhorrent to the nation. Let those who had done it pay the price. This somewhat unheroic solution was found to be in harmony with that spirit of compromise which has played so invaluable a part in British affairs.

Monk's advice was accepted by Charles's faithful Chancellor, Hyde, who had shared his master's exile and was soon to be rewarded with the Earldom of Clarendon. Hyde drafted Charles's manifesto called the Declaration of Breda. In this document the King promised to leave all thorny problems for future Parliaments to settle. It was largely due to Hyde's lawyerly concern for Parliament and precedent that the Restoration came to stand for the return of good order and the revival, after Cromwell's experiments, of the country's ancient institutions.

While the negotiations reached their final form the elections for a new Parliament were held. Nominally those who had borne arms against the Republic were excluded, but the Royalist tide flowed so strongly that this ban had no effect.

Presbyterians and Royalists found themselves in a great majority, and the Republicans and Anabaptists went down before them in every county. In vain did they rise in arms; in vain did they propose to recall Richard Cromwell who was about to seek refuge in France. They were reminded that they themselves had cast him out. Lambert, escaping from the Tower, in which he had been confined, prepared to dispute the quarrel in the field. His men deserted him, and he was recaptured without bloodshed. This fiasco sealed the Restoration. Monk, the bulk of his army, the City militia, the Royalists throughout the land, the great majority of the newly elected House of Commons, the peers, who assembled again as if nothing had happened, were all banded together, and knew that they had the power. The Lords and Commons were restored. It remained only to complete the three Estates of the Realm by the recall of the King.

Parliament hastened to send the exiled Charles a large sum of money for his convenience, and soon concerned itself with the crimson velvet furniture of his coaches of State. The Fleet, once so hostile, was sent to conduct him to his native shores. Immense crowds awaited him at Dover. There on May 25, 1660, General Monk received him with profound reverence as he landed. The journey to London was triumphal. All classes crowded to welcome the King home to his own. They cheered and wept in uncontrollable emotion. They felt themselves delivered from a nightmare. They now dreamed they had entered a Golden Age. Charles, Clarendon, Nicholas, the well-tried secretary, and a handful of wanderers who had shared the royal misfortunes gazed about them in astonishment. Could this be the same island from which they had escaped so narrowly only a few years back? Still more must Charles have wondered whether he slept or waked when on Blackheath he saw the dark, glistening col-

umns of the Ironside Army drawn up in stately array and
dutiful obedience. It was but eight years since he had hidden
from its patrols in the branches of the Boscobel oak. It was
but a few months since they had driven his adherents into
rout at Winnington Bridge. The entry to the City was a blaze
of thanksgiving. The Lord Mayor and Councillors of rebel
London led the festival. The Presbyterian divines obstructed
his passage only to have the honour of presenting the Bible
amid their fervent salutations. Both Houses of Parliament
acknowledged their devotion to his rights and person. And all
around the masses, rich and poor, Cavalier and Roundhead,
Episcopalian, Presbyterian, and Independent, framed a scene
of reconciliation and rejoicing without compare in history. It
was England's supreme day of joy.

*　　*　　*　　*　　*

The wheel had not however swung a full circle, as many
might have thought. This was not only the restoration of the
monarchy; it was the restoration of Parliament. Indeed, it was
the greatest hour in Parliamentary history. The House of Commons had broken the Crown in the field; it had at length
mastered the terrible Army it had created for that purpose.
It had purged itself of its own excesses, and now stood forth
beyond all challenge, or even need of argument, as the dominant institution of the realm. All that was solid in the constitutional claims put forward against Charles I had become so
deeply rooted that it was not even necessary to mention it. All
the laws of the Long Parliament since Charles I quitted
London at the beginning of 1642, all the statutes of the
Commonwealth or of the Protectorate, now fell to the ground.
But there remained the potent limitations of the Prerogative to which Charles I had agreed. The statutes to which
he had set his seal were valid. The work of 1641 still stood.
Above all, everyone now took it for granted that the Crown

was the instrument of Parliament and the King the servant of his people.

Though the doctrine of Divine Right was again proclaimed, that of Absolute Power had been abandoned. The criminal jurisdiction of the Privy Council, the Star Chamber, and the High Commission Court were gone. The idea of the Crown levying taxes without the consent of Parliament or by ingenious and questionable devices had vanished. All legislation henceforward stood upon the majorities of legally elected Parliaments, and no royal ordinance could resist or replace it. The Restoration achieved what Pym and Hampden had originally sought, and rejected the excesses into which they had been drawn by the stress of conflict and the crimes and follies of war and dictatorship. The victory of the Commons and the Common Law was permanent.

A new conception of sovereignty had now been born. In their early conflicts with Charles I and his father the Parliamentarians had not aimed at abolishing the Prerogative altogether. The Common Lawyers had borne the brunt of the struggle, and the principles for which they had contended were in the main Common Law principles. They had struggled to ensure that the King should be under the law. This meant the law for which Magna Carta was felt to stand—traditional law, the kind of law which made Englishmen free from arbitrary arrest and arbitrary punishment; the law that had for centuries been declared in the courts of Common Law. Parliament had not striven to make itself omnipotent, nor to destroy the traditional powers of the Crown, but to control their exercise so that the liberties of Parliament and of the individual were safeguarded and protected. Coke had claimed that judges were the highest interpreters of the law. During the years without a King, and without the Royal Prerogative, the idea had emerged that an Act of Parliament was the final authority. This had no root in the past, nor was it part of the lawyers' case. Power had passed from the lawyers to the leaders of cavalry, and they had left their mark upon the Constitution. Coke's claim that the fundamental law of custom and tradition could not be overborne, even by Crown and Parliament together, and his dream of judges in a Supreme Court of Common Law declaring what was or what was not legal, had been extinguished in England for ever. It survived in New England across the ocean, one day to emerge in an American revolution directed against both Parliament and Crown.

* * * * *

Finance at the Restoration was, as ever, an immediate and thorny subject. Large sums were needed, apart from the ordinary charges, for paying off the Army and the debts contracted by the King in exile. The debts of the Protectorate were heartily repudiated. The King relinquished his feudal dues from wardships, knight service, and other medieval survivals. Parliament granted him instead revenues for life which, with his hereditary property, were calculated to yield about £1,200,000. This was keeping him very strait, and in fact the figure proved optimistic, but he and his advisers professed themselves content. The country was impoverished by the ordeal through which it had passed; the process of tax collection was grievously deranged; a settlement for life was not to be disdained. For all extraordinary expenditure the King was dependent upon Parliament, and both he and Clarendon accepted this. The Crown was not to be free of Parliament.

But both Crown and Parliament were to be free of the Army. That force, which had grown to forty thousand men, unequalled in fighting quality in the world, was to be dispersed, and nothing like it was on any account to be raised ever again. "No standing Army," was to be the common watchword of all parties.

Such decisions of the united nation, which laid the scalpel on so many festering wounds, could not, however necessary, be received without pain and wincing by those affected. The Cavaliers were mortified that the vindication of their cause brought them no relief from the mulctings of which they had been the victims. In vain they protested that the Act of Oblivion and Indemnity was in fact one of oblivion for past services and indemnity for past crimes. They were scandalised that only those who had actually condemned the Royal Martyr should be punished, while those who had compassed and achieved his ruin in bloody war and wreaked their malice on his faithful friends should escape scot-free and even be enriched. Everyone however, except the soldiers, was agreed about getting rid of the Army; and that this could be done, and done without bloodshed, seemed a miracle. The Ironside soldiers were abashed by public opinion. Every hand was turned against them. After all the services they had rendered, the victories they had won in the field, the earnest efforts they had made to establish a godly Government for the realm, the restraints of personal conduct they had observed, they found themselves universally detested. They were to be thrust out into the darkness. But they yielded themselves to the tide of opinion. They were paid their dues. They returned to their homes and their former callings, and within a few months this omnipotent, invincible machine, which might at any moment have devoured the whole realm and society of Britain, vanished in the civil population, leaving scarcely a trace behind. Henceforward they showed themselves examples of industry and sobriety, as formerly of valour and zeal.

Of about sixty men who had signed the late King's death warrant a third were dead, a third had fled, and a bare twenty remained. King Charles strove against his loyal Parliament to save as many as possible. Feeling ran high. The King fought for clemency for his father's murderers, and Parliament, many of whose Members had abetted their action, clamoured for retribution. In the end nine suffered the extreme penalty of treason. They were the scapegoats of collective crime. Nearly all of them gloried in their deed. Harrison and other officers stepped upon the scaffold with the conviction that posterity would salute their sacrifice. Hugh Peters, the fiery preacher, alone showed weakness, but the example of his comrades and a strong cordial sustained him, and when the executioner, knife in hand, covered with blood, met him in the shambles with "How does that suit you, Dr Peters?" he answered steadfastly that it suited him well enough.

The numbers of those executed fell so far short of the public demand that an addition was made to the bloody scene which at any rate cost no more life. The corpses of Cromwell, Ireton, and Bradshaw were pulled out of their coffins in Westminster Abbey, where they had been buried a few years earlier in solemn state, drawn through the streets on hurdles to Tyburn, hanged upon the three-cornered gibbet for twenty-four hours, their heads spiked up in prominent places, and the remains cast upon the dunghill. Pym and twenty other Parliamentarians were also disinterred and buried in a pit. Such ghoulish warring with the dead was enforced by the ferocity of public opinion, to which the King was glad to throw carcasses instead of living men.

Only two other persons in England were condemned to death, General Lambert and Sir Harry Vane. Lambert had a wild career behind him, and in the last year of the Republic might at any moment have laid his hands upon supreme power. We have seen the plans which he had indulged for his daughter's marriage. He had imagined himself as the Constable of the Restoration, forestalling Monk, or alternatively as a successor of His Highness the Lord Protector after destroying Monk. He was a man of limitless audacity and long experience in military revolution. But all just failed. Now Lambert, the Ironside general, hero of a dozen fields, humbled himself before his judges. He sought mercy from the King. He found in the King's brother, the Duke of York, a powerful advocate. He was pardoned, and lived the rest of his life in Guernsey, "with liberty to move about the island," and later in Plymouth, consoling himself with painting and botany.

Vane was of tougher quality. He scorned to sue for mercy, and so spirited was his defence, so searching his law and logic, that he might well have been indulged. But there was one incident in his past which now proved fatal to him. It was remembered that twenty years before he had purloined, and disclosed to Pym, his father's notes of the Privy Council meeting, alleging that Strafford had advised the bringing of an Irish army into England, thus sealing Strafford's fate. If debts were to be paid, this was certainly not one to be overlooked. Charles showed no desire to spare him. "He is too dangerous to let live," the King said, "if we can honestly put him out of the way." He met his death with the utmost alacrity and self-confidence, and the blare of trumpets drowned the cogent arguments he sought to offer to the hostile crowd.

Almost the only notable in Scotland to suffer death at the Restoration was the Marquess of Argyll. He came to London to join in the royal welcome, but was immediately arrested. Charles, wishing to be rid of the burden, sent him back to Scotland to be tried by his peers and fellow countrymen. The restored King had had a long fight to minimise these gruesome deeds. "I am weary of hanging," he said. But the Scottish Parliament in the temper of the new hour made haste to send their former guide and mentor to the block. He too died with unflinching courage and with exemplary piety; but everyone felt it was quits for Montrose. In all therefore, through Charles's exertions, and at some expense to his popularity, less than a dozen persons were put to death in this intense Counter-Revolution. By an ironic contrivance which Charles must have enjoyed, they were made to be condemned by some of the principal accessories to and profiteers by their crimes. Leading figures of the Parliamentary party, peers and commoners, high officers under the Republic or Cromwell, made ready shift to sit upon the tribunals which slaughtered the regicides; and it is upon these that history may justly cast whatever odium belongs to these melancholy but limited reprisals.

The Merry Monarch

THE Parliament which recalled the King was a balanced assembly, and represented both sides of the nation. It surmounted the grave political difficulties of the Restoration with success. It had however no constitutional validity, since it had not been summoned by royal writ. This was considered to be a fatal defect. The King, who thought he might well go farther and fare worse, cast his royal authority over the assembly, endorsing retrospectively the action taken in calling them together. But this was felt not to achieve a perfect legality. The House could not claim to be a Parliament, but only a Convention. At the end of 1660 it was thought necessary to dissolve it. This concession to a newly recovered respect for law prevented all chance of a religious settlement which would embrace the whole nation. The elections expressed the delight of a liberated people. The Royalists had done nothing at the Restoration. They had been completely beaten and cowed. Their turn had now come. An overwhelming anti-Puritan majority presented itself at Westminster; and from their ruined homes and mutilated estates, where they had been glad to bury themselves during Cromwell's tyranny, came the men or their sons who had charged with Rupert.

The longest Parliament in English history now began. It lasted eighteen years. It has been called the Cavalier Parliament—or, more significantly, the Pension Parliament. It was composed at first of men well past their prime and of broken veterans of the war, but when it was eventually dissolved all except two hundred of them had been replaced at by-elections, often by Roundheads or their heirs. From the moment when it first met it showed itself more Royalist in theory than in practice. It rendered all honour to the King. It had no intention of being governed by him. The many landed gentry who had been impoverished in the royal cause were not blind monarchists. They did not mean to part with any of the Parliamentary rights which had been gained in the struggle. They were ready to make provision for the defence of the country by means of militia; but the militia must be controlled by the Lord-Lieutenants of the counties. They vehemently asserted the supremacy of the Crown over the armed forces; but they took care that the only troops in the country should be under the local control of their own class. Thus not only the King but Parliament was without an army. The repository of force had now become the county families and gentry. Having established this as the result of bitter experiences and long meditation, the Cavalier Parliament addressed itself to religion, with special regard to the political and social aspects, and to its own interests.

From the days of Queen Elizabeth down to the Civil War the aim of the monarchy had been the establishment of an all-including National Church, based upon the Prayer Book and Episcopacy. There was also the desire to unite the life and faith of England and Scotland. These aims, even extending to Ireland, had been achieved under totally different forms in a brutal fashion by the sword of Cromwell. Against all this, both in Church and State, in Parliament and the Court, there was now a profound reaction.

Since Clarendon as Lord Chancellor was the chief Minister, and preponderant in the Government, his name is identified with the group of Acts which re-established the Anglican Church and drove the Protestant sects into enduring opposition. Charles would have preferred to take the way of

toleration, Clarendon that of comprehension. But the zeal of
the Cavalier Parliament, of the followers of Laud, now returned from exile, and of some recalcitrant Presbyterian leaders baffled them both. Parliament recognised that there were
religious bodies definitely outside the National Church, and
determined, if not to extirpate them, at least to leave them
outside under grievous disabilities. In so doing it consolidated
Nonconformity as a political force with clear objectives: first,
toleration, which was secured at the Revolution of 1688; and
thereafter the abolition of the privileged status of the Church.
But this latter was only attained, and that partially, when in
the nineteenth century the vote of the commercial and industrial middle class became a decisive factor in political
combinations. An exact assessment of the influence of Nonconformity on English political thought would be difficult to
make. It carried forward much of the old Puritan austerity
and stubbornness, with much of its narrowness. Its learning was
often great. Perhaps a comprehensive Church with wide
terms of subscription would best have served the cause of religion. But it is also possible that the variety of religious
thought which Nonconformity provided could not have been
contained within a State Church however broadly based, and
that the Three Bodies, as they came to be called—Presbyterians with their rationalism, Congregationalists with their
independence, Baptists with their fervour—were expressions
of deeply seated and divergent tendencies of the English
mind.

For good or for ill, the "Clarendon Code" was a parting of
the ways. It destroyed all chance of a United National
Church. The Episcopacy, unconsciously perhaps, but de-
cidedly, accepted the position not of the leaders of a nation-
wide faith but of a sect. It was "the Great Sect," "the official
sect," "the established sect"; but still a sect. Outside were all

the forms of Dissent or Nonconformity. The Convention Parliament might well have made a compromise which would have joined together the great majority of Christians of the Protestant faith in England. The Cavalier Parliament accepted the schism, and rejoiced in belonging to the larger, richer, and more favoured section. They built upon their system not a nation but a party. The country gentlemen and landowners who had fought for God and King should have their own Church and bishops, as they now had their own militia and their own Commission of the Peace.

The Clarendon Code of 1662 went some way beyond the ideas of Clarendon himself. He had hoped for a union in Church and State, inspired by the heart-melting of the Restoration. Neither did Charles will this great separation. He walked by the easy path of indifference to the uplands of toleration. He was certainly not spiritually minded. If a gentleman was going to be religious perhaps Rome would give him the greatest satisfaction. But then what trouble that would make, and was not the Anglican Church the mainstay of the Throne? He wished to see all the religious fervour cooled and abated. Why distract this world for the sake of the next? Why ill-use people because they would not agree upon the various doubtful and disputable methods of obtaining salvation? He would have liked to anticipate and appropriate the blunt declaration of Frederick the Great: "In Prussia everyone must get to Heaven in his own way." But he did not intend to make trouble about his personal view. He did his best at every stage for toleration and shrugged his shoulders at the rest. "Of this you may be sure," he said to a deputation of Quakers during the Convention Parliament, "that you shall none of you suffer for your opinions or religious beliefs, so long as you live peaceably, and you have the word of a King for it."

The Cavalier Parliament sternly corrected this deplorable laxity. The Clarendon Code consisted of a series of statutes: the Corporation Act of 1661 required all persons holding municipal office to renounce the Solemn League and Covenant—a test which excluded many of the Presbyterians; to take the oath of non-resistance—which excluded Republicans; and to receive the Sacrament according to the rites of the Church of England—which excluded Roman Catholics and some of the Nonconformists. The object of this Act was to confine municipal office, closely connected with the election of Members of Parliament, to Royalist Anglicans. The Act of Uniformity of 1662 imposed upon the clergy the Prayer Book of Queen Elizabeth, with some excisions and certain valuable additions. It required from them a declaration of unfeigned assent and consent to all and everything contained in the Prayer Book, and extracted from them and all teachers in schools and universities a declaration "to conform to the Liturgy of the Church of England as it is now by law established." One fifth of the clergy, nearly two thousand ministers, refusing to comply, were deprived of their livings. These sweeping decisions were followed by other measures of enforcement. The Conventicle Act of 1664 sought to prevent the ejected clergy from preaching to audiences of their own, and the Five Mile Act of 1665 forbade them to go within five miles of any "City or Town Corporate or Borough or any parish or place where they had preached or held a living."

This Code embodied the triumph of those who had been beaten in the field and who had played little part in the Restoration. Its echoes divide the present-day religious life of England. It potently assisted the foundation of parties. The Royalist party in possession of power planned to bind together its affiliated interests. All the other elements in the nation, including those who had lately ruled and terrified it, drew instinctively together. A large group of villages where modern Birmingham now stands happened to be more than five miles from any "City, Town Corporate or Borough." The nonconformity of the Midlands focused itself here, and can be seen to-day in high repute. Thus from the Restoration there emerged no national settlement, but rather two Englands, each with its different background, interests, culture, and outlook. Of course there were crosscurrents. As Macaulay wrote, and later writers have confirmed his view, "there was a great line which separated the official men and their friends and dependents, who were sometimes called the Court party, from those who were sometimes honoured with the appellation of the Country party." Those who enjoyed official patronage, or hoped to do so, naturally had different interests from those who did not. But alongside this distinction another cleavage was opening. The lines were being drawn in political life between the Conservative and Radical traditions which have persisted down to our own day. We enter the era of conflict between broad party groups, soon to bear the names of Tory and Whig, which shaped the destinies of the British Empire till all was melted in the fires of the Great War of 1914.

*　　*　　*　　*　　*

For these far-reaching fissures Charles II had no responsibility. Throughout his reign he consistently strove for toleration. In May 1663 he tried to suspend the operation of the Act of Uniformity for three months; but the reinstated bishops and the constitutional lawyers frustrated him. In December he issued his first Declaration of Indulgence, claiming to exercise a dispensing power inherent in the Crown to relieve Dissenters from the laws enforcing religious conformity or requiring oaths; but the Commons, unconscious that it was what they themselves were doing, protested vehemently against any scheme for "establishing schism by a law." In March 1672 he ran great risks with a second Declaration of Indulgence, which sought to suspend "the execution of all manner of penal laws in matters ecclesiastical against whatsoever classes of Nonconformists and Recusants," as the Roman Catholics were called. "Penal statutes in matters ecclesiastical," rejoined the House of Commons severely, "cannot be suspended but by Act of Parliament." This admonition was coupled with a threat of refusal of supply, and the King, with the memory of Cromwell's sword, now so oddly invoked, before his eyes, submitted as a constitutional sovereign ought to do. Partisans of Parliament should realise that in this crucial period the King's was the only modern and merciful voice that spoke.

But Charles II had need of an Act of Indulgence for himself. Court life was one unceasing flagrant and brazen scandal. His two principal mistresses, Barbara Villiers, created Countess of Castlemaine, and Louise de Kérouaille—"Madame Carwell," as the English called her—created Duchess of Portsmouth, beguiled his leisure and amused themselves with foreign affairs. His marriage with Catherine of Braganza, who brought a rich dowry of eight hundred thousand pounds and the naval bases of Tangier and Bombay, in no way interrupted these dissipations. His treatment of his wife was cruel in an extreme degree; he forced her to accept Barbara as her Lady-in-Waiting. The refined, devout Portuguese princess on one occasion was so outraged that the blood gushed from her nostrils and she was borne swooning from the Court. It was with relief that the public learned that the King had taken a mistress from the people, the transcendently beautiful and good-natured Nell Gwyn, who was lustily cheered in the streets as "the Protestant whore." But these were only the more notorious features of a life of lust and self-indulgence which disgraced a Christian throne, and in an Asiatic Court would have been veiled in the mysteries of the seraglio.

The King's example spread its demoralisation far and wide, and the sense of relief from the tyranny of the Puritans spurred forward every amorous adventure. Nature, affronted, reclaimed her rights with usury. The Commonwealth Parliament had punished adultery by death; Charles scourged chastity and faithfulness with ridicule. There can however be no doubt that the mass of the nation in all classes preferred the lax rule of the sinners to the rigorous discipline of the saints. The people of England did not wish to be the people of God in the sense of the Puritan God. They descended with thankfulness from the superhuman levels to which they had been painfully hoisted. The heroic age of the constitutional conflict and of the Civil Wars and the grim manifestation of the Puritan Empire were no more. All shrank to a smaller size and an easier pace. Charles noticed how much weaker was the type of manhood of the new generation he found about him than the high-spirited Cavaliers and rugged Roundheads who were dying off.

It is inevitable that after a period of intense effort there should follow one of exhaustion and disarray. But this was a fleeting view. The race endured, and in Charles's Court, at his side, there was already a young man, an ensign in his Guards, a partner in his games at tennis, an intruder, as he learned with some displeasure, in the affections of Lady Castlemaine, who would one day grasp a longer and a brighter sword than Cromwell's and wield it in wider fields only against the enemies of British greatness and freedom. A Dorsetshire squire, Winston Churchill, along with his father, had fought in the Royalist ranks and had been wounded, mulcted, and expropriated by the Roundheads. The King could do little for his faithful adherent. He tried without success to persuade Clarendon to include Sir Winston in his private committee of Parliamentary managers. But he found a place at Court for his son as one of his own pages, and for his daughter Arabella in the household of the Duchess of York. Both improved their advantage. John Churchill obtained a commission in the Guards; Arabella became the mistress of the Duke of York, and bore him a son, James Fitz James, afterwards famous as the warrior Duke of Berwick.

Two personalities of force and capacity, vividly contrasted in character, Clarendon and Ashley, afterwards Earl of Shaftesbury, swayed the Privy Council. Shaftesbury had plunged into the Revolution in the Short Parliament when he was but eighteen. "I no sooner perceived myself in the world but I found myself in a storm." He had fought on the Roundhead side. He had worked with Cromwell. As a leader of Presbyterians he had influenced and aided Monk in bringing about the Restoration. It took him time to rise, but he was still young, and he had deeply ingrained convictions. No one understood better the anatomy of the convulsive forces which had devastated the country, but had at length for the time being worn themselves out upon each other. Shaftesbury was the most powerful representative of the vanished domination. Although he had headed the Presbyterians against the Army in the year of anarchy no one knew more about the spirit of the Independents. He was therefore the foremost advocate of toleration in the Council, and no doubt fortified the King in all he did to that end. He was always conscious of the fierce Ironside dogs who now seemed to sleep so quietly. He knew where they lay and how to put his hands on them. His other care was the City of London, of whose decisive weight on great occasions he had a lively recollection. Throughout the reign he stood by the City of London, and the City stood by him. The legislation of the Cavalier Parliament vexed the King almost as much as Shaftesbury, but neither could withstand in practice or in principle the obstinate will power of a large Parliamentary majority.

For the first seven years of the reign Clarendon continued First Minister. This wise, venerable statesman wrestled stoutly with the licentiousness of the King and Court, with the intrigues of the royal mistresses, with the inadequacy of the revenue, and with the intolerance of the House of Commons. He was also confronted with the intrigues of Henry Bennett, Charles's favourite, who was made Secretary of State and Earl of Arlington. An important and sometimes sinister part in the politics of the reign was played by this flamboyant figure. "He was a proud and insolent man," his contemporary, Bishop Burnet, wrote of Arlington. "He had the art of observing the King's temper, and managing it beyond all the men of the time." Clarendon's daughter however had won the heart of the Duke of York, and in spite of all that could be done to prevent it, and many imputations against the lady, the marriage had been solemnised. The Chief Minister was now father-in-law to the King's brother. His grandchildren might succeed to the throne. The jealousy of the nobles was inflamed and Clarendon's sense of his own greatness was inflated by this royal connection.

The acquisition of Tangier as part of the dowry of Catherine of Braganza turned the eyes of the Government to Mediterranean and Oriental trade. Money was so short that the defence of Tangier against the Moors and of commerce in the Mediterranean against the pirates could only be achieved if some great economy were made. Cromwell's capture of Dunkirk had imposed upon the royal exchequer an annual cost of no less than £120,000 a year, or one tenth of the normal revenue. To Cromwell, with his ideas of great interventions for the Protestant cause in Europe, Dunkirk had seemed an invaluable bridgehead. The Tory policy already looked to "trade and plantations" in the outer seas rather than to action in Europe. Charles, on Clarendon's advice, sold Dunkirk to the French for £400,000. This transaction, by no means unreasonable in itself, was much condemned. Clarendon was accused of having taken a heavy bribe. The large house he was building for himself in London was mockingly called "Dunkirk House." The accusation seems to have been unjust, but the stigma remained, and in later years, when Dunkirk became a nest of French privateers, much blame was cast upon his memory.

The rivalry of England and Holland upon the seas, in fishery, and in trade had become intense, and the strength of the Dutch had revived since Cromwell's war. The commerce of the East Indies flowed to Amsterdam, that of the West Indies to Flushing; that of England and Scotland passed to the Continent through Dort and Rotterdam. The herrings caught off Scottish coasts produced rich revenues for the States-General. The Dutch East India Company gathered the wealth of the Orient. Since the Portuguese Governor of Bombay was recalcitrant in yielding that part of Catherine's dowry, the English as yet had no sure base in India. Meanwhile great Dutch fleets, heavily laden, doubled the Cape of Good Hope several times a year. On the West African coast also the Dutch prospered, and their colonies and trading stations grew continually. They had a settlement on the Hudson, thrust among the colonies of New England. It was too much. Parliament was moved by the merchants; the King was roused to patriotic ardour, the Duke of York thirsted for naval glory. The great sum of over two and a half millions was voted. More than a hundred new ships were built, armed with new and heavier cannon. Former Cavalier and Cromwellian officers joined hands and received commissions from the King. Rupert and Monk commanded divisions of the Fleet. War at sea began off the West African coast in 1664, and spread to home waters in the following year.

In June the English fleet of more than 150 ships, manned by 25,000 men and mounting 5,000 guns, met the Dutch in equal strength off Lowestoft, and a long, fierce battle was fought, in which many of the leaders on both sides perished. The old Cromwellian admiral, John Lawson, who used to dress like a common sailor, was mortally wounded. By the side of the Duke of York his friends Lords Falmouth and Muskerry were killed by a single cannon ball. But the Dutch admiral Kortenaer and their Commander-in-Chief, Opdam, shared their fate. At the height of the action the *Royal Charles* (formerly the *Naseby*), with the Duke on board, engaged the Dutch flagship at close quarters. Opdam, cool and resolute, was directing the battle from a chair on his quarterdeck when a salvo from the English fired the magazine and blew him and his ship into the air. The English artillery was markedly superior in weight and skill, and the Dutch withdrew worsted though undismayed.

The return of Admiral De Ruyter from the West Indies restored the fortunes of the Republic. Lord Sandwich, who had temporarily succeeded the Duke of York, hoped to capture the Dutch merchant fleets from the Mediterranean and from both of the Indies, with cargoes of immense value on board, but, avoiding the Channel and sailing north-about, they took refuge in the harbour of Bergen. The King of Denmark and Norway, who had been at odds with the Dutch, promised in consideration of half the booty to remain inactive if the English attacked the Treasure Fleet in his harbour. However, the necessary orders had not reached the Danish commander when the English fleet attacked; he opened fire with the shore batteries and repulsed the assailants. England, indignant, declared war upon the Danes, who became the allies of the Dutch. De Ruyter arrived on the coast, and escorted the bulk of the Treasure Fleet safely into Texel. It was thought remarkable on the Continent that the Dutch should have maintained themselves so effectually against the far greater sea-power of England during the first year of the war.

An even greater battle than Lowestoft was fought in June 1666. Louis XIV had promised to aid Holland if she were attacked. Although Charles protested that the Dutch were the aggressors, France declared war on England. For four days the English and Dutch fleets battled off the North Foreland. De Ruyter commanded the Dutch, whose ships now mounted heavier cannon. The sound of the guns was heard in London, and men realised with dismay that Rupert, having to watch for the French fleet in the Channel, was separated from Monk. At the close of the second day's cannonading the English were outmatched; then Rupert, arriving on the third day, restored the balance. But the fourth day was adverse, and Monk and Rupert, with heavy losses, retired into the Thames. De Ruyter had triumphed.

The English were no more daunted by their defeat than the Dutch had been in the previous year. By great exertions the Fleet was refitted, and soon put to sea even stronger than before. Again they met their redoubtable antagonists, and on August 4, 1666, gained a clear victory over them. However, the Republic for the third time brought their fleet to sea in good order, and at last the French Fleet also appeared in the Channel.

England was now isolated, and even her power at sea was uncertain. Both sides bent beneath the financial strain. But other calamities drained the strength of the Island. From the spring of 1665 the Great Plague had raged in London. Never since the Black Death in 1348 had pestilence spread such ravages. In London at the climax about seven thousand people died in a single week. The Court retired to Salisbury, leaving the capital in the charge of Monk, whose nerves were equal to every kind of strain. Daniel Defoe's *Journal of the Plague Year* reconstructs for us in vivid, searing style the panic and horror. The worst of the plague was over when in September 1666 the Great Fire engulfed the tormented capital. It broke out near London Bridge, in a narrow street of wooden houses, and, driven by a strong east wind, the flames spread with resistless fury for four whole days. Wild suspicions that the fire was the work of Anabaptists, Catholics, or foreigners maddened the mob. The King, who had returned to London, acquitted himself with courage and humanity. When the fire was at length stopped outside the City walls by blowing up whole streets more than thirteen thousand dwelling-houses, eighty-nine churches, and St Paul's Cathedral had been devoured. The warehouses containing the merchandise for months of trade and many warlike stores were destroyed. The yield of the chimney tax, then so important to the revenue, was ruined. Yet the fire extinguished the plague, and to later times it seems that the real calamity was not so much the destruction of the insanitary medieval city as the failure to carry through Wren's plan for rebuilding it as a unity of quays and avenues centred on St Paul's and the Royal Exchange. The task of reconstruction was none the less faced with courage, and from the ashes of the old cathedral rose the splendid dome of St Paul's as it stands to-day.

Although the war dragged on till 1667 Charles now sought peace both with France and Holland. Want of money prevented the English battle fleet from keeping the sea, and while the negotiations lingered the Dutch, to spur them, sailed up the Medway under Admiral De Witt, brother of the famous John, Grand Pensionary of Holland, broke the boom which guarded Chatham harbour, burnt four ships of the line, and towed away the battleship *Royal Charles,* which had destroyed Admiral Opdam in the Battle of Lowestoft. The sound of enemy cannon, this time loud and near, rolled up the Thames. In the general indignation and alarm even Cavaliers remarked that nothing like this had happened under Cromwell. Among the Puritans the plague, the fire, and the disaster at sea were regarded as direct visitations by which the Almighty chastised the immorality of the age, and especially of the Court.

Peace, of which both sides had equal need, was made on indifferent terms. England's chief gain in the war was New Amsterdam, now renamed New York. But recriminations began. The Court asked how the country could be defended when Parliament kept the King so short of money. Parliament retorted that he had spent too much on his mistresses and luxuries. Clarendon, expostulating with all sides, was assailed by all. He had fallen out with Parliament, rebuked the mistresses, and, worst of all, bored the King. An impeachment was launched against him, and he went into exile, there to complete his noble *History of the Rebellion,* which casts its broad and lasting illumination on the times through which he lived. After Clarendon's fall the King was for a while guided chiefly by Arlington, and in his lighter moods by his boon companion Buckingham, son of James I's murdered favourite, a gay, witty, dissolute nobleman, whose sword was stained with the blood of an injured husband whom he had slain in a duel. The growing discontents of the Cavalier Parliament at the morals and expense of the Court made it necessary to broaden the basis of the Government, and from 1668 five principal personages began to be recognised as the responsible Ministers. There had been much talk of Cabinets and Cabals; and now, by chance, the initials of these five men, Clifford, Arlington, Buckingham, Ashley, and Lauderdale, actually spelt the word "Cabal."

* * * * *

The dominant fact on the continent of Europe, never realised by Cromwell, was the rise of France at the expense of Spain and Austria. Among men born to a throne few have outshone Louis XIV in natural capacity. He was now in his youthful prime. The French people, consolidated under the sagacious government of Cardinal Mazarin, were by far the strongest nation in Europe. They numbered twenty millions, four times as many as the population of England. In possession of the finest and fairest regions of the globe, at the head of European culture in art and learning, and with a magnificent army and centralised executive, France towered above her neighbours, and offered herself willingly to the leadership of her ambitious, masterful King. The Thirty Years War, which had ended only in 1648, had broken the Imperial power in Germany. The house of Habsburg presided in a spiritual and historical sense over a loose association of divided Germanic principalities, without exerting authority or receiving more than ceremonial allegiance. Even in his own hereditary Austrian lands the Holy Roman Emperor was distracted by the hostility of the Magyars of Hungary and the unceasing threat of Turkish invasion. Thus along the French frontiers stood no strong state nor solidly joined confederation. Flanders, Brabant, Liége, Luxembourg, Lorraine, Alsace, Franche-Comté, and Savoy, all lay open to the ambition, force, and diplomacy of France.

At the same time to the southward the evident decay of Spain and of the Spanish ruling family cast a lengthening shadow of disturbance upon the world. Mazarin had schemed to unite, if not at first the Crowns, at least the royal families of France and Spain, with all that that promised in world dominion. He had induced Louis XIV to marry the Infanta of Spain; but though as Queen of France she had had to renounce her rights in the Spanish succession the renunciation was conditional on the payment of a large sum of money included in her dowry. The Spaniards could not pay, and Louis already looked to the union of the two Crowns of France and Spain as the main goal of his life.

But King Philip of Spain married a second time, and when he died in 1665 he left a sickly son, who as Charles II of Spain lingered for thirty-five years as a flickering obstruction to the French design. Louis, his claims postponed indefinitely, resolved to compensate himself in the Netherlands. He declared that by the ancient custom of the Duchy of Brabant children of a first marriage should suffer no loss if their father married again, and that the Queen of France accordingly had sovereignty over the Spanish Netherlands, of which Brabant formed a large part. These pretensions were asserted in the first war into which Louis led his people. The Spanish Government did not greatly resent, and could not at all resist, the French demands upon the Belgic provinces. But if Belgium fell to France the Dutch Republic could not survive. John De Witt, at the head of the Dutch oligarchy, had been willing to fight England at sea, but a war on land against France was beyond the strength of the Republic. Moreover, it might reinforce the Orange party, who were De Witt's rivals. Their head, Prince William, was aged seventeen and was astonishingly able. Since the days of William the Silent members of the house of Orange had held the office of Stadtholder, or Chief Magistrate, and in wartime the Captain-Generalship of the armed forces. Conflict with France would give Prince William the opportunity to claim the honours of his ancestors, so far denied him. De Witt tried to negotiate; he offered large concessions. But Louis XIV sent Marshal Turenne into Flanders, occupied a large part of the Spanish Netherlands, and placated the Emperor by a partition treaty which to some extent safeguarded Imperial interests. Thus harassed, De Witt made peace with England. Charles and the Cabal, aided by their envoy Sir William Temple at The Hague, concluded a triple alliance with Holland and Sweden against France. The Protestant combination was hailed with delight by the whole country. The King and Ministers found themselves for a time borne up by public favour. This, the first of the long series of coalitions against France, checked Louis XIV for a while. He was forced to make peace with Spain. By the Treaty of Aix-la-Chapelle in 1668 he restored Franche-Comté to the Spanish King, but advanced his own frontiers in Flanders. This brought him, among other acquisitions, the thriving city of Lille, which he converted into the largest and strongest of French fortresses.

The success and popularity in London of the Dutch and Swedish alliance had done nothing to quell commercial friction between England and Holland. Sweden, under a boy ruler, was weak, and before long changed sides. The Triple Alliance crumbled. Louis XIV was determined to buy off one of the two maritime powers before resuming war. He addressed himself to England and in 1670 began secret negotiations with Charles II. Charles's sister Henriette, the charming "Minette," was the wife of Louis' brother, the Duke of Orleans, and provided a channel of intimate communication. Above all things Charles needed money. He pointed out to Louis that Parliament would give him ample funds to oppose France; how much would Louis pay him not to do so? If he paid enough Charles would have no need to call the dreaded Parliament together. Here was the basis of the shameful Treaty of Dover.

Besides the clauses which were eventually made public, there was a secret clause upon which Arlington and Clifford were Charles's only confidants. "The King of Great Britain, being convinced of the truth of the Catholic Faith, is determined to declare himself a Catholic . . . as soon as the welfare of his realm will permit. His Most Christian Majesty promises to further this action by giving to the King of Great Britain two million livres tournois . . . and to assist His Britannic Majesty with six thousand foot-soldiers." The King was also to receive a subvention of £166,000 a year. Charles undertook to betray his country for money, some of which he devoted to his pleasures and mistresses. But it is doubtful if he ever intended to keep so unnatural a promise. At any rate he made no attempt to do so, and spent most of the cash on the Fleet.

The Treaty of Dover contemplated a third Dutch war, in which France and England would combine when Louis XIV felt the moment opportune. In March 1672 Louis claimed fulfilment of the pact. There was no lack of pretexts for quarrel between England and Holland. "Our business," wrote an English diplomatist at The Hague, "is to break with them and yet to lay the breach at their door." Contrary to established convention, the Dutch Fleet did not salute the yacht which was bringing home Sir William Temple's wife. The Dutch were conciliatory when the English protested, and so an act of provocation was devised. The English made an unsuccessful attack on the Dutch fleet coming from Smyrna as it sailed up the Channel past Portsmouth. War began. At sea the English and French mustered ninety-eight warships to the enemy's seventy-five. They had 6,000 guns and 34,000 men against 20,000 Dutchmen with 4,500 guns. But the genius of Admiral De Ruyter maintained the honour of the Republic. In a great battle at Sole Bay on June 7, 1672, De Ruyter surprised the English and French, who were ten ships stronger, as they lay at anchor. Grievous and cruel was the long battle. The Suffolk shores were crowded with frantic spectators, and the cannonade was heard many miles away. The French squadron put out to sea, but the wind prevented them from engaging. The Duke of York's flagship, the *Prince,* was beset on every side. Upon her decks stood the first company of the Guards, in which Ensign Churchill was serving. She became such a wreck that the Duke, who fought with his usual courage, was forced to shift his flag to the *St Michael,* and, when this ship was in turn disabled, to the *London.* Lord Sandwich, in the second flagship, perished when the *Royal James* sank, burnt almost to the water's edge. Nevertheless the Dutch drew off with very heavy losses of their own.

On land Louis struck with terrible force at the hard-pressed Republic. Suddenly, without cause or quarrel, his cavalry swam the Rhine and his armies invaded Holland. A hundred and twenty thousand French troops, armed for the first time with a bayonet which fitted around instead of blocking the muzzle of the musket, were irresistible. Eighty-three Dutch strongholds opened their gates. The Dutch people, faced with extermination, turned in their peril to William of Orange. The great-grandson of William the Silent, now Captain-General, did not fail them. He uttered the famous defiance, "We can die in the last ditch." The sluices in the dykes were opened; the bitter waters rolled in a deluge over the fertile land, and Holland was saved. At The Hague a revolution took place and William of Orange became Stadtholder. De Witt resigned. He and his brother were torn to pieces by an Orange mob in the capital.

All through 1673 De Ruyter sustained the Dutch arms at sea, and many fierce battles were fought, with varying success. In a great action off Texel on August 21 De Ruyter frustrated an Anglo-French invasion and successfully brought in the Dutch East India fleet. On land Louis XIV took the field in person. While Condé with weak forces occupied the Dutch in the north and Turenne engaged the Emperor's forces in Alsace, the King, accompanied by the Queen and his mistress Madame de Montespan, with an enormous Court, advanced in the centre behind the magnificence of the French army. It soon appeared that Maestricht, a strong Dutch fortress garrisoned by about five thousand men, had been selected for his triumph. "Big sieges," he remarked, "please me more than the others." They certainly suited his military disposition better than battles. Maestricht surrendered after a long struggle, but the campaign was in no sense decisive.

The Popish Plot

THE meeting of Parliament in February of 1673 had apprised Charles of his subjects' loathing for the war against the Dutch Protestant Republic, in which he had allowed himself to become engaged, not as the champion of English commerce, but as the lackey of Louis XIV. Resentment of the Dutch affronts at sea and jealousy of their trade were overridden by the fear and hatred of Papist France and her ever-growing dominance in Europe. Whispers ran afoot through London that the King and his Ministers had been bribed by France to betray the freedom and the faith of the Island. The secret article in the Dover Treaty had only to be known to create a political explosion of measureless violence. Shaftesbury, though not privy to it, must have had his suspicions. Early in 1673 Arlington seems to have confessed the facts to him. With dexterity and promptitude Shaftesbury withdrew himself from the Government, and became the leader of an Opposition which was ultimately as violent as that of Pym. The growing antagonism of the Commons to France, the fear of the returning tides of Popery, the King's "laxity towards Papists," the conversion of the Duke of York to Rome, all stirred a deep and dangerous agitation throughout the whole country, in which the dominant Anglican forces were in full accord with Presbyterian and Puritan feeling. Everywhere there was the hum of political excitement. Coffee-houses buzzed; pamphlets circulated; by-elections were scenes of uproar. A Bill was forced upon the King for a Test. No man could hold office or a King's commission afloat or ashore who would not solemnly declare his disbelief in the doctrine of Transubstantiation. This purge destroyed the Cabal. Clifford, a Catholic, refused to forswear himself; Arlington was dismissed because of his unpopularity; Buckingham had a personal quarrel with the King. Shaftesbury had already voted for the Test Act, and was the leader of the Opposition. Lauderdale alone remained, cynical, cruel, and servile, master of Scotland.

All eyes were now fixed upon James, Duke of York. His marriage, after the death of his first wife, Anne Hyde, to the Catholic princess Mary of Modena had rendered him suspect. Would he dissemble or would he give up his offices? Very soon it was known that the heir to the throne had laid down his post of Lord High Admiral rather than submit to the Test. This event staggered the nation. The Queen was unlikely to give King Charles an heir. The crown would therefore pass to a Papist King, who showed that for conscience sake he would not hesitate to sacrifice every material advantage. The strength of the forces now moving against the King and his policy rose from the virtual unanimity which prevailed between the Anglicans and the Dissenters, between the swords which had followed Rupert and the swords which had followed Cromwell. All the armed forces were in the hands of the Royalist gentry, and there were many thousands of Cromwell's old soldiers in London alone. They were all on the same side now, and at their head was the second great Parliamentary tactician of the century, Shaftesbury. This was of all combinations the most menacing to the King.

Dryden has recorded his biased but commanding verdict upon Shaftesbury in lines and phrases which are indelible:

> For close designs and crooked counsels fit,
> Sagacious, bold, and turbulent of wit,

Restless, unfixed in principles and place,
In power unpleased, impatient of disgrace;
A fiery soul which, working out its way,
Fretted the pigmy body to decay
And o'er-informed the tenement of clay.
A daring pilot in extremity,
Pleased with the danger, when the waves went high,
He sought the storms; but, for a calm unfit,
Would steer too nigh the sands to boast his wit.
Great wits are sure to madness near allied,
And thin partitions do their bounds divide.

The power of the Cavalier Parliament had been made plain in every dispute with the Crown. It had exerted itself in foreign policy, had completely controlled domestic affairs, and had compelled the King to change his advisers by the hard instruments of the Test Act or Impeachment. A new departure was now made. Sir Thomas Osborne, a Yorkshire landowner, had gathered great influence in the Commons, and was to a large extent forced upon the King for his own salvation. His policy was the union into one strong party with a popular programme of all those elements which had stood by the monarchy in the Civil War and were now deeply angered with the Court. Economy, Anglicanism, and independence from France were the principal ideals of this party, and Osborne now carried them to the King's Council. He was very soon raised to the peerage as Earl of Danby, and began an administration which was based on a party organisation possessing a small but effective majority in the House of Commons. In order to rally his followers to the Crown and to break with the Opposition, Danby proposed in 1675 that no person should hold any office or sit in either House without first declaring on oath that resistance to the royal power was in all cases criminal. This was deliberately intended to draw a hard line against the Puritan elements and traditions. The plan was to vest the whole Government, national and local, in the Court party and fight the rest. In this design, which Danby pursued by corrupt party management and in unprecedented by-election activity, he was countered in the Lords by Shaftesbury and Buckingham; and so vigorous was the opposition of these two ex-Ministers that Danby had to abandon his new retaliatory Test.

In foreign affairs the new Minister publicly differed from his master. He opposed French ascendancy and interference, and gained general support thereby; but he was forced to become privy to the King's secret intrigues with Louis XIV, and, holding strongly to the Cavalier idea that the King should have considerable personal power, he was lured into asking the French monarch for money on Charles's behalf. The height of his precarious popularity was reached when he contrived a marriage between Mary, the Duke of York's daughter by his first wife, and the now famous Protestant hero, William of Orange. This match was of the highest consequence. Dread of a Papist King had already turned all eyes to the formidable, gleaming figure of the Stadtholder of Holland, Charles I's grandson by his daughter. William's inflexible Protestantism, grave demeanour, high gifts, and noble ancestry had raised him already to a position of eminence in Europe. Married now to the daughter of the Duke of York, the English heir presumptive, he seemed to offer an alternative succession to the Crown. This was by no means the outlook of King Charles II, still less of his brother, James. They did not regard the danger as serious. Charles was led to believe that Shaftesbury's opposition might be diminished by such a marriage, and the Duke of York's self-confidence was proof against so remote a menace to his title. Thus the marriage was made, and the two maritime nations, which had recently contended in fierce, memorable battles in the Narrow Seas, became united by this remarkable tie. Since then the Dutch and English peoples have seldom been severed in the broad course of European events.

* * * * *

It was at this moment that Louis XIV, dissatisfied with his English investments and indignant at a marriage which threatened to carry England into the Dutch system and was a strong assertion of Protestant interests, resolved to ruin Danby. He revealed to the Opposition, most of whom took his bribes while opposing his interests, that the English Minister had been asking for French money. The revelation was made in the House of Commons with careful preparation, and in the most dramatic fashion. It exploded at a frightful moment. The tale of dark designs to subjugate Protestant England to Rome was on every lip. Rumours about a secret treaty with the French king and the bugbear of the Duke of York's seemingly inevitable succession were now inflamed and fanned by what was called the "Popish Plot."

A renegade priest of disreputable character, Dr Titus Oates, presented himself as the Protestant champion. He had acquired letters written by Catholics and Jesuits in England to their co-religionists in St Omer and other French Catholic centres. From these materials he accused the Duchess of York's private secretary, Coleman, of a conspiracy to murder the King, bring about a French invasion, and cause a general massacre of Protestants. Many responsible men in both Houses of Parliament believed Oates's accusations, or pretended that they did. An order was issued for Coleman's arrest. It is certain that he had no intent against Charles, but he was a centre of Catholic activity and correspondence. He succeeded in burning the bulk of his papers; but those that were seized contained indiscreet references to the restoration of the Old Faith, and to the Catholic disappointment at Charles's attitude, which in the rage of the hour gave colour to Oates's accusations. Coleman was examined in October 1678 before a magistrate, Sir Edmund Berry Godfrey, and while the case was proceeding Godfrey was found dead one night at the foot of Greenberry Hill, now Primrose Hill. Although three men, whose names by odd coincidence were Green, Berry, and Hill, were hanged for the reputed murder, the mystery of his death has never been solved. This cumulative sensation drove English society into madness. Anglicans and Puritans alike armed themselves with swords or life preservers, and in London everyone talked about expecting a Papist dagger. Oates rose in a few months to be a popular hero; and being as wicked as any man who ever lived, he exploited his advantage to the full. Meanwhile Shaftesbury, long versed in revolutions, saw his opportunity to ride the storm.

Montagu, a former Ambassador to France, in collusion with the Whig and Puritan leaders, had exposed letters written by Danby in which there was mention of six million livres as the price of English assent to the proposed Treaty of Nimwegen between the French and the Dutch, and also the King's desire to be independent of Parliamentary grants. By this treaty the French were to make considerable gains. Danby, in reply, read other letters which mitigated but did not overturn the crude facts. His impeachment was resolved. Even Strafford had not been in a more perilous plight. Indeed, it seemed hardly possible that he could save his head. Charles, wishing to stay the capital proceedings instituted against his Minister, partly unjustly, and anyhow for actions which Danby had taken only to please the King, at length, in December 1678, dissolved the Cavalier Parliament.

This Parliament had sat, with a number of intervals, for

eighteen years. It had been born in the Cavalier fervour of the Restoration; it ended when the King was convinced it would reduce him to the status of a Venetian Doge. In length of life it had surpassed the Long Parliament. In fidelity to the Constitution as against the Crown it had rivalled over a long period the early vigour of its predecessor. It had confirmed in a Royalist victory all the gains made by the Great Rebellion. It had restored within limits, and under fictions which were henceforward understood, the repute of the Royal Prerogative and the monarchical system. It had also established Parliamentary control of finance and brought nearer the responsibility of Ministers to the Lords and Commons. It was founded upon a rock—the Parliamentary and Protestant character of the English Constitution. It presents us with the massing of those forces, themselves so bitterly estranged, which upon the main issue produced the Revolution of 1688.

*　　*　　*　　*　　*

Charles, in breaking this prop which had so long sustained him, did not intend to put his trust in a different party. He hoped that the new set of Members would be less rigid, less grooved and opinionated than the old. He supposed that the country was more friendly to him than the London hive in which Shaftesbury was now supreme. But all this was illusion. The country was more adverse than the capital. Everywhere the voters enjoyed the election. They ate, drank, and argued with gusto at the expense of the candidates. As happened after the Short Parliament of Charles I, all the prominent opponents of the King were returned. The trusty followers of the Court, who hitherto had mustered a hundred and fifty, now returned barely thirty. The situation was not unlike that of 1640; but with one decisive difference. Both the King and the country had gone through an experience which neither wished to repeat. Over England hung the dread of civil war, and all the Cromwellian atrocities that might spring therefrom. The shadow of his father's fate fell ever upon the King's footsteps. And by now the idea of saving the Kingship and of saving himself at all costs was dominant. Charles II yielded to the wish of the nation; he bowed to the hostile Parliament. Danby, threatened by attainder, was glad to be forgotten for five years in the Tower. He had still a part to play.

The brunt fell upon James, Duke of York. The King had already asked him not to attend the Privy Council, and now advised him to leave the country. The Duke retired to the Low Countries, carrying with him on his staff the very young captain in the British and colonel in the French Army, John Churchill, his trusted aide-de-camp and man of business. Charles, thus relieved at home, faced the fury of the anti-Popish hurricane. Oates and other perjurers who followed in his train instituted a reign of terror against the English Catholic notables. By perjury and suborned evidence they sent a number of blameless Catholics to the scaffold. The King made every effort in his power to protect them. When this was in vain he resigned himself to letting the bloody work go on. His cynical but profound knowledge of men and the vicissitudes of his years of exile served him well. Not for mean motives he endured the horrible ordeal which his subjects imposed upon him, of signing the death warrants of men he knew were guiltless. But there was a great change in his conduct. He abandoned his easy, indolent detachment from politics. He saw that his life and dynasty were at stake; he set himself with all his resources and with all the statecraft which modern research increasingly exalts to recover the ground that had been lost. The last five years of his reign are those most honourable to his memory. His mortal duel with Shaftesbury was a stirring episode. It was diamond cut diamond. At the beginning the King seemed at the mercy of this

terrible subject; but by using time and letting passions find
their vent, as well as by strokes of dæmonic ingenuity,
Charles II emerged the victor, and the merciless Shaftesbury,
stained with innocent blood, eventually died in exile.

The struggle centred upon the Exclusion Bill. To keep the
Papist heir from the throne was the main object of the majority of the nation. Anything rather than that. But who then
should succeed? Shaftesbury looked to William of Orange;
but he also looked, with more favour, upon the Duke of Monmouth, Charles's illegitimate son by Lucy Waters. Here was
a young man, charming, romantic, brave, gleaming, our beloved Protestant Duke—was he born in wedlock or was he a
bastard? Some form of marriage it was widely believed had
been solemnised between the King and Lucy. There was a
"black box" in which the marriage lines were said to repose.
It had been spirited away by emissaries of the Pope. What
had now become the more powerful party in England longed
to establish Monmouth's legitimacy. They wanted a King, a
Protestant King, an Anglican King bred in constitutional
ways, with a strain of common blood to give him sense, and
a clear-cut policy of organising Protestantism against the
Catholic overlordship of Europe which Louis XIV was trying to achieve. Only one man could decide this issue.
Charles had only to recognise Monmouth as his heir to free
himself from every trouble and assure the future of his country. Nothing would induce the King to betray the succession.
Sensualist, libertine, agnostic, dilettante, he had one loyalty
—the royal blood, the legitimate succession. However painful it might be for himself and his realm, he conceived it his
sacred duty to pass the crown to a brother whose virtues and
whose vices alike rendered him of all others the man, as he
knew well, least fitted to wear it. Nevertheless the legend of
the "black box" has persisted, and in our own time we have
been told how a Duke of Buccleuch, descended from the un-

fortunate Monmouth, discovered and destroyed, as dangerous to the monarchy, the marriage certificate of Lucy Waters.

The new House of Commons met more fierce than the old one had parted. There was an overwhelming anti-Catholic majority. It proceeded immediately to impeach, and, when this lagged, to attaint Danby. It concentrated its efforts upon the Exclusion Bill. There was grave logic behind this measure. When Papists were excluded by law from every post in the realm, how should the kingly power and prerogative be wielded by one of the proscribed faith? Charles laboured to present a compromise. He could not admit that Parliament should alter the lineal succession to the Crown. Out of such courses had sprung the Wars of the Roses. But he offered remarkable limitations which, were they accepted, and could they be enforced, would create a narrowly limited constitutional monarchy in England. All ecclesiastical patronage would be withdrawn from a Popish sovereign. No Papist should sit in either House of Parliament, or hold any office or place of trust. The Parliament sitting at the King's death should remain sitting for a certain time, or reassemble without further summons if it was not in session. The judges should only be appointed with the consent of Parliament. Finally, he formally abandoned the claim for which his father had fought so long—the power of the sword. Lord-Lieutenants who controlled the militia, their deputies, and the officers of the Navy would be nominated by Parliament. But in the prevailing temper no one would believe that any restrictions could be imposed upon a Popish King. The Exclusion Bill passed its second reading by an overwhelming vote, and the King descended upon the Parliament with another dissolution.

Nevertheless this short-lived legislature left behind it a monument. It passed a Habeas Corpus Act which confirmed and strengthened the freedom of the individual against arbitrary arrest by the executive Government. No Englishman, however great or however humble, could be imprisoned for more than a few days without grounds being shown against him in open court according to the settled law of the land. The King did not object to this. The balance of forces in the country at this time seemed so equal that his own courtiers, servants, or former Ministers might well have need of this protection. He pronounced the traditional words in Norman French, "Le Roi le veult," and wherever the English language is spoken in any part of the world, wherever the authority of the British Imperial Crown or of the Government of the United States prevails, all law-abiding men breathe freely. The descent into despotism which has engulfed so many leading nations in the present age has made the virtue of this enactment, sprung from English political genius, apparent even to the most thoughtless, the most ignorant, the most base.

The Protestant tide again swept the country, and in all parts men voted against the Duke of York becoming King. Earnest and venerable divines tried to induce James to return to the Church of his fathers and his future subjects. He remained obdurate. To the warrior quality of his nature was added the zeal of a convert. Not for him the worldly-wise compliances to which Henry of Navarre had stooped to gain an earthly crown. Better exile, poverty, death, for himself; better the ruin of the land by civil war. The dominant motives of both sides deserve a high respect, and led inexorably to vast and long distresses. In these days, when the Catholic Church raises her immemorial authority against secular tyranny, it is hard to realise how different was the aspect which she wore to the England of 1679, with lively recollection of the fires of Smithfield, the Massacre of St Bartholomew, the Spanish Armada, and the Gunpowder Plot.

Whig and Tory

AS soon as the King saw that the election gave him no relief he prorogued the meeting of the resulting Parliament for almost another year. And it is in this interval that
we first discern the use of those names Whig and Tory which
were to divide the British Island for nearly two hundred
years. Although the root of the quarrel was still religious, the
reign of Charles II saw the detachment of liberal ideas from
their sectarian basis. The collective mind of England was
moving forward from the ravines of religious entanglement
to broader if less picturesque uplands. The impulse of religious controversy, which had hitherto been vital to political
progress, henceforth took the second place. To the sombre
warfare of creeds and sects there succeeded the squalid but
far less irrational or uncontrollable strife of parties.

During this year 1680, before the new Parliament had
met, the gentry, who had the main power in the land, began
to be disturbed at the violence of the Protestant Movement.
The Royalist-Anglican elements increasingly recognised in
Shaftesbury's agitation the terrible lineaments of Oliver
Cromwell. The loathed memory of the Civil War and the so-
called "Commonwealth" obsessed the older generation. If petitions for the exclusion of the Duke of York were signed by
many thousands in the cities and towns, so also abhorrence of
these demands upon the Crown was widespread in the country. But no parties could live under such labels as Petitioners
and Abhorrers. Instead of naming themselves they named
each other. The term "Whig" had described a sour, bigoted,

canting, money-grubbing Scots Presbyterian. Irish Papist bandits ravaging estates and manor-houses had been called "Tories." Neither side was lacking in power of abuse. "A Tory is a monster with an English face, a French heart, and an Irish conscience. A creature of a large forehead, prodigious mouth, supple hams, and no brains. They are a sort of wild boars, that would root out the Constitution, . . . that with dark lanthorn policies would at once blow up the two bulwarks of our freedom, Parliaments and Juries; making the first only a Parliament of Paris, and the latter but mere tools to echo back the pleasure of the judge." [1] The Whig, on the other hand, "talks of nothing but new light and prophecy, spiritual incomes, indwellings, emanations, manifestations, sealings, . . . to which also the zealous twang of his nose adds no small efficacy. . . . This little horn takes a mouth to himself, and his language is Overturn, Overturn. His prayer is a rhapsody of holy hickops, sanctified barkings, illuminated goggles, sighs, sobs, yexes, gasps, and groans. He prays for the King, but with more distinctions and mental reservations than an honest man would in taking the Covenant." [1]

One can see from these expressions of scorn and hatred how narrowly England escaped another cruel purging of the sword. Yet the names Whig and Tory not only stuck, but became cherished and vaunted by those upon whom they were fastened. They gradually entered into the whole life of the nation, and represented in successive forms its main temperamental types. They were adorned by memorable achievements for the welfare of England, and both had their share in the expansion and greatness which were to come. Party loyalties and names came to be transmitted by families across the gen-

[1] Both quotations from David Ogg, *England in the Reign of Charles II*, (1934), pp. 609–10.

erations, though the issues changed with the times and the party groupings varied. Orators and famous writers, sure of their appeal, pointed to them in terms of pride.

The harassed King, rather than face his fourth Parliament, adopted an expedient which recalls the futile *Magnum Consilium* to which his father had been drawn forty years before. Sir William Temple, envoy at The Hague, a leading advocate of an anti-French policy and architect of the triple alliance which had checked Louis XIV at Aix-la-Chapelle, proposed a plan for a Privy Council, reduced in numbers but clothed with power. Thirty magnates of both parties, half officeholders, half independent, would replace the old secret Cabal or Cabinet which had connived at the Treaty of Dover. For good or ill the royal policy should be open; there was to be an end, it was thought, of secret diplomacy. Charles was now in full breach with Louis XIV, who scattered his bribes widely among the Opposition. He accepted the plan. A glorified Privy Council assembled. Shaftesbury, the leader of the Opposition, was appointed its president by the King. These well-meant endeavours came to nought. The stresses were too great, and inside the Council of thirty there soon developed an inner ring which conducted all the business. Shaftesbury was in no wise placated by his readmission to official life. He did not abandon the movement and party of which he was head. On the contrary, he used his position to advance their interests. When Parliament met in October 1680 he again championed the Exclusion Bill, and at this moment he reached his zenith. He seemed to combine in himself the power of a Minister of the Crown and the popularity of a leader of incipient revolt. The Exclusion Bill was carried through the Commons, and the struggle was fought out in the Lords.

That it ended bloodlessly was largely due to the statesman who has rendered the word "Trimmer" illustrious. George

Savile, Marquis of Halifax, was the opponent alike of Popery and of France. He was one of those rare beings in whom cool moderation and width of judgment are combined with resolute action. He could defend a middle course with a constancy usually granted only to extremists. He could change from side to side, with or against the current, without losing his force or the esteem in which he was held. He never shrank from the blasts of public frenzy, and rose above all taunts and aspersions of time-serving. In the immortal pen-pictures which Dryden has drawn of the personalities of these turbulent days none is more pleasing than that of Jotham, who

> only tried
> The worse awhile, then chose the better side,
> Nor chose alone, but changed the balance too.
> So much the weight of one brave man can do.

Halifax, who had been so hot against Danby, broke the Exclusion Bill in the House of Lords. His task was rendered easier by the difficulty of advancing an alternative successor to the Crown. Of those who were against James some were for his eldest daughter, Mary, wife of the renowned Prince of Orange, in whose veins the royal blood of England also flowed. Shaftesbury had played with this idea, but in the end decided for the bastard Monmouth. He procured his admission to the Privy Council. He wove him into the texture of his party. The Whigs propagated the fiction that he was legitimate after all. Anyhow, the King dearly loved his handsome, dashing son. Might he not, as pressures and perils gathered about him, take the safe and easy course of declaring him legitimate? But this complaisant solution, which Charles would never tolerate, did not appeal to an assembly every man of which owned lands, wealth, and power through the strictest

interpretations of hereditary right. The Anglican Church refused to resist Popery by crowning bastardy. By sixty-three
votes to thirty the Peers rejected the Exclusion Bill.

*　*　*　*　*

The fury against the Popish Plot was gradually slaked in
the blood of its victims. In November 1680 one of the last of
them, Lord Stafford, declared his innocence on the scaffold,
and the crowd cried, "We believe you, my lord." The fabric
of lies in which Oates and others had decked themselves was
wearing thin. The judges began to look pointedly at contra-
dictions and irrelevances in the evidence by which the lives of
Catholics were sworn away. The mood of panic had been too
keen to last. The fact that the King was obviously severed
from Louis XIV mitigated political passion. Charles saw in
this new temper the chance of a more favourable Parliament.
Halifax, fresh from rendering him the highest service, opposed the dissolution. He thought there was still something to
be made of the Parliament of 1680. But the King, after a
full debate in his Privy Council, overrode the majority. "Gentlemen," he said, "I have heard enough," and for the third
time in three years there was an electoral trial of strength.
But this was challenging the electors to go directly back on
what they had just voted. Again there was no decisive change
in the character of the majority returned.

Presently it was learned that Parliament was to meet in
Oxford, where the King could not be bullied by the City of
London and Shaftesbury's gangs of apprentices called "White
Boys." To Oxford then both sides repaired. Charles moved
his Guards to the town, and occupied several places on the
roads from London with troops. The Whig lords arrived
with bodies of armed retainers, who eyed the Household Cavalry and gallants of the Court with the respectful hostility of
gentlemen upon a duelling ground. The Members came

· 371 ·

down in parties of forty or fifty, the London M.P.s being escorted by armed citizens. A trial of strength impended, and none could tell that it would not take a bloody form. The large majority of the Commons was still resolved upon the Exclusion Bill.

It would seem that the King kept two courses of action open, both of which he had prepared. He had caused Lawrence Hyde, Clarendon's son, the Duke of York's brother-in-law, a competent financier, to examine precisely the state of the normal revenue granted to the Crown for life. Could the King by strict economies "live of his own"? In this calculation his foremost thought was the upkeep of the Navy, which he consistently set even in front of his mistresses and his own comfort. Hyde reported that it was impossible to discharge the royal services upon the original grant of customs and excise and such further taxes as Parliament had conceded. With strict economy however the deficit would not be large. Hyde was next employed in negotiating with Louis XIV, and eventually a hundred thousand pounds a year was obtained upon the understanding that England would not act contrary to French ambitions on the Continent. With this aid it was thought the King could manage independently of the ferocious Parliament. England had now reached a point in its history as low as when King John, in not dissimilar stresses, had made it over as a fief to the Pope. Modern opinion, which judges Charles's actions from the constitutional standpoint, is revolted by the spectacle of a prince selling the foreign policy of his country for a hundred thousand pounds a year. But if present-day standards are to be applied the religious intolerance of Parliament and the party violence of Shaftesbury must also be condemned.

Moreover, the King did not intend to adopt this ignominious policy which he had in his pocket, or almost in his pocket, unless he found no hope in Parliament. He made a show of going to extreme lengths to meet the national fear of a Popish King. The sacred principle of hereditary succession must not be destroyed, but short of this every security should be given. James, when he succeeded, should be King only in name. The kingdom would be governed by a Protector and the Privy Council. The accident of the conversion of the heir presumptive to Rome should not strip him of his royalty, but should deprive him of all power. The administration should rest in Protestant hands. If a son was born to James he would be educated as a Protestant and ascend the throne on coming of age. In default of a son, James's children, the two staunch Protestant princesses, Mary and after her Anne, would reign. The Protector meanwhile was to be no other than William of Orange.

There is no doubt that the King might have agreed to such a settlement, and could then have defied France and made an alliance with the Dutch and the Protestant princes of Germany. Not one can lightly censure this scheme, and the fact that it was framed reveals the grinding conflicts in Charles's mind. But Shaftesbury thought otherwise. He and all his party were set upon Monmouth for the Crown. Parliament had no sooner met than its hostile temper was apparent. The King in his speech deplored the factious, unreasonable behaviour of its predecessor. The House of Commons re-elected the old Speaker, who hinted in his humble address that they saw no need for change in their demeanour. Shaftesbury, still a member of the Privy Council, in a sense part of the Government, held a hard conversation with the King in the presence of many awestruck notables. A paper was handed to Charles demanding that Monmouth should be declared successor. Charles replied that this was contrary to law and also to justice. "If you are restrained," said Shaftesbury, "only by law and justice, rely on us and leave us to act. We will make laws which will give legality to measures so necessary to the quiet of the nation." "Let there be no delusion," rejoined the King. "I will not yield, nor will I be bullied. Men usually become more timid as they become older; it is the opposite with me, and for what may remain of my life I am determined that nothing shall tarnish my reputation. I have law and reason and all right-thinking men on my side. I have the Church"— here he pointed to the bishops—"and nothing will ever separate us."

The sitting of the Commons two days later, on March 26, 1681, was decisive. A private Member of importance unfolded to the House the kind of plan for a Protestant Protectorate during James's reign which the King had in mind. Charles would perhaps have been wise to let this discussion proceed. But Oxford was a camp in which two armed factions jostled one another. At any moment there might be an outbreak. Just as James would sacrifice all for his religious faith, so Charles would dare all for the hereditary principle. There was no risk he would not run to prevent his beloved son, Monmouth, from ousting a brother who was the main source of all his troubles.

The Commons passed a resolution for excluding the Duke of York. On the Monday following two sedan chairs made their way to Parliament. In the first was the King, the crown hidden beneath his feet; in the second, which was closed, were the sceptre and the robes of State. Thus Charles wended his way to the House of Lords, installed in the Geometry School of the university. The Commons were debating a question of jurisdiction arising out of a Crown prosecution for libel, and a Member was declaiming about the bearing of Magna Carta upon the point, when Black Rod knocked at the door and summoned them to the Peers. Most Members thought that this portended some compliance by the King with their wishes. They were surprised to see him robed, upon his throne, and astounded when the Chancellor declared in his name that Parliament was again dissolved.

No one could tell what the consequences would be. Forty years before the Scottish Assembly had refused to disperse upon the warrant of the Crown. A hundred years later the National Assembly of France was to resort to the tennis court at Versailles to affirm its continued existence. But the dose of the Civil War still worked in the Englishmen of 1681. Their respect for law paralysed their action. The King withdrew under a heavy escort of his Guards to Windsor. Shaftesbury made a bid to convert the elements of the vanished Parliament into a revolutionary Convention. But no one would listen. Charles had hazarded rightly. On one day there was a Parliament regarding itself as the responsible custodian of national destiny, ready to embark upon dire contention; the next a jumble of Members scrambling for conveyances to carry them home.

From this time Shaftesbury's star waned and the sagacious Halifax entered the ascendant. The reaction against the execution of the Catholic lords and others was now apparent, and the submission of Parliament to a third dissolution gave it substance. Within two months the King felt strong enough to indict Shaftesbury for fomenting rebellion. This strange man was now physically almost at the last gasp. His health, though not his spirit, was broken. His appearance—he could hardly walk—dismayed his followers. The Middlesex Grand Jury, faithful to his cause, wrote "Ignoramus" across the bill presented against him. This meant that they found the evidence insufficient. He was liberated according to law. But meanwhile one of his followers had been hanged at Oxford on charges similar to those which Shaftesbury had escaped in London. He could no longer continue the struggle. He counselled insurrection; and it seemed that a royal murder would be one of its preliminaries. Shaftesbury at this point fled to Holland, hoping perhaps for Dutch support, and died at The Hague in a few weeks. He cannot be ranked with the chief architects of the Parliamentary system. As a Puritan revolutionary he understood every move in the party game, but he deliberately stained his hands with innocent blood. He sought above all the triumph of his party and his tenets. His life's work left no inheritance for England. He was as formidable as Pym, but his fame sinks to a different level.

*　*　*　*　*

The absorbing question now was whether there would be civil war. All the Cromwellian forces were astir; indeed, there was a terror in men's hearts that if James came to the throne they would have to choose between turning Papist and being burnt at the stake. Their fears increased when James returned from exile in May 1682. It was only a generation since Cornet Joyce had carried off the King from Holmby House. An ex-officer of the Roundheads, "Hannibal" Rumbold, who had been on duty around the scaffold at Whitehall on the memorable 30th of January, dwelt in the Rye House by the Newmarket Road, where it ran through a cutting. Fifty zealous Ironsides could easily overpower the small travelling escort of the King and the Duke of York on their return from their pastime of horse racing. Above this dark design, and unwitting of it, was a general conspiracy for armed action. Many, but by no means all, of the forces which were to hurl James from the throne a few years later were morally prepared to fight. Various Whig noblemen and magnates had taken counsel together. The lucky accident of a fire in Newmarket, by which much of the town was destroyed, led Charles and

James to return some days before the expected date. They passed the Rye House in safety, and a few weeks later the secret of the plot was betrayed. It compromised the much wider circles in which armed resistance had been considered.

When the news spread through the land it caught the Royalist reaction upon its strong upturn. It transformed everything. Hitherto the Whigs had exploited the Popish Plot and made common folk believe that the King was about to be butchered by the Roman Catholics. Here was the antidote. Here was a Whig or Puritan plot from the other side to kill the King. All the veneration which Englishmen had for the monarchy, and the high personal popularity of Charles, with his graceful manners and dangerously attractive vices, were reinforced by the dread that his death would make his Papist brother King. From this moment Charles's triumph was complete. Halifax urged the summoning of another Parliament. But the King had had enough of such convulsions. With Louis' subsidy he could just manage to pay his way. When thirty Catholic victims had been slaughtered on false perjured evidence and Charles had had to sign the death warrants it is not surprising that he let himself swim with the vengeance of the incoming tide.

Two famous men were engulfed. Neither William Lord Russell nor Algernon Sidney had sought the King's life; but Russell had been privy to preparations for revolt, and Sidney had been found with an unpublished paper, scholarly in character, justifying resistance to the royal authority. The Tory Cavalier party, relieved of its fears and now roused in its turn, clamoured for vengeance. Charles classed Russell, and to a lesser extent Sidney, with Sir Harry Vane as enemies of the monarchy. After public trial both went to the scaffold. Russell refused to attempt the purchase of his life by bowing to the principle of nonresistance. Sidney affirmed with his last breath the fundamental doctrines of what had now become the Whig Party. Intense discussion was held by Church and State with both these indomitable men. Nothing was yielded by them. Ranke, in a moving passage, says: "In this lies the peculiar mark of this century, that in the clash of political and religious opinions, which struggled for supremacy, unalterable convictions are formed which lend the character a firm inward bearing, which again raises it above the strife of party struggle. As the die falls, so men either obtain power and gain scope for their ideas, or they must offer their neck to the avenging axe."

These executions were of lasting significance. Martyrs for religion there had been in plenty. Protestant, Catholic, Puritan, Presbyterian, Anabaptist, Quaker, had marched the grisly road unflinching. Great Ministers of State and public men had fallen in the ruin of their policies; the Regicides had faced the last extremity with pride. But here were the first martyrs for the sake of Party. The whole Bedford family, in its widespread roots and branches, vindicated the honour of Russell; and the Whigs, already content with their name, revered from one generation to another these champions of their doctrine and interest. Long did they extol the cause for which "Hampden died upon the field and Sidney on the scaffold." The Whig Party has passed from life into history. When we consider how the principles of free government, then struggling for acceptance and authority in a world of cross-purposes and misunderstanding, are precious to those now living we too must salute the men who testified so early and so plainly.

The power of Charles at home remained henceforth unchallenged. He was able to make a counter-attack. The Whig strongholds were in the boroughs and cities. These depended on their charters for the control of local government and the benches of magistrates. Influence at Parliamentary elections was also at stake. By pressure and manipulation Tory sheriffs were elected in London, and henceforth through that agency City juries could be trusted to deal severely with Whig delinquents. Nothing like Shaftesbury's acquittal could occur again. Success in London was followed up in the Provinces. The Whig corporations were asked by writs of *Quo Warranto* to prove their title to their long-used liberties. These titles were found in many cases, to the satisfaction of the royal judges, to be defective. Under these pressures large numbers of hitherto hostile corporations threw themselves on the mercy of the Crown and begged for new charters in accordance with the royal pleasure. The country gentlemen, ever jealous of the privileges of the boroughs, lent their support to the Government. Thus the Whigs, overborne in the countryside, now saw their power crippled in the towns as well. It is remarkable that they should have survived as a political force and that the course of events should so soon have restored them to predominance.

Against his own wishes the triumphant King followed meekly the foreign policy which his French paymaster prescribed. He lived with increasing frugality; his mistresses became concerned for their future, and scrambled for pensions solidly secured upon the revenues of the Post Office. Only the Fleet was nursed. Louis continued his aggressions and waged war upon freedom and the Protestant faith. His armies overran the Spanish Netherlands; he laid his hands on Strasbourg; he made inroads upon the German principalities. He ruled splendid and supreme in Europe. England, which under Elizabeth and Cromwell had played a great European part, for a while shrank, apart from domestic politics, to a quiescent and contented community, busy with commerce and colonies, absorbed in its own affairs and thankful they were easier.

Across the seas widespread thrusts were taking place, often on the initiative of the men on the spot rather than by planned direction from London. English commerce was expanding in India and on the West Coast of Africa. The Hudson Bay Company, launched in 1669, had set up its first trading posts and was building up its influence in the northern territories of Canada. On the coasts of Newfoundland English fishermen had revivified the earliest colony of the Crown. On the American mainland the British occupation of the entire eastern seaboard was almost complete. The capture of New York and the settlement of New Jersey had joined in contiguity the two existing groups of colonies that lay to the north and south. Inland the state of Pennsylvania was beginning to take shape as an asylum for the persecuted of all countries under the guidance of its Quaker proprietor, William Penn. To the south the two Carolinas had been founded and named in honour of the King. At the end of Charles's reign the American colonies contained about a quarter of a million settlers, not counting the increasing number of Negro slaves, transhipped from Africa. The local assemblies of the colonists were sturdily asserting traditional English rights against the interventions of the King's Ministers from London. Perhaps not many Englishmen at the time, absorbed in the pleasures and feuds of Restoration London, foresaw the broad prospects that stretched out before these comparatively small and distant American communities. One who caught a glimpse was Sir Winston Churchill. Towards the close of his life he published a book called *Divi Britannici* which has been unfavourably referred to by Macauley, in praise of the greatness and antiquity of the British monarchy. Churchill wrote with pride of the new horizons of seventeenth-century Britain, "extending to those far-distant regions, now become a part of us and growing apace to be the bigger part, in the sunburnt America." But all this lay in the future.

*　　*　　*　　*　　*

Talk of excluding James from the throne died away. He had now become the vehement supporter of French aims in Europe. Unchastened by the past, he dreamed of reconverting England to Rome under the sword of France. Nevertheless, his own popularity revived. His conduct afloat was not forgotten.

> The glory of the British line,
> Old Jimmy's come again,

sang the Tory rhymesters. He resumed his functions. In all but name he became again Lord High Admiral. He dilated to Charles, who had no illusions, upon the proved efficacy of a strong policy. He braced himself and hardened his heart for the mission which lay before him.

The King was only fifty-six, and in appearance lively and robust, but his exorbitant pleasures had undermined his constitution. To represent him as a mere voluptuary is to underrate both his character and his intellect. His whole life had been an unceasing struggle. The tragedy he had witnessed and endured in his youth, the adventures and privations of his manhood, the twenty-five years of baffling politics through which he maintained himself upon the throne, the hateful subjugations forced on him by the Popish Plot, now in his last few years gave place to a serene experience. All the fires of England burned low, but there was a genial glow from the embers at which the weary King warmed his hands.

Halifax, now more than ever trusted, still urged him to the

adventure of a new Parliament, and Charles might have consented, when suddenly in February 1685 an apoplectic stroke laid him low. The doctors of the day inflicted their tormenting remedies upon him in vain. With that air of superiority to death for which all mortals should be grateful he apologised for being "so unconscionable a time in dying." James was at hand to save his soul. Old Father Huddleston, the priest who had helped him in the days of the Boscobel oak, was brought up the backstairs to rally him to Rome and give the last sacrament. Apart from hereditary monarchy, there was not much in which Charles believed in this world or another. He wanted to be King, as was his right, and have a pleasant life. He was cynical rather than cruel, and indifferent rather than tolerant. His care for the Royal Navy is his chief claim upon the gratitude of his countrymen.

The Catholic King

THE struggle between Crown and Parliament which had dominated English life since the reign of James I had now come back to its starting point. Eighty years of fearful events and the sharpest ups and downs of fortune had brought the monarchy, in appearance and for the practical purposes of the moment, to almost Tudor absolutism. In spite of Marston Moor and Naseby, after the execution of a King, after Oliver Cromwell, after the military anarchy, after the enthusiasm of the Restoration, after the savage incipient revolution which raged around the Popish Plot, Charles II had been able to reign for three years without the aid of Parliament and to transmit the crown of a Protestant country to a Catholic successor. So vital did the institution of monarchy appear to those who had lived in this strenuous age that even the barrier of a hostile religion could not prevent the lawful heir from ascending the throne amid the respectful homage of his British subjects.

For the last two years of his brother's reign James had played a leading part in the realm. He had exploited the victory which Charles, by compliance, by using time, by an ignominious foreign policy, had gained for the house of Stuart. His accession to the throne seemed to him to be the vindication of the downright conceptions for which he had always stood. All he thought he needed to make him a real king, on the model now established in Europe by Louis XIV, was a loyal Fleet and a standing Army, well trained and equipped. Warlike command appealed strongly to his nature. He had fought under Turenne; he had fought in the forefront of bloody actions at sea. To form land and sea forces devoted to the royal authority and to his person was his first object. Here was the key by which all doors might be opened. Prating Parliaments, a proud, politically minded nobility, the restored, triumphant Episcopacy, the blatant Whigs, the sullen, brooding Puritans, all would have to take their place once the King of England possessed a heavy, tempered, sharpened sword. Everyone was awestruck or spellbound by the splendour of France under absolute monarchy. The power of the French nation, now that its quarrels were stilled and its force united under the great king, was the main fact of the age. Why should not the British islands rise to equal grandeur by adopting similar methods?

But behind this there swelled in the King's breast the hope that he might reconcile all his people to the old faith and heal the schism which had rent Christendom for so many generations. He was resolved that there should at least be toleration among all English Christians. It is one of the disputes of history whether toleration was all he sought. James was a convert to Rome. He was a bigot, and there was no sacrifice he would not make for his faith. He lost his throne in consequence, and his son carried on after him the conscientious warfare, to his own exclusion. Toleration was the natural first step to the revival of Catholicism. The King was determined that the Catholics should not be persecuted, and for tactical reasons, at a later date, he extended his protection to the Dissenters. It is possible that he fortified himself inwardly by asserting that all he wanted was toleration, and by the enlightened use of the dispensing power to be the true father of all his people.

These large plans filled James's resolute and obstinate mind. Protestant opinion has never doubted that if he had gained despotic power he would have used it for his religion in the same ruthless manner as Louis XIV. In the very year of James's accession the King of France revoked the Edict of Nantes, and by the persecutions known as the Dragonnades quelled the last resistance of the Huguenots. James, in letters which are still preserved, approved the persecutions practised by the French monarch. On the other hand, in his reign he never dared transgress the limits of toleration. He was hurled from his throne before he could complete the first phase of his policy, so that it cannot be proved that it would not have been final. Afterwards in exile he entered into a correspondence, of which sixty letters have been preserved, with Rancé, the Prior of the Trappists, in which devotion to the Catholic faith is combined with toleration. But by then toleration was the most he could hope for if he ever returned to England. The English Protestant nation would have been very foolish to trust themselves to the merciful tolerances of James II once he had obtained the absolute power he sought.

They did not do so. They viewed with intense distrust every step he took in the name of toleration. They were quite sure, from his character, from his record, from his avowed unshakeable convictions, from the whole character of the Catholic Church at this time, that once he wielded the sword their choice would be the Mass or the stake.

Events rolled forward on their unresting course. The sudden death of Charles II came as a shattering blow to his well-loved bastard, Monmouth. He was in Holland, a gay prince, dancing and skating, happy with his beautiful mistress, Lady Wentworth. Thus he beguiled the time till Protestant feeling in England and his father's love should win him what he believed was his birthright. Suddenly he found that he must deal henceforward not with a father who would forgive anything, but with an uncle who forgave nothing, and had a long score in his ledger. William of Orange had entertained him agreeably at The Hague, but on the day when Charles's death was known reasons of State supervened and he ordered him to leave the country. He gave him good advice to take a commission from the Emperor against the Turks. But Monmouth was in the grip of the exiles. Around him were the desperate fugitives from the Rye House Plot. "Claim your rights," they said. "Now or never !" Monmouth might well have been content to lead a happy life with Lady Wentworth, but these morose and frantic men drove him to his doom. They all thought of the England they had quitted in 1681. Before Monmouth's eyes, too, there shone the scenes of his progress through the West Country. Would not all England rise for "our beloved Protestant Duke" against a Popish King? Three little ships with Argyll, son of the Covenanting Earl, and "Hannibal" Rumbold were prepared for Scotland. Three others, with other Rye House conspirators or followers of Shaftesbury, would carry Monmouth upon his perilous challenge.

James ascended the throne with all the ease of Richard Cromwell. He took every measure which forethought could enjoin to grasp the royal power, and his earliest declarations carried comfort to an anxious land. He tried to dispel the belief that he was vindictive or inclined to arbitrary rule. "I have often heretofore ventured my life in defence of this nation, and I shall go as far as any man in preserving it in all its just rights and liberties." He declared himself resolved to maintain both in State and Church a system of government established by law. "The laws of England," he said, "are sufficient to make the King a great monarch." He would maintain the rights and prerogative of the Crown, and would not invade any man's property. He is even reported to have said that "as regards his private religious opinions, no one should perceive that he entertained them." Nevertheless, from the moment he felt himself effectively King, on the second Sunday after his accession, he went publicly to Mass in his chapel. The Duke of Norfolk, who carried the sword of state before him, stopped at the door. "My lord," said the King, "your father would have gone farther." "Your Majesty's father would not have gone so far," rejoined the Duke.

His public practice of the Roman faith immediately disquieted the Anglican clergy; but its effects did not reach the country for some time. The royal proclamation was generally accepted. The calling of a Parliament to vote such revenues as expired with Charles II was indispensable. The electors returned a House of Commons loyal and friendly to the new King. They voted him a revenue for life which, with the growth of trade, amounted to nearly £2,000,000 a year. Sir Edward Seymour, High Tory, who was out of temper with the management of the elections in his own West Country, alone warned the House of its imprudence and urged delay. Encouraged by the attitude of Parliament, James decided at first to pursue constitutional methods. He knew what he meant to have, and he hoped it might be given him by agreement. No decisive change was made in the Ministers. Halifax continued for a while to be the leading Counsellor, and everyone looked forward to the coronation.

It was at this moment, on June 11, 1685, that Monmouth landed. He had been nineteen days at sea, using up his luck in escaping the English warships. He entered the Harbour of Lyme Regis, not far from Portland Bill. He was at once welcomed by the populace. He issued a proclamation asserting the validity of his mother's marriage and denouncing James as a usurper who had murdered Charles II. In one day fifteen hundred persons signed the rolls of enlistment in his army. But when the messengers brought the news at a gallop to Whitehall James was found in the first flush of his power. He

had no large army; but there were the Household Cavalry
and a regiment of Dragoons under his long-trusted officer
and agent, Lord Churchill. There were also two regiments of
regular infantry under Colonel Kirke which had been withdrawn from Tangier when that outpost was abandoned. All
the ruling forces rallied round the Crown. Parliament swore
to live and die with the King. Monmouth was attainted and a
price was placed upon his head. Extraordinary supplies were
voted. The militia was called out, and almost everywhere responded. A French emigrant, Louis Duras, long resident in
England, who had been created Earl of Feversham, was
placed in command of the royal troops; but Churchill by
forced marches had already reached the spot. Monmouth and
his rebels, who by then amounted to six or seven thousand
ardent men, made a long march through Taunton and Bridgwater towards Bristol, which closed its gates against him,
then circled back by Bath and Frome, and finally, a month
after his landing, reached Bridgwater again. Churchill, now
joined by Kirke, hung close upon him from day to day, while
Feversham and the royal army approached.

Despite the enthusiasm for his cause among the common
people the unhappy Duke knew that he was doomed. He had
learned that Argyll and Rumbold, landing in Scotland, had
been overpowered and captured. Their execution was imminent. One last chance remained—a sudden night attack upon
the royal army. Feversham was surprised in his camp at
Sedgemoor; but an unforeseen deep ditch, called the Bussex
Rhine, prevented a hand-to-hand struggle. Churchill, vigilant
and active, took control. The West Country peasantry and
miners, though assailed by sixteen pieces of artillery and
charged in flank and rear by the Household troops, fought
with Ironside tenacity. They were slaughtered where they
stood, and a merciless pursuit, with wholesale executions,

ended their forlorn endeavour. Monmouth escaped the field only to be hunted down a few days later. He could claim no mercy, and none did he receive. The King has been censured for according him an interview when his offence was mortal and his fate was certain. "I die a Protestant of the Church of England," he declared on the scaffold. "If you be of the Church of England, my lord," interposed the divines who attended him, "you must acknowledge the doctrine of non-resistance to be true." To this point had the Anglicans carried their abject theory.

Chief Justice Jeffreys was sent into the West to deal with the large number of prisoners. This cruel, able, unscrupulous judge made his name for ever odious by "the Bloody Assizes." Between two and three hundred persons were hanged, and about eight hundred transported to Barbados, where their descendants still survive. The ladies of the Court scrambled for the profits of selling these poor slaves, and James marked the ruthless judge for advancement to Lord Chancellor. Churchill, upon whom the light now from time to time begins to fall, was appealed to on behalf of two young Baptists—the Hewlings—under sentence of death. Could he gain access for their sister to the King? He used his influence on her behalf. "But, madam," said he, putting his hand upon the mantelpiece, "I dare not flatter you with hopes; that marble is as capable of feeling compassion as the King's heart." The Hewlings were executed.

The conduct of William of Orange showed his statecraft. He was under treaty to send three regiments of infantry to James's aid. He fulfilled his obligation with alacrity. He even offered to come in person to command them. On the other hand, he had not tried too hard to stop Monmouth's expedition from sailing. If the Duke won there would be a Protestant King of England, who would certainly join a coalition against

Louis XIV. If he failed the last barrier which stood between William and his wife Mary and the succession to the English throne would be for ever removed. Of the two alternatives that which he most desired came to pass.

*   *   *   *   *

James was now at the height of his power. The defeat of the rebels and the prevention of another civil war had procured a nation-wide rally to the Crown. Of this he took immediate advantage. As soon as Jeffreys' "campaign," as James called it, was ended he proposed to his Council the repeal of the Test Act and the Habeas Corpus Act. These two hated relics of his brother's reign seemed to him the main objects of assault. In the emergency he had given many commissions to Catholic officers. He was determined to retain them in his new, tripled army. Halifax, as Lord President of the Council, pointed to the statutes which this would affront; Lord Keeper North warned his master of the dangers he was incurring. Halifax was removed, not only from the Presidency of the Council, but from the Privy Council altogether; and when North died soon after, Chief Justice Jeffreys, red-handed from "the Bloody Assizes," was made Lord Chancellor in his stead. Robert Spencer, Earl of Sunderland, later in the year became Lord President in the place of Halifax, as well as Secretary of State, and was henceforward James's chief Minister. Sunderland is a baffling figure who served in turn Charles, James, and later William III. He throve by changing sides. Now he had become a Papist to please his master. No one knew better than he the politics and inclinations of the leading families in the country, and that is what made him indispensable to successive sovereigns.

Parliament met for its second session on November 9, and the King laid his immediate purpose before it. In his blunt way he declared, with admitted reason, that the militia was useless. They had twice run away before Monmouth's half-armed peasantry. A strong standing Army was indispensable to the peace and order of the realm. He also made it plain that he would not dismiss his Catholic officers on the morrow of their faithful services. These two demands shook the friendly Parliament to its foundations. It was deeply and predominantly imbued with the Cavalier spirit. Its most hideous nightmare was a standing Army, its dearest treasure the Established Church. Fear and perplexity disturbed all Members, assaulted both in their secular and religious feelings; and beneath their agitation anger grew. While the old loyalties, revived by recent dangers, still inspired the Tory nobles and country gentlemen, the doctrine of nonresistance dominated the Church. Both were prepared to condone the breach of the Test Act committed by Catholic officers during the rebellion. The Commons offered an additional grant of £700,-000 to strengthen the royal forces. They only asked, with profuse expressions of devotion, for reassurance that Acts of Parliament should not be set aside by the Prerogative, and for comforting words about the security of the Protestant religion. The King gave a forbidding answer.

In the House of Lords Devonshire, the hardy Whig; Halifax, the renowned ex-Minister; Bridgwater and Nottingham, actually members of the Privy Council; and, not the least, Henry Compton, Bishop of London, son of a father who had died for Charles I at Newbury, asserted the rights of the nation. A day was fixed for further discussion, and the judges were invited to pronounce upon the lawfulness of the King's proceedings. James had not yet packed the Bench with his partisans. He saw plainly that the declaration which must now be expected from the judges and the House of Lords would constitute a massive obstacle to that very dispensing power for the relief and preferment of the Catholics upon which his heart was set. He therefore repeated the stroke by which Charles II had dispersed the Parliament at Oxford in 1681. On November 20 he suddenly appeared in the House of Lords, summoned the Commons to the Bar, and prorogued Parliament. It never met again while he was King.

Freeing himself from Parliamentary opposition by repeated prorogations, King James proceeded throughout 1686 to relieve his fellow religionists. First he desired to dispense with the Test against Catholics in the Army. The judges whom he consulted were adverse, but after various dismissals and appointments the Bench assumed a new complexion, and a test case, Hales *versus* Godden, was arranged. Hales, a Catholic, appointed Governor of Portsmouth, was sued by collusion, by his coachman, Godden, who claimed £500 reward as a common informer against a violator of the Test Act. Hales pleaded the royal dispensing power as his defence. The court agreed. Thus armed, James granted a dispensation to the Curate of Putney, although he had become a Catholic, to continue in his benefice. At the same time Roman Catholic peers were admitted to the Privy Council. The King went further. He set up an Ecclesiastical Commission, almost identical with the old Court of High Commission destroyed by the Long Parliament, the main function of which was to prevent Anglican clergy from preaching against Catholicism. Bishop Compton had already been dismissed from the Privy Council. He was now suspended from his functions as Bishop of London.

These actions disturbed the whole realm. The methods of absolutism were being used to restore the Catholic religion, more dreaded than absolutism itself. Lawyers discerned that a direct conflict between statutory law and Royal Prerogative had arisen. Moreover, they now asserted that the King should not only be under the law, but under the law made in Parliament, the law of statute. The Common Lawyers all ranged themselves behind the new claim.

By the end of the year James had driven away many of his most faithful friends and disquieted everybody. Halifax, who had saved him from the Exclusion Bill, was brooding in the country. Danby, only liberated from the Tower in 1684, had perforce abandoned his dream of Church and King. He saw it could never be realised with a Papist sovereign. Albemarle, son of General Monk, had quitted the royal service. The loyal Parliament which had rallied to James against Monmouth and Argyll could be brought together no more without the certainty of a quarrel. Its lords and squires sat sullen and anxious amidst their tenantry. The Church, the bulwark of legitimacy, the champion of nonresistance, seethed with suppressed alarms, and only the powerful influence of Lawrence Hyde, now Earl of Rochester, upon the bishops and clergy prevented a vehement outburst. It was plain that the King, with all the downright resolution of his nature, was actively and of set purpose subverting the faith and Constitution of the land.

During the whole of 1686 and 1687 James held Parliament in abeyance, and used his dispensing power to introduce Roman Catholics into key positions. Whigs and Tories drew closer together. James was uniting the party that had challenged his brother with the party that had rallied so ardently to his brother's defence. He now embarked upon a political manœuvre at once audacious, crafty, and miscalculated. Hitherto he had striven only to relieve his Catholic subjects. He would now bid for the aid of the Dissenters, who were equally oppressed. If Whigs and Tories were combined he would match them by a coalition of Papists and Nonconformists under the armed power of the Crown. In William Penn, the Quaker courtier and founder of the state of Pennsylvania across the seas, influential in both this and the former reign, he found a powerful and skilled agent. Thus did the King break down the national barriers of his throne and try to shore it up with novel, ill-assorted, and inadequate props.

In January 1687 came the fall of the Hydes. For a long time both had been unhappy in their offices. Clarendon, the elder brother, in Ireland, had been overawed by James's faithful follower, the Roman Catholic Earl of Tyrconnel; Rochester, in Whitehall, was subdued by Sunderland. On January 7, 1687, Rochester was dismissed from the Treasury, and three days later Clarendon was replaced by Tyrconnel. The friend of the Hydes who governed Scotland in His Majesty's name was superseded by two Catholics. These changes marked another definite stage in the reign of James II. The prorogation of Parliament at the end of 1685 had been the beginning of Cavalier and Anglican discontent against the Crown. With the dismissal of Rochester began the revolutionary conspiracy.

Meanwhile James was raising and preparing his Army. Charles II's forces of about seven thousand men had cost £280,000 a year. Already James was spending £600,000 upon the upkeep of more than twenty thousand men. Three troops of Life Guards, each as strong as a regiment, the Blues, ten regiments of horse or dragoons, two battalions of foot-guards and fifteen of the line, besides garrison troops, were under arms by February 1686. Every summer a great camp was formed at Hounslow to impress the Londoners. In August 1686 this contained about ten thousand men. A year later Feversham could assemble fifteen thousand men and twenty-eight guns. The King went often to the camp, seeking to make himself popular with the officers and all ranks. He allowed Mass to be celebrated in a wooden chapel borne on wheels and placed in the centre of the camp between the horse and foot. He watched the drill of the troops, and dined with Feversham, Churchill, and other generals. He continued his infusion of Catholic officers and Irish recruits. He had a parson, Johnson, pilloried and whipped from Newgate to Tyburn for a seditious pamphlet addressed to Protestant soldiers. He comforted himself with the aspect of this formidable Army, the like of which had not been seen since Cromwell, and against which nothing could be matched in England. He increasingly promoted Catholics to key posts. The Duke of Berwick, now eighteen years old, was made Governor of Portsmouth, and Catholics commanded at both Hull and Dover. Eventually a Catholic admiral ruled the Channel Fleet.

The Revolution
of 1688

WILLIAM OF ORANGE watched the King's proceedings with close attention. Soon after the dismissal of the Hydes, Dykevelt, a Dutchman of the highest character, arrived in London as his envoy, partly to exhibit William as pleading with James to moderate his measures, and partly to sound the Opposition leaders. Dykevelt saw all the statesmen opposed to the Court, and made it clear that they could count upon William and Mary for help. For some months past King James and the Catholic party had been toying with a plan to make the Princess Anne next in succession to the Crown on condition that she would turn Catholic. Anne's circle at her house, the Cockpit, was firmly Protestant. Bishop Compton was her spiritual guide, John Churchill her trusted adviser, and his wife Sarah her bosom friend. The mere rumour of such designs locked the whole of this group together, and Anne, convulsed with fear and anger at the suggestion that her faith would be tampered with, roused herself to a mood of martyrdom. The strong, sincere, and natural attitude of this closely knit group was to play an important part in later events. After Dykevelt's departure Churchill wrote to William on May 17, 1687, giving him assurances "under my own hand, that my places and the King's favour I set at nought, in comparison of being true to my religion. In all things but this, the King may command me; and I call God to witness, that even with joy I should expose my life for his service, so sensible am I of his favours." But he declared that, "although I cannot live the life of a saint, I am resolved if there be ever occasion for it, to show the resolution of a martyr."

The provocations of the royal policy continued. The first Declaration of Indulgence was issued. It did precisely what James's Parliament had objected to in advance: it set aside statutory acts by Royal Prerogative. Meanwhile an attempt to force a Catholic President upon Magdalen College, Oxford, and the expulsion of the Fellows for their resistance, added to the stir. In July James planned the public reception of the Papal Nuncio, d'Adda. The Duke of Somerset, when commanded to conduct the ceremonial, objected on the ground that the recognition of Papal officials had been declared illegal at the Reformation. "I am above the law," said James. "Your Majesty is so," replied the Duke, "but I am not." He was at once dismissed from all his offices.

The King had, in modern parlance, set up his political platform. The second step was to create a party machine, and the third to secure by its agency a Parliament with a mandate for the repeal of the Tests. The narrow franchise could be manipulated in the country to a very large extent by the Lord-Lieutenants and by the magistrates, and in the towns and cities by the corporations. Upon these therefore the royal energies were now directed. Lord-Lieutenants, including many of the greatest territorial magnates, who refused to help pack a favourable Parliament, were dismissed, and Catholics or faithful nominees of the Court installed in their places. The municipal corporations and the benches of magistrates were drastically remodelled so as to secure the fullest representation, or even the preponderance, of Papists and Dissenters. The Government tried to extort from all local authorities a pledge to support the King's policy. The process of setting Papists and Dissenters over or in place of Anglicans and Cavaliers ruptured and recast the whole social structure of English life as established at the Restoration. Not only the proudest and wealthiest nobles but the broad strength of the people were equally offended. The rich and powerful, in resisting the Crown, felt themselves upborne by the feelings of the voteless masses.

Defenders of James's conduct are concerned to exaggerate the number of English Catholics. It is even claimed that one eighth of the population still adhered, in spite of generations of persecution, to the Old Faith. The old Catholic families in England however, apart from favoured individuals, were deeply apprehensive of the headlong adventure upon which the King was launching them. The Pope himself, in accordance with the policy of the Holy See, deprecated James's excessive zeal, and his Legate in England urged caution and prudence. But the King hardened his heart and strengthened his Army.

For many months there was still parley. The parsons preached against Popery. Halifax issued his cogent *Letter to a Dissenter* to offset James's attempt to rally the Nonconformists. Bishop Burnet wrote from The Hague appealing to the Anglicans to stand steadfastly against the King's policy despite their doctrine of nonresistance. William of Orange made no secret of his own sentiments. The national fear and hatred of Catholicism were inflamed by the daily landing on the British shores of miserable victims of Catholic "toleration" as practised in France by the most powerful sovereign in the world. All classes and parties knew the close sympathy and co-operation of the French and the English Courts. They saw all they cared for in this world and the next threatened. They therefore entered, not without many scruples and hesitations, but with inexorable resolve, upon the paths of conspiracy and rebellion.

* * * * *

During the ten years which followed the Treaty of Nimwegen Louis XIV reached his zenith. England, rent by her domestic quarrels, had ceased to be a factor in European affairs. The Habsburg Empire was equally paralysed for action in the West by the Ottoman invasion and Hungarian revolts. Louis, conscious of his dominating power, sought to revive the empire of Charlemagne on a vaster scale. He contemplated himself as a candidate for the Imperial throne. He was deep in schemes which would secure the reversion of Spain and her New World empire to a French prince. His inroads upon his neighbours were unceasing. In 1681 he had swooped across the Rhine and occupied Strasbourg. In 1684 he bombarded Genoa, besieged Luxembourg, massed troops upon the Spanish frontier, and laid claims to large territories in North-West Germany. His neighbours cowered beneath his unrelenting scourge in pain and fear. His flail fell upon the Huguenots, but he also engaged in a most grievous quarrel with the Papacy. He marshalled and disciplined the French clergy with the same thoroughness as his armies. He grasped all ecclesiastical revenues and patronage. He claimed not only temporal but in many directions spiritual control. The Gallican Church yielded itself with patriotic adulation to his commands. All who diverged fell under the same heavy hand which had destroyed the Huguenots.

The Pope, Innocent XI, stands high in the long line of pontiffs. The virtues of this eminently practical and competent cleric, who began life as a soldier, shine with a modern glow across the generations. In manner gentle, in temper tolerant, in mood humane, in outlook broad and comprehending, he nevertheless possessed and exercised an inflexible will and an imperturbable daring. He understood the political balances of Europe as well as any statesman then alive. He disapproved of French persecution of the Protestants. He condemned conversions effected by such means. Christ had not used armed apostles. "Men must be led to the temple, not dragged into it." He withdrew all spiritual authority from the French episcopacy. He pronounced decrees of interdict and excommunication, and finally he wove himself into the whole European combination which was forming against the predominance of France. While on the one hand he comforted the Catholic Emperor, he also consorted with the Calvinist Prince of Orange. Thus slowly, fitfully, but none the less surely, the sense of a common cause grew across the barriers of class, race, creed, and self-interest in the hearts of millions of men.

In England during the autumn of 1688 everything pointed, as in 1642, to the outbreak of civil war. But now the grouping of the forces was far different from the days when Charles I unfurled his standard at Nottingham. The King had a large, well-equipped regular Army, with a powerful artillery. He believed himself master of the best, if not at the moment the largest, Navy afloat. He could call for powerful armed aid from Ireland and from France. He held the principal seaports and arsenals under trusty Catholic governors. He enjoyed substantial revenues. He assumed that the Church of England was paralysed by its doctrine of nonresistance, and he had been careful not to allow any Parliament to assemble for collective action. Ranged against him on the other hand were not only the Whigs, but almost all the old friends of the Crown. The men who had made the Restoration, the sons of the men who had fought and died for his father at Marston Moor and Naseby, the Church whose bishops and ministers had so long faced persecution for the principle of Divine Right, the universities which had melted their plate for King Charles I's coffers and sent their young scholars to his armies, the nobility and landed gentry whose interests had seemed so bound up with the monarchy—all, with bent heads and burning hearts, must now prepare themselves to outface their King in arms. Never did the aristocracy or the Established Church face a sterner test or serve the nation better than in 1688. They never flinched; they never doubted.

In this wide and secret confederacy there were two main divisions of policy. The moderates, led by Halifax and Nottingham, urged caution and delay. The Ministry, they pleaded, was breaking up. There had been no widespread conversions to Catholicism, as James had hoped, and he would never get a Parliament to support him. No case had yet arisen to warrant actual treason. Remember, they enjoined, how a standing army rallies to its duty once fighting has begun. Remember Sedgemoor. "All is going well, if you do not spoil it." On the other hand stood the party of action, headed by Danby. He was the first man of great position who definitely set himself to bring William and a foreign army into England. With Danby were the Whig leaders—Shrewsbury, Devonshire, and some others. As early as the spring of 1688 they invited William to come over; and William replied that if he received at the right moment a formal request from leading English statesmen he would come, and that he would be ready by September. A nation-wide conspiracy was on foot by the end of May. Detailed plans were made, and the land was full of whisperings and of mysterious comings and goings.

Much now turned upon the Army. If the troops obeyed orders and fought for the King England would be torn by civil war, the end of which no man could foresee. But if the Army refused to fight, or was prevented from fighting by any means, then the great issues at stake would be settled bloodlessly. It seems certain, though there is no actual proof, that the general revolutionary conspiracy had a definite military core; and that this formed itself in the Army, or at least among the high officers of the Army, step by step with the designs of the statesmen. The supreme object of all the conspirators, civil or military, was to coerce the King without using physical force. This was certainly Churchill's long-formed intention. With him in secret consultation were the colonels of the two Tangier regiments, Kirke and Trelawny, the Duke of Grafton, commanding the Guards, the Duke of Ormonde, and a number of other officers. And now events struck their hammer blows.

*   *   *   *   *

At the end of April James issued a second Declaration of Indulgence. He ordered that the Declaration should be read in all the churches. On May 18 seven bishops, headed by the Primate, the venerable William Sancroft, protested against this use of the dispensing power. The clergy obeyed their ecclesiastical superiors and the Declaration was left unread. James, furious at disobedience, and apparently scandalised at this departure, by the Church he was seeking to undermine, from its doctrine of nonresistance, demanded that the bishops should be put on trial for seditious libel. His Minister, Sunderland, now thoroughly alarmed, endeavoured to dissuade him from so extreme a step. Even Lord Chancellor Jeffreys told Clarendon that the King was going too far. But James persisted, the trial was ordered, and the bishops, all of whom refused the proffered bail, were committed to the Tower.

Up to this moment there always lived the hope that the stresses which racked the nation would die with the King. The accession of either Mary, the heir-presumptive, or Anne, the next in order, promised an end to the struggle between a

Catholic monarch and a Protestant people. Peaceable folk could therefore be patient until the tyranny was past. The doctrine of nonresistance did not seem a principle of despair. But on June 10, while the trial of the bishops was still pending, the Queen gave birth to a son. Thus there lay before the English people the prospect of a Papist line, stretching out indefinitely upon the life of the future.

The bishops, formerly detested, never popular, now became the idols of the nation. As they stepped on board the barge for the Tower they were hailed by immense crowds with greetings in which reverence and political sympathy were combined. Now for the first time the Episcopacy found itself in alliance with the population of London. The same scenes were repeated when they were brought back to Westminster Hall on June 15, and at their trial on June 29. The sitting lasted until late in the evening, and the jurors remained together throughout the night. When on the following day the bishops were declared "Not Guilty" the verdict was acclaimed with universal joy. As they left the court masses of people, including lifelong foes of the Episcopacy, knelt down and asked their blessing. But the attitude of the Army was more important. The King had visited them at Hounslow, and as he departed heard loud cheering. "What is that clamour?" he asked. "Sire, it is nothing; the soldiers are glad that the bishops are acquitted." "Do you call that nothing?" said James.

On the same night, while cannon and tumults proclaimed the public joy, the seven leaders of the party of action met at Shrewsbury's town house, and there and then signed and dispatched their famous letter to William. It was cool and businesslike in tone. "If the circumstances stand so with your Highness," it said, "that you believe you can get here time enough, in a condition to give assistance this year, . . . we, who subscribe this, will not fail to attend your Highness upon your landing." The signatories were Shrewsbury, Danby, Russell, Bishop Compton, Devonshire, Henry Sidney, and Lumley. The letter was conveyed to The Hague by Admiral Herbert, disguised as a common sailor, and its signatories spread throughout the Island for the purpose of levying war upon the King. Shrewsbury, a former Catholic, converted Protestant, after mortgaging his estates to raise £40,000, crossed the sea to join William. Danby undertook to raise Yorkshire; Compton toured the North "to see his sisters." Devonshire, who had lain since 1685 in obscurity at Chatsworth, formed his tenantry into a regiment of horse. William, stricken in his ambition by the birth of a male Stuart heir, exclaimed, "Now or never!" and began to prepare his expedition.

The birth of the baby prince struck so cruel a blow to the hopes of the nation that it was received with general incredulity, sincere or studiously affected. From the beginning doubts had been thrown upon the belated pregnancy of the Queen. The prayers and intercessions of the Catholics, and their confident predictions that a son would be born as a result, led to a widespread conviction that a trick had been practised. The legend that a child had been smuggled into St James's Palace in a warming pan was afoot even before the ashes of the official bonfires had been cleared from the streets. By the King's improvidence the majority of persons present at the birth were Papists, the wives of Papists, or foreigners. The Archbishop of Canterbury was absent; he had that day been conducted to the Tower. Neither of the Hydes had been summoned, though as Privy Counsellors, brothers-in-law of the King, and uncles to the two princesses, whose rights to the Crown were involved, their presence would have been natural. The Dutch Ambassador, who had a special duty to William, was not invited. It is more important, perhaps, that

Princess Anne was not there. She was at Bath with the Churchills. It was vital to the nation to prove that the child was an impostor. Sincerely attached to the principle of legitimacy, the English Protestants had no other means of escape from the intolerable fact of a Papist heir. They enshrined the legend of the warming pan as a fundamental article of political faith. It was not discarded until after many eventful years, and when the question had ceased to have any practical importance.

Churchill in August renewed his pledge to William, given fifteen months before, and wrote in his own handwriting a signed letter, still extant, which if betrayed would have cost him his life. "Mr Sidney will let you know how I intend to behave myself; I think it is what I owe to God and my country. My honour I take leave to put into your Royal Highness's hands, in which I think it safe. If you think there is anything else that I ought to do, you have but to command me, and I shall pay an entire obedience to it, being resolved to die in that religion that it has pleased God to give you both the will and power to protect." Nevertheless this extraordinary man, who at this time played only a subordinate part, continued to hold all his offices and commands in the Army, and no doubt intended to use all his influence with the troops against James when the time came. He hoped in this way either to compel the King to submit or to deprive him of all means of resistance. His sincerity of purpose and duplicity of method were equal. He acted as if he was conducting a military operation. Moreover, deceit is inseparable from conspiracy.

Across the sea, watching from day to day the assembled armies of France, lay William of Orange with the troops and Fleet of Holland. He had in his service six Scottish and English regiments, which formed the core of his expedition.

Protestant Europe and England alike looked to him as their champion against the tyrannies and aggression of Louis. But before he could invade England he had to obtain the sanction of the States-General. At a moment when the whole of the French Army was massed and ready for immediate advance it was not easy to persuade the anxious burghers of Holland or the threatened princes of Germany that their best chance of safety lay in sending a Dutch army into England. However, William convinced Frederick III of Brandenburg, and received from him a contingent under Marshal Schomberg. The other German princes acquiesced in the Prussian view. Most of Catholic Spain set political above religious considerations and made no difficulty about attempting to dethrone a Catholic king. The Emperor's religious scruples were removed by the Pope. All these diverse interests and creeds were united in a strategy so far-seeing and broad-minded as is only produced by an overpowering sense of common danger.

All however turned upon the action of France. If the French armies marched against Holland William and the whole Dutch strength would be needed to face them, and England must be left to her fate. If, on the other hand, Louis struck upon the Rhine at Brandenburg and the German coalition, then the expedition could sail. Louis XIV kept all in suspense till the last moment. Had James been willing to commit himself finally to a French alliance Louis would have invaded Holland. But James had patriotic pride as well as religious bigotry. To the last he wavered so that in Holland they thought he was allied to France, and in France to Holland. Louis therefore decided that the best he could hope for would be an England impotent through civil war. At the end of September he turned his armies towards the middle Rhine, and from that moment William was free to set forth. The States-General granted him authority for his English descent and James's hour was come.

* * * * *

As the autumn weeks slipped by excitement and tension grew throughout the Island, and the vast conspiracy which now comprised the main strength of the nation heaved beneath the strain of affairs. The King's attempt to bring in some of the Irish Roman Catholic regiments which Tyrconnel had raised for him produced symptoms so menacing that the project was abandoned. The hatred and fears of all classes found expression in an insulting, derisive ballad against the Irish and the Papists. *Lilliburlero,* like *Tipperary* in our own times, was on all lips, in all ears, and carried a cryptic message of war to all hearts. The doggerel lines, written by Lord Wharton, with deep knowledge of the common folk and their modes of thought and expression, had no provable relation to William, nor to invasion or revolt. But the jingle of the chorus made an impression upon the Army "that cannot," said Bishop Burnet, "be imagined by those that saw it not." Everyone watched the weathercock. All turned on the wind. Rumour ran riot. The Irish were coming. The French were coming. The Papists were planning a general massacre of Protestants. The kingdom was sold to Louis. Nothing was safe, and no one could be trusted. The laws, the Constitution, the Church—all were in jeopardy. But a deliverer would appear. He would come clad with power from over the seas to rescue England from Popery and slavery—if only the wind would blow from the east. And here one of Wharton's couplets, which nominally applied to Tyrconnel, gained a new and indeed an opposite significance:

> O, why does he stay so long behind?
> Ho! by my shoul, 'tis a Protestant wind.

The Protestant wind was blowing in the hearts of men, rising in fierce gusts to gale fury. Soon it would blow across the North Sea!

The scale and reality of William's preparations and the alarming state of feeling throughout England had terrified Sunderland and Jeffreys. These two Ministers induced the King to reverse his whole policy. Parliament must be called without delay. All further aggressive Catholic measures must be stopped and a reconciliation made with the Episcopal Church. On October 3 James agreed to abolish the Ecclesiastical Commission, to close the Roman Catholic schools, to restore the Protestant Fellows of Magdalen College, to put the Act of Uniformity into force against Catholics and Dissenters. The dismissed Lord-Lieutenants were invited to resume their functions in the counties. Their charters were restored to the recalcitrant municipalities. The bishops were begged to let bygones be bygones. The Tory squires were urged to take their old places in the magistracy. In the last few months of his reign James was compelled to desert the standard he had himself set up and try in vain by the sacrifice of all his objectives to placate the furies he had aroused. But it was too late.

On October 19 William set out upon the seas. His small army was a microcosm of Protestant Europe—Dutch, Swedes, Danes, Prussians, English, and Scotch, together with a forlorn, devoted band of French Huguenots, to the number of fourteen thousand, embarked upon about five hundred vessels, escorted by sixty warships. William had planned to land in the North, where Danby and other nobles were in readiness to join him. But after he had been once driven back by a gale the wind carried him through the Straits of Dover, which he passed in full view of the crowded coasts of England and France. On November 5 he landed at Torbay, on the coast of Devon. Reminded that it was the anniversary of the Gunpowder Plot, he remarked to Burnet, "What do you think of Predestination now?"

James was not at first greatly alarmed at the news. He hoped to pen William in the West and to hamper his communications by sea. The troops which had been sent to Yorkshire were recalled to the South, and Salisbury was fixed as the point of assembly for the royal Army. At this crisis the King could marshal as large an army as Oliver Cromwell at his height. Nearly forty thousand regular soldiers were in the royal pay. The Scottish troops, about four thousand strong, had only reached Carlisle, the bulk of the three thousand Irish were still beyond Chester, and at least seven thousand men must be left to hold down London. Still, twenty-five thousand men, or nearly double the number of William's expedition, were around Salisbury when the King arrived on November 19. This was the largest concentration of trained full-time troops that England had ever seen.

But now successive desertions smote the unhappy prince. Lord Cornbury, eldest son of the Earl of Clarendon, an officer of the Royal Dragoons, endeavoured to carry three regiments of horse to William's camp. James, warned from many quarters, meditated Churchill's arrest. On the night of November 23, having failed to carry any large part of the Army with them, Churchill and the Duke of Grafton, with about four hundred officers and troopers, quitted the royal camp. At the same time the Princess Anne, attended by Sarah Churchill, and guided by Bishop Compton, fled from Whitehall and hastened northwards. And now revolt broke out all over the country. Danby was in arms in Yorkshire, Devonshire in Derbyshire, Delamere in Cheshire. Lord Bath delivered Plymouth to William. Byng, later an admiral, representing the captains of the Fleet, arrived at his headquarters to inform him that the Navy and Portsmouth were at his disposal. City after city rose in rebellion. By one spontaneous, tremendous convulsion the English nation repudiated James.

The King, finding resistance impossible, assembled such peers and Privy Counsellors as were still in London, and on their advice entered into negotiations with the Prince of Orange. Meanwhile the invading army moved steadily forward towards London. James sent his wife and son out of the kingdom, and on the night of December 11 stole from the palace at Whitehall, crossed the river, and rode to the coast. He endeavoured to plunge his realm into anarchy. He threw the Great Seal into the Thames, and sent orders to Feversham to disband the Army, and to Dartmouth to sail to Ireland with what ships he could. The wildest rumours of Irish massacres spread through the land. The London mob sacked the foreign embassies, and a panic and terror, known as "Irish Night," swept the capital. Undoubtedly a complete collapse of order would have occurred but for the resolute action of the Council, which was still sitting in London. With some difficulty they suppressed the storm, and, acknowledging William's authority, besought him to hasten his marches to London.

James in his flight had actually got on board a ship, but, missing the tide, was caught and dragged ashore by the fishermen and townsfolk. He was brought back to London, and after some days of painful suspense was allowed to escape again. This time he succeeded and left English soil for ever. But though the downfall and flight of this impolitic monarch were at the time ignominious, his dignity has been restored to him by history. His sacrifice for religion gained for him the lasting respect of the Catholic Church, and he carried with him into lifelong exile an air of royalty and honour.

INDEX

INDEX

INDEX

INDEX

Louis XI, King of France, 23, 27
Louis XII, King of France, 38
Louis XIII, King of France, 163, 246
Louis XIV, King, 350; aids Holland against England, 347; marriage of, 351; invades Netherlands, 351–2; secret negotiations of, with Charles II, 352, 356, 360, 372; invades Holland, 353–4; before Maestricht, 355; reveals bribes, 360; aims of, 364; bribes Opposition, 369; successes of, 379, 399; power of France under, 384; religious intoleration of, 385
Lowestoft, Battle of, 346
Ludovic, Duke of Milan, 25
Luther, Martin, 5–6, 55
Lutheran Church, 115
Luxembourg, 399
Lyme Regis, 254, 387

Macaulay, Lord, on the origin of parties, 340
Maestricht, siege of, 355
Magellan, Ferdinand, 13
Magnum Concilium, King summons, 210, 369
Magyars of Hungary, 350
Man, Isle of, 299
Manchester, Edward Montagu, second Earl of, 251, 255
Margaret of Austria, Regent of Netherlands, 29, 37
Margaret Tudor, Queen of James IV of Scotland, 22, 37
Maria Theresa, Queen of Louis XIV of France, 351, 355
Marie de Médicis, Queen of Henry IV of France, 163
Marston Moor, Battle of, 251–3, 257
Martial law, under Charles I, 183
Martin Marprelate, 116
Mary I, Queen of England, question of succession of, 46, 62, 65, 94; banished from Court, 57; Anne Boleyn accused of trying to poison, 69; and Catherine Parr, 81; question of marriage of, 84, 96–7; succeeds to throne, 95; restores Roman faith, 77, 101; marries Philip of Spain, 98; martyrdoms in reign of, 99, 101; death of, 100
Mary II, Queen of England, 359, 370, 373

Mary, Queen of Scots, 109–10; marriages of, 82, 104, 109; claim of, to English throne, 104, 109, 117; in England, 110–1; conspires against Elizabeth, 118; execution of, 118–9; son of, 147
Mary of Guise, Queen of James V of Scotland, 82, 104, 108
Mary of Modena, Queen of James II, 357; birth of son to, 403–4
Mary Tudor, Queen of Louis II—see Suffolk, Duchess of
Maryland, 176–7
Massachusetts, 170–5
Massachusetts Bay Company, 171–5
Massey, Governor of Gloucester, 242–4
Maurice, Prince of the Rhine, 236, 240
Maximilian I, Holy Roman Emperor, marries Mary of Burgundy, 27; fights for Henry VIII, 36, 38
Mayflower, the, 169
Mazarin, Cardinal, 295, 304, 350–1
Medina-Sidonia, Duke of, 124–5, 128–31
Mediterranean, loses land route to East, 9, 13; English campaign against pirates of, 301, 305; English interest in, 344
Medway, river, 348
Mexico, mineral treasures of, 14, 120
Middlesex, Lionel Cranfield, Earl of, 163
Monasteries, dissolution of smaller, 72–3; and enclosure, 73, 88; resistance to dissolution of, 75–7; dissolution of larger, 77
Mongols, invasion of Europe by, 9
Monk, General George, commands in Scotland, 322–3; invited to come to London, 323; Commander-in-Chief, 325; advises Charles II on terms for Restoration, 325–6; receives King, 327; in command at sea, 346; in London during plague, 348; mentioned, 343
Monmouth, James Scott, Duke of, and succession to throne, 364, 370, 374; on Privy Council, 370; rising of, 386–8; execution of, 389
Monopolies, under Elizabeth, 143; under Charles I, 195
Montespan, Madame de, 355

DESIGN BY AVERY FISHER

IT IS FITTING THAT BOTH THE DISPLAY
AND TEXT TYPE FACES USED IN THIS BOOK
ARE OF ENGLISH ORIGIN. THE BINDING,
TITLE PAGE AND IMPORTANT HEADINGS
ARE SET IN PERPETUA, THE CREATION OF
ERIC GILL. THE ORIGINAL FORMS FROM
WHICH THE TYPE WAS CUT BY THE MONO-
TYPE CORPORATION WERE SIMPLY LET-
TERS DRAWN WITH BRUSH AND INK.

THE TEXT HAS THROUGHOUT BEEN SET
IN TIMES ROMAN, INITIALLY DESIGNED
BY STANLEY MORISON FOR USE IN THE
LONDON TIMES. ITS EXTREME LEGIBIL-
ITY AND ATTRACTIVE 'COLOR' IN MASS
ARE ITS MOST DISTINCTIVE CHARACTER-
ISTICS.

MAPS BY JAMES MACDONALD